W9-AVY-704

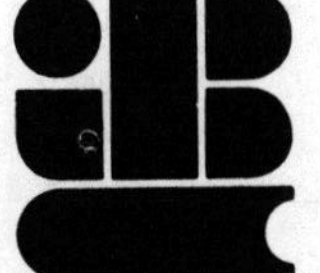

Training for Impact

Dana Gaines Robinson
James C. Robinson

Training for Impact

How to Link Training to Business Needs and Measure the Results

Jossey-Bass Publishers · San Francisco

Jossey-Bass books and products are available through most bookstores. To contact Jossey-Bass directly, call (888) 378-2537, fax to (800) 605-2665, or visit our website at www.josseybass.com

Substantial discounts on bulk quantities of Jossey-Bass books are available to corporations, professional associations, and other organizations. For details and discount information, contact the special sales department at Jossey-Bass.

For sales outside the United States, please contact your local Simon & Schuster International Office.

Manufactured in the United States of America.

JACKET DESIGN BY WILLI BAUM

Library of Congress Cataloging-in-Publication Data

Robinson, Dana Gaines, date.
Training for impact : how to link training to business needs and measure the results / Dana Gaines Robinson, James C. Robinson.
p. cm — (The Jossey-Bass management series)
Bibliographies: p.
Includes index.
ISBN 1-55542-153-9 (alk. paper)
1. Employees, Training of. 2. Employees, Training of—Evaluation.
HF5549.5T7R527 1989
658.3'124—dc19 88-46088

HB Printing 20 19 18 17 16 15 14 13

The Jossey-Bass Management Series

Consulting Editors
Human Resources

Leonard Nadler
Zeace Nadler
College Park, Maryland

Contents

Preface xiii

The Authors xix

Part One: Moving from Activity Training to Impact Training **1**

1. The Training-for-Activity Trap 3

2. The Training-for-Impact Approach 10

Part Two: Creating Strategic Partnerships with Management **31**

3. Identifying Business Needs and Clients 33

4. Forming a Collaborative Relationship with Clients 48

5. Conducting Initial Project Meetings 66

Part Three: Diagnosing Organizational Needs and Making Training Decisions 83

6. Assessing Performance Effectiveness 85

7. Analyzing Causes of Performance Gaps 108

8. Tabulating, Interpreting, and Reporting Results to Clients 132

Part Four: Building Evaluation and Tracking Systems into Training Programs 161

9. Participant Reactions: Going Beyond "Smile Sheets" 163

10. Participant Learning: Assessing Development of Knowledge and Skills 185

11. Behavioral Results: Evaluating Transfer of Learning to the Job 208

12. Nonobservable Results: Identifying Changes in Values, Beliefs, and Cognitive Skills 244

13. Operational Results: Measuring Impact on the Business 255

Part Five: Using the Training-for-Impact Approach 281

14. How and Where to Begin 283

References 295

Annotated Bibliography 297

Index 301

To human resources development professionals who strive to make a difference

Preface

Does any of these situations sound familiar?

- Your training function delivers an increasing number of programs each year, yet you do not know what impact this training is having on your organization.
- You are continually frustrated by the lack of management support for training in your company. Managers say that training is important, but it is an ongoing battle to gain the needed resources, time, and support to do the job right.
- On the basis of conversations you have had with past participants, you wonder whether people are really using on the job many of the skills learned in your programs. This question is especially pertinent when you continue to hear your participants say, "This is great; you should send my boss"—and you know their bosses have already attended.
- The number of people who call at the last minute to cancel out of a training program is increasing. They cite work

pressures as the reason, but you wonder. Could it be that they see training as nice but not essential? What you do know is that the courses are being conducted with fewer people than intended.

- Your management is asking for more justification of your operating budget. Other than showing managers your activity report (number of programs taught, number of people attending), you have little to provide.

Should any or all of these situations strike a familiar chord, this book is for you. With the increasing focus on human resources as the organizational element that can provide a competitive edge, we—the people in the human resources development (HRD) profession—are being challenged as never before.

In this book, we provide strategies and how-to's for implementing results-oriented, business-related training efforts that result in impacts on organizations. Too often, training is conducted as an activity; trainers report only on the number of people who attended and the number of courses offered in a year. We address the need to move away from such an activity approach and toward an impact approach in what we do as HRD professionals. You will learn the how-to's of linking your training to business needs, obtaining management support, and measuring the results.

The entire book will discuss how to gain impact from training programs. We define *training* as techniques that "focus on learning the skills, knowledge, and attitudes required to initially perform a job or task or to improve upon the performance of a current job or task" (Nadler and Wiggs, 1986, p. 5).

You will also note the use of the terms *business* and *business need* throughout our book. We use these terms broadly, to refer to the organization's mission or its reason to exist. For example, if you work in a not-for-profit agency, your business needs may involve obtaining volunteer help, collecting contributions, or influencing legislation that affects your agency. If you work in the public sector, your business needs could involve obtaining resources to meet the needs of the public or identifying ways to serve the public more efficiently. And, of course, if you work in the for-profit sector, business needs exist in the areas of increasing revenue, reducing costs, and maximizing the quality of output. For us, the term *business* is applicable to any organization, whether that organization is public, private, or not for profit. Training must be linked to the business of an organization, whatever that business may be.

The approach we use to implement results-oriented training is unique, because it:

- Uses a consultative approach to line managers, requiring that the HRD professional form a partnership with such managers for the duration of any training project
- Increases management support for training efforts, because management understands that training is directly linked to the business needs of the organization
- Requires working with management to ensure that the work environment is ready to support the skills to be taught
- Provides the HRD professional with a framework to measure the impact of training efforts on the organization, whether those results are behavioral, nonobservable, or operational
- Informs managers about the roles they must play to get results from training, acknowledging that training alone will be insufficient to bring about results

For Whom Is This Book Written?

We have written this book for people whose primary professional responsibility is the training of others. Such job titles as director of training, human resources development manager, staff instructor, program designer, or consultant to the training profession would qualify their holders for inclusion in our audience. We frequently use the term *HRD professional* to mean anyone involved in the planning, design, and delivery of training and educational programs, in an association, organization, or institution. Even though you may not actually deliver training programs, if you are involved in some manner in the process of building skills and knowledge in others, then you will find this book relevant.

When we wrote this book, we primarily considered the needs of HRD professionals working in organizations. This focus may not be readily apparent from some of the terminology we use throughout the book. We refer to line managers as clients and to HRD professionals as consultants. This is a purposeful use of terms. It is our opinion that HRD professionals can no longer view their role as designing and delivering training programs. Rather, such professionals must view their role as one that increases performance effectiveness within the organization. Such an enlarged venue requires some additional skills: consultation, organizational assessment, and measurement of results.

Scope of This Book

One focus is the strategies required to establish training programs in organizations so that they are linked to business needs and provide measurable results. We do not address the how-to's of training design and delivery; instead, we focus on what must happen before and after the program is delivered.

Another focus of this book is the transfer of behavior or skills from the training program to the job. For us, behavior and skills are actions that can be seen or heard. They are observable. Through people's use of skills and behavior, operational results become possible. Much of the content of this book is relevant to HRD professionals involved in the communicating of information (for example, courses on policy or law) and to professionals involved in training that addresses the raising of awareness or the changing of values, but most of our examples address the transfer of behavior or skills. For us, this is where the real payoff from training lies.

Overview of the Contents

In Chapter One, we describe in some detail the activity trap in which many HRD professionals find themselves. In

Chapter Two, we contrast the activity trap to the Training-for-Impact approach. Chapter Two gives a complete overview of the model that is discussed in detail throughout the book.

In Chapters Two through Five, you will learn techniques for identifying and working with the key decision makers in your organization. You need to be partnered with these people if business-related training is to occur. In Chapters Six and Seven, you will learn the how-to's of assessing training needs and the work environment's readiness for the new skills to be taught. In Chapter Eight, we discuss how to interpret and report this type of information to your managers so that they will want to take appropriate action.

Chapters Nine through Thirteen provide specific guidelines for evaluating your business-related training efforts. Two chapters address evaluation of training: One chapter is on reaction evaluation and the other is on learning evaluation. Three chapters discuss the tracking of training efforts—specifically, the measurement of behavioral results, nonobservable results, and operational impacts.

In Chapter Fourteen, we provide some additional tips and techniques for getting started in the delivery of training that has impact. We also provide guidelines for when you should (and should not) use the approaches described in this book.

Our intent is to provide you with as many steps, techniques, and instructions as possible. Many examples come from our own experience as consultants. Throughout the book, you will find actual samples of questions and practical tips. We want this book to be a resource for you to use in your day-to-day job. Our objective is to provide you with pragmatic, proven ideas that you can apply either in their entirety or in part.

Acknowledgments

Like any other major project, this book would not have become a reality without the aid and support of many people. We wish to extend sincere thanks and appreciation to several colleagues who encouraged us through the three years it took to complete the manuscript. Many of these people reviewed the entire manuscript and provided us invaluable feedback. They include Dan Hupp, Gary Martini, Tom Newman, Valerie Phillips, Tony Roithmayr, and Dennis Sweeney. We extend special thanks to Dana Robinson's mother, Martha Larson, for her enthusiastic encouragement over the years, as well as for her invaluable feedback on the completed manuscript.

Three people deserve special recognition for sitting in front of the word processor and inputting all these words over and over and over again. To Barbara Martin, Terri Osthoff, and Betsy Selig, a big "Thanks." While many people have influenced and guided us professionally through the years, we particularly want to thank Peter Block, Tom Gilbert, Arnold Goldstein, Robert Mager, Pat McLagan, Geary Rummler, and Ron Zemke for their wisdom and contributions to the HRD field.

Finally, we wish to thank our consulting editors, Leonard and Zeace Nadler. Both of these people were with us every chapter of the way, letting us know that we were moving forward, although it seemed at times that we were standing still. They provided the type of feedback we could understand and use, so that the manuscript became continually better. Thanks for your tenacity in sticking with us—and for your belief that this book was possible.

Pittsburgh, Pennsylvania
March 1989

Dana Gaines Robinson
James C. Robinson

The Authors

Dana Gaines Robinson is president and founder of the consulting firm Partners in Change, Inc., with offices in Pittsburgh and Toronto. She received her bachelor's degree (1965) from the University of California, Berkeley, in sociology and her master's degree (1979) from Temple University in psychoeducational processes.

Before becoming an external consultant, Robinson was an internal HRD professional for nine years. She knows firsthand the pressures and issues that face the internal practitioner, having managed the training and development functions for two corporations: Mellon East Bank (formerly Girard Bank) and Merck Sharp and Dohme. While working in these organizations, she developed an evaluation technology known as Tracking for Change. This process measures the results of training efforts and is described in detail in this book. *TRAINING: The Magazine of Human Resources Development* has recognized her as an "HRD Master" because of her work in this area.

Robinson is also recognized for her diagnostic skills and

her ability to design and implement front-end assessments that identify the developmental needs of people. She has assisted corporations in determining the competencies that will be required of successful managers in the 1990s, and she is a frequent speaker on this subject.

An active contributor to the American Society for Training and Development (ASTD), Robinson was chair of the HRD careers committee and is currently working on the design committee to design the 1989 national ASTD conference. With Robert Younglove, she coauthored *Making Your Career Transition into External HRD Consulting* (1986) for ASTD. She is a frequent speaker at both ASTD and TRAINING national conferences and appeared in a nationally televised videoconference, which addressed how to introduce change into an organization.

James C. Robinson is a recognized leader in the areas of program design, skill development, skill transfer, and trainer development, and he is currently chairman of Partners in Change, Inc. Robinson received his bachelor's degree (1951) from the University of Massachusetts in animal science, a master's degree (1957) from the University of Wisconsin in animal genetics, and a second master's degree (1973) from Syracuse University in adult education. He has served on several ASTD projects, including the task forces on professional standards and on competency and standards.

The training programs Robinson has developed have been used to build skills in over two million supervisors in over twenty countries around the world. Robinson was a pioneer in developing behavior-modeling programs for supervisors and has authored a book on that subject: *Developing Managers Through Behavior Modeling*. That book was described by *TRAINING* magazine as a "must" for training practitioners. He also designed, tested, and implemented the first criteria-referenced, competency-based instructor training workshop for behavior-modeling instructors.

For over twelve years, Robinson has worked in the area of skill transfer. Since 1976, he has surveyed over 350 training managers to determine the most commonly occurring barriers to and enhancers of skill transfer. For the past seven years, he has conducted workshops and seminars on strategies for increasing skill transfer. Acknowledging the importance of the individual's manager to skill transfer, he designed a management reinforcement workshop that has become a model for many similar workshops.

Robinson was a line manager for ten years and was a training director for six years in a *Fortune* 100 company. For several years, he was vice-president at Development Dimensions International, and he was chief architect of its most successful training program, *Interaction Management*.

Training for Impact

Part One

Moving from Activity Training to Impact Training

For many years HRD professionals have successfully been designing and delivering training programs—the more, the better. A company training catalogue, thick with training opportunities, was viewed as a desirable goal. Growth in the number of participant and instructor days was a sure sign of success.

Such an approach to training we call Training for Activity. The training program became the end; while thought might have been given to what happened after the training course, very little (if any) time was spent considering that question. Such an approach is sufficient if the role of the HRD professional is to deliver training courses.

But what if you view your role as one of contributing to organizational effectiveness or assisting in performance improvement? Then conducting courses in an activity mode is insufficient. An approach we call Training for Impact becomes the desirable option. Considering the lean-and-mean, highly competitive times of the 1990s, it may be the only option.

In the next two chapters, we provide a more complete overview of each of these two approaches to training.

One

The Training-for-Activity Trap

Meet Alan Douglas, the manager of human resources development (HRD) for a major financial institution with five thousand employees. Alan is responsible for all training, education, and development in this company, including teller skills training, sales training, customer contact training, technical/operational training, and supervisory/managerial development. He reports to the director of human resources and has a staff of six training professionals reporting to him.

Alan has been in this position for five years, having been recruited from outside the bank. When he began as manager of HRD, he had a secretary and one professional reporting to him. Over the intervening years, he has increased both the number of training programs offered and the number of people on his staff who deliver them. The annual training catalogue, which has steadily increased in size, indicates all the programs offered, together with a calendar of times when people can attend. Individual employees, with their supervisors' approval, register for any desired program.

Over the years, Alan has been rewarded by his management for increasing both the number and types of programs offered in the bank. Each year, his management expects to see greater variety and an increased number of training programs from his function.

Alan has just concluded his annual goal-setting meeting with his manager and has agreed to add some additional programs to the training catalogue. These new programs will focus on influencing skills for managers and selling skills for branch personnel. He is also to offer, on an annual basis, a two-day off-site conference with topics of interest for high-level managers of the company. This conference will be a combination of educational programming and organizationally endorsed "rest and recreation" (providing managers a chance to informally socialize away from the office).

Alan is not enthusiastic about these commitments. Over the past two years, he has begun to suspect that something is amiss. There is an increasing number of cancellations from training programs at the last minute. Last year, the department actually had to cancel five programs because of poor enrollment. It is not uncommon for at least one person in a program to leave for lunch and not return. Such individuals say that they are needed in their units because of pressing issues, but Alan wonders if the reason is something more. Training evaluations, completed at the conclusion of the programs, indicate high levels of satisfaction among those who attend, but when Alan or his staff follow up with participants, they often learn that little of what was taught has been applied to the job. Alan also continues to experience the problem of learning about business plans only after they are final. Rather than being brought in early in the planning cycle to help managers determine the HRD implications of their decisions, he is informed after the fact and told how to respond.

The final alert to Alan that something is wrong occurred just two weeks ago. While having lunch with a colleague from the commercial banking department, he learned that the senior vice-president of that department may be creating a training function that will report to her directly. She believes that her

Figure 1. Training-for-Activity Approach.

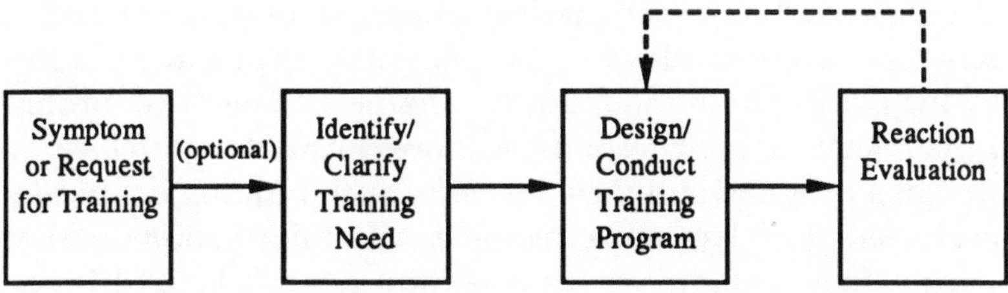

business needs for training are not being met sufficiently by the corporate function. While Alan is still investigating that rumor, there does appear to be some truth to it, and it is a cause of real concern to Alan.

Alan believes that more could be done by his function, but he seems trapped by a monster of his own creation. He worked hard to develop his list of programs, and that is what management now expects of him and his staff. Delivering these programs requires most of his staff's time and leaves little time available for other things. As a result, management views Alan's function as being responsible for running training courses, not for assisting managers in meeting their business objectives. Alan is viewed as a business overhead, not as a business partner. He would like to change that—but where to begin?

Characteristics of Training for Activity

Alan may not be aware of it, but much of his frustration stems from the approach he has used to implement his training programs for the past five years. His problem is probably not with the quality of program design or delivery. It is more likely that the problem centers on how Alan has chosen to introduce and implement his programs. His approach has been one of *Training for Activity* and is illustrated by Figure 1.

In Training for Activity, the training process begins with some symptom or request for training. For example, a line manager may indicate that supervisors in his area of responsibility need a time-management program. From that start, needs assessment becomes an optional item. In Training for Activity, the individual requesting training often wants it "next week," a schedule that precludes the possibility of collecting information to further clarify or substantiate the need. The HRD professional, wanting to be responsive, moves forward to purchase or design a program and then deliver it. Such training is typically evaluated by end-of-course critiques only. Information on what participants thought was most helpful or least helpful is collected, as is information on the competence of instructors and the pacing of the workshop. Such information is used to modify the design of the program, so that the next time it is delivered it will be more effective. Training for Activity exhibits the following five characteristics.

1. *The HRD department is held accountable for its activity, not for its results.* In corporate America today, getting results is what matters. The structures for accountability and rewards in most business units reinforce the achievement of results. Manufacturing lines are held accountable for rate of output and high quality; selling functions, for increased sales and earnings; engineers, for the design of new machinery, which increases productivity. The HRD function, however, usually reports on its activity (number of programs offered, number of participants who attend) and its costs (for materials, external vendors, audiovisual equipment). There is no accounting of the results of those activities and costs. Managers are left to deduce their own opinions about payback.

2. *The HRD staff is held accountable for design and delivery of training programs.* In Training for Activity, trainers are held accountable for the number of programs they deliver or design. The more activity completed, the better. In certain instances, trainers know they are to spend a portion of their time in delivery. For some people, this portion is 80 percent or higher. There is little time to do needs assessments or research, which require out-of-classroom time. In an organization operating under Training for Activity, it is generally believed that if one is called a trainer, one should be in the classroom; otherwise, one is not really working.

3. *Skill transfer from the classroom to the job is unknown or*

absent. When using Training for Activity, the HRD function's major purpose is to offer and deliver courses that provide attendees with skills and knowledge in a high-quality learning environment. Whether this learning experience is delivered in a classroom or by other means, the end-of-course reaction evaluation is often the only evaluation tool. While they do provide valuable information about a program, such evaluations do not collect data about application of the new knowledge or skills to the job. Furthermore, the HRD department that uses the Training-for-Activity approach rarely considers implementation strategies that would ensure a high degree of skill transfer. On-the-job application is viewed as the responsibility of the participant and his or her boss; the HRD department is responsible for providing the participants with skills and knowledge. Our experience has shown that little transfer occurs under such conditions.

4. *There is a lack of clear alignment with business needs.* In Training for Activity, it is common to see unconnected courses offered for a variety of reasons. For example, a needs assessment completed five years ago indicated that the course would be helpful, and now that course has a life of its own, or perhaps everyone in the industry is conducting this program, and so it makes sense for the organization to do likewise. Again, the course may address a skill needed by some, and so it is thought useful to have everyone go through it, or maybe the HRD department has decided that people will benefit from the course.

Absent from all these rationales is a direct link to a business problem (reduced market share, increasing customer complaints) or a business opportunity (the introduction of new high-tech equipment, the launching of a new product or service). Without such tight tethering to business needs, is it any wonder that management is unenthusiastic about training programs?

5. *There is a lack of identified management responsibility for results.* In Training for Activity, the HRD department comes to be viewed as the place where people go to get repaired or recharged: Send unskilled supervisors to Supervisory Course 101, and they will come back competent and able. When that does

not occur, the HRD function is vulnerable to blame from management. What is missing here is identification of what management must contribute in order to achieve results. No one person or group of people has accepted accountability for ensuring that the skills taught will be used on the job.

The Business Need for an Alternative Training Approach

One of the criticisms most commonly leveled at HRD professionals today is that they lack business savvy and do not speak the language of business. Business language requires HRD professionals to consider the return to the organization for dollars spent on training. Current estimates nationwide indicate that projected training and development budgets for 1989 will be close to $40 billion for U.S. corporations of one hundred people or more (Feuer, 1988). This figure represents actual direct expenses anticipated; when you add to this figure the expense of people attending training programs on company time, the expense quickly rises to more than $200 billion (American Society for Training and Development, 1986). What is gained by U.S. corporations because of this investment? What benefits accrue?

If HRD professionals want to be seen as business partners, then training programs must be tied to business needs, problems, or opportunities, and these links must be clearly understood by management. Moreover, the business outcomes to be derived from any training effort should be articulated before the program is implemented. Cost per participant for a training program should also be calculated, and management should be offered the opportunity to determine whether anticipated benefits will be worth the investment. Furthermore, the joint responsibilities of HRD professionals and line management should be spelled out, to ensure that these outcomes occur. Finally, data should be provided to managers to help them know if the desired business outcomes have occurred.

The Training-for-Impact approach described in this book

provides the how-to's for making this business partnership a reality. This approach requires HRD professionals to have skills in addition to those they need to design and deliver training programs. Let us look now in more detail at the approach we call *Training for Impact.*

Two

The Training-for-Impact Approach

So far, we have indicated that HRD professionals should avoid Training for Activity because of its inherent disadvantages. Instead, the focus should be on results-oriented training that is driven by business needs, helps the organization achieve its goals, provides people with the skills and knowledge they need to improve their performance, assesses readiness of the work environment to support learned skills, has management accepting the responsibility for a supportive work environment that encourages skill transfer, and has measurable results that can be tracked.

Where to begin? That is the question we asked eight years ago, as we began developing the Training-for-Impact approach. This approach is a composite of the strategies just mentioned

Note: Portions of this chapter are drawn from "Training for Impact (How to Stop Spinning Your Wheels and Get into the Race), by Dana Gaines Robinson. Reprinted with permission from the Feb. 1984 issue (pp. 42–47) of *TRAINING: The Magazine of Human Resources Development*. Copyright Lakewood Publications, Minneapolis, Minn. All rights reserved.

and is to be used as a guide for achieving the needs-driven, results-oriented training described in this book. Training for Impact is applicable to any situation where training's purpose is to help the organization achieve its objectives. The approach can be used by any HRD professional who wishes to move out of the Training-for-Activity trap and into results-oriented training.

Before we take an in-depth look at the approach, we need to examine a fundamental concept, which can be summarized by this formula:

Learning Experience × Work Environment = Business Results

Business results occur when skills taught in a training program are applied on the job, yielding improved performance. For this to happen, the HRD professional must provide a well-designed and skillfully delivered training program in which participants learn what was intended; thus, the "learning experience" side of the results equation is 100 percent. That learning by itself, however, will be insufficient to produce on-the-job results. What must also be present is a work environment that reinforces the use of skills taught in the program by holding people accountable for using those skills and by coaching those skills (generally through the direct boss) when people need additional guidance. If this supportive work environment is not present, then we will have a 0 on the "work environment" side of our equation. Recalling basic arithmetic, 100 multiplied by 0 will yield 0 in terms of on-the-job results. The HRD professional, acting alone and without the assurance that the work environment (which management controls) is supporting skills, will probably experience limited business results from training efforts. Again, this dilemma is a common failing in the activity approach to training, where the concentration of the HRD professional is on the "learning experience" side of the equation; little effort is given to ensuring that the work environment will support new skills. We have personally experienced hundreds of situations where either the "learning experience" or the "work environment" side of the results equation was inoperative.

For example, there was a bank that trained its tellers in

cross-selling and introducing additional bank services to customers who came to their teller windows. The training program was very successful, with the teller participants consistently evidencing the new skills in simulations. When tellers attempted to use the skills on the job, however, service to customers slowed, and lines started to form in the bank. After all, if a teller not only handles a transaction but also attempts to have a conversation about additional services, the time per transaction increases. Branch management, concerned when the lines became longer, instructed tellers to speed up their servicing of customers. What disappeared, of course, was the time spent cross-selling. The work environment in this bank did not support what the learning experience of the training program had provided.

In another organization, personal computers were being introduced to all the administrative and managerial staff. The training department provided an "Introduction to Computers" course. The problem was that this course did not provide specific skills and hands-on opportunities regarding operation of the computer and its software. Instead, the program provided an overview of general computer concepts and terms. Management in this instance was eager to support what was needed to maximize the investment made in personal computers (in other words, the work environment was receptive to the skills needed). Nevertheless, the training program had not provided the appropriate skills (the "learning experience" side of the equation had a 0). When these staff members had completed the program, they knew how to turn on a computer but not how to operate it. They were left to their own devices to figure it out back on the job, when work pressures were high. Results from this training effort were minimal, largely because of a training program that did not provide specific application skills.

Interdependence between the HRD function and management is essential. Together, they can achieve a great deal, but when mutual support and partnership are absent, there is low probability that efforts to develop people will be successfully transferred to the job.

Training for Impact

In Training for Impact, the HRD professional, as the project begins, creates a partnership with key line managers associated with the training project. This partnership is often formed through the initiative of the HRD professional. It ensures that both the "learning experience" and the "work environment" sides of the results equation will be operative. The HRD professional most directly influences and controls the learning experience, while key line managers (people we refer to in this book as *clients*) influence and control the work environment.

With the project's clients, the HRD professional identifies the business need that is driving a request for training. Training is viewed as a means to an end, rather than as an end in itself. In Training for Activity, the end result is often thought of in terms of increased skills or knowledge; in Training for Impact, the business results that will occur because of increased skills or knowledge are identified. Figure 2 illustrates the difference between Training for Activity and Training for Impact with respect to results.

To ensure that the business need can be met (and that the skills and knowledge being delivered can be transferred to the job), some assessment on the front end of training delivery must occur. In the Training-for-Impact approach, such assessment efforts are mandatory, not optional. Here is where the HRD professional determines requirements for specific skills and knowledge, as well as whether the work environment of the potential learners will support such skills and knowledge. The HRD professional can deliver on the need to improve skills; the client manager must deliver on ensuring that the work environment will support new skills.

In the Training-for-Impact approach, measurement of results is also a requirement. How do we know that skills were transferred? How do we know that people did learn? Is the business need being met as desired? These are the questions to be addressed through collection of information once the training program has been launched. To recapitulate, this approach

Figure 2. Results from Activity Training and Impact Training.

TRAINING PROGRAM	— (leads to) →	PROGRAM RESULTS	— (leads to) →	BUSINESS RESULTS
		• increased skill		• improved work performance
		• increased knowledge		• improved quality of service
		• increased awareness		• increased revenue
				• reduced cost-of-sales
			ACTIVITY TRAINING	IMPACT TRAINING

to training implementation requires a partnership with a client-manager, identification of a business need for the training, assessment of the situation to specifically identify required skills and knowledge, preparation of the work environment to ensure that it will support the new learning, and measurement of results.

Let us take a closer look at what the Training-for-Impact approach involves. The model is displayed in Figure 3. To illustrate the major steps in the process, we will describe a fictitious organization known as Nu-Karparts, Inc. This company is a wholesale organization that supplies automobile parts to independent retail stores throughout the United States. (While this company does not really exist, the various results you will read about have occurred in projects with which we have been associated.)

Step 1: Identify Business Need. The need for training is sometimes revealed in the form of a request: "Please conduct a program on problem solving for my supervisors." Many times, the HRD department identifies a potential training need in a more proactive manner. However the need is revealed, if train-

Figure 3. Training for Impact.

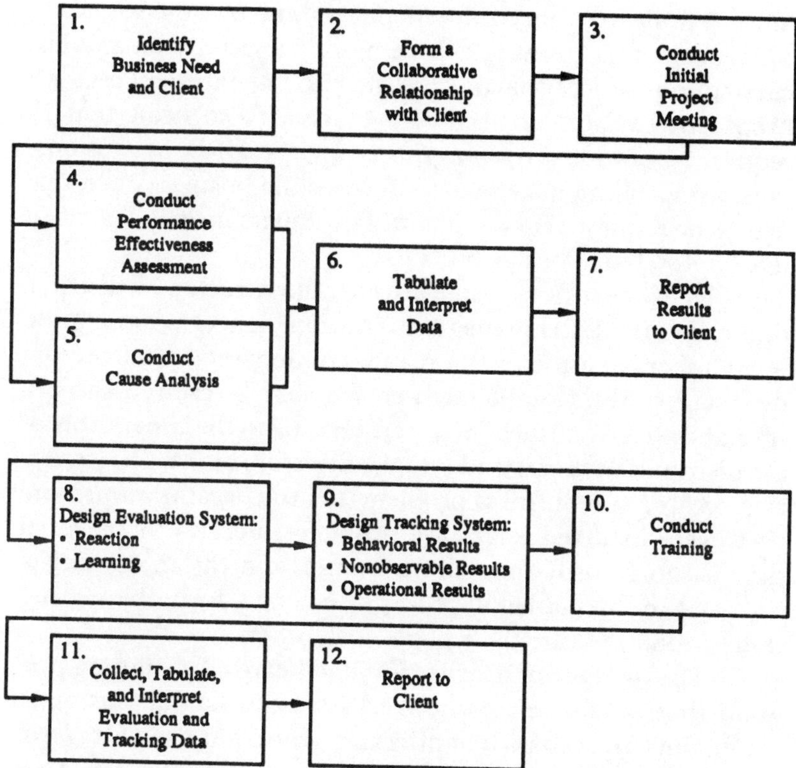

ing is to be linked to business needs, then the association of those two items must be made early in the process.

Some business needs are problems; they are focused on the past and indicate that there is a deviation between what should be and what is. Generally, such problems are causing concern in the minds of some line managers (who probably need to be the clients for the project).

Other business needs are actually opportunities, for they are looking to the future and to something that is about to happen. For example, perhaps a new retail outlet is to be opened, or a new product or service is about to be launched. In these cases, managers want to maximize opportunities, so that projected benefits will be realized.

Training that is strategically linked to business needs must be done in connection with one or both of those scenarios. This means that training will be more project-driven and less curriculum-based. It means that the HRD department must be prepared to respond to needs as they arise. It also means that if a request comes for a training program, the HRD professional must ask probing questions to uncover the business need that drives the request. (How to identify a business need is described in Chapter Three of this book.)

NU-KARPARTS: At Nu-Karparts, the director of distribution called the HRD manager to indicate concern over a growing number of customer complaints coming into his office from the retail stores. Complaints were not being resolved successfully at the clerical level. They were moving to the supervisors of the distribution center and into the director's office. This escalation created two business problems for the organization: More costs were incurred to resolve problems (because managerial time is more costly than clerical time), and the image of Nu-Karparts in the marketplace was threatened, for unhappy customers tend to share their plight with others.

The director of distribution had heard of a training program that taught telephone clerks how to handle customer complaints. He wanted that program to be conducted for two of the centers. On the basis of the results of that pilot effort, he would implement it throughout the United States.

Step 2: Identify and Form a Collaborative Relationship with the Client. For the training effort to be successful and have results, both the learning experience and the work environment must be examined and managed in a manner that will produce the desired results. As we indicated earlier, HRD professionals are responsible for and can control only the learning experience, and so a partnership with a client who has responsibility for the work environment is necessary. This client is usually the individual who has the power to make decisions about the work environment, has something to gain or lose from the success or failure of a training effort directed toward a business problem or opportunity, and has a need to be actively involved in the project.

HRD professionals must seek out these clients and influence them to work collaboratively to resolve the business needs in question. Selecting the right client or client group is crucial to the success of a project. Without a client, you are liable to operate under a Training-for-Activity approach, whose results will be doubtful. Effective client teams can enable you to provide results-oriented, needs-driven training (the Training-for-Impact approach). (Identifying and consulting with clients is discussed in Chapters Three and Four of this book.)

NU-KARPARTS: The HRD professional assigned to customer relations determined that the appropriate client group would be the director of distribution and the two distribution center managers who would be involved in the pilot. These were the people who had the most to gain or lose from the program's success or failure. After a discussion of the advantages a client team offered, it was decided to move forward.

Step 3: Conduct an Initial Project Meeting. This is a pivotal step in any training project that is being established as a Training-for-Impact effort. In this meeting, the HRD professional must influence a client manager to see the benefits of not conducting a training course immediately. Here is where the benefits of involving other key managers, on an as-needed basis, are identified. Most important, in this meeting the HRD professional begins to raise the client manager's awareness that training by itself will not meet a business need. It is the partnership of training with management that will provide the desired results. When this meeting concludes, the training project in question will be either firmly on the road to an impact effort or headed toward an activity approach. (This meeting and what needs to occur in it are described in detail in Chapter Five.)

NU-KARPARTS: From the initial contact, it was clear that the director of distribution felt that a training program was the answer to his business problem (escalating customer complaints). It was also understood that the director wanted to move forward rapidly with a training program. Therefore, the HRD manager determined that, as a result of his initial project meeting with the director, two things needed to be accomplished. First, the director needed to understand that a more thorough investigation was required to identify why these complaints were escalating. To conduct such an analysis would mean that training could not be implemented as rapidly as the director expected. Second, the director had to see the value of bringing in the two distribution center managers (who would be a part of the pilot effort) as part of the client team.

The HRD manager prepared for this meeting by developing many questions and reviewing the training program in which the director expressed an interest. During the meeting, questions like the following were asked:

- When did the customer complaints begin to escalate?
- Does this escalation of complaints occur in all centers or only in some?
- What leads the director to believe that lack of skills is the cause of this escalation?

Often, the director responded to such questions with a thoughtful "I'm not certain" or "That's a good question – I'll need to check into that." The HRD manager then commented that collecting such information would be vital, to make certain that any actions taken would be attacking the cause of the problem, and not just the symptom itself. If lack of skills was the only reason why complaints were escalating, then a training program would be the answer; but it would also be beneficial to determine whether there were other problems.

The director agreed that more information should be collected. He also saw the value of holding a meeting with the distribution center managers involved in this project. It was agreed that a meeting of all parties would occur in two weeks, when the managers would be on site anyway.

Step 4: Conduct a Performance Effectiveness Assessment. Once you and your client have determined which business need is driving the request for training, it becomes important to complete some assessments. These occur at the front end of training. In the Training-for-Impact approach, front-end work is not optional; it is mandatory. The issue is not whether to do it, but rather what specific information is required for any particular project.

In a performance effectiveness assessment, the HRD professional determines what should be happening (What skills and knowledge are required for people to perform successfully? What should operational results indicate?), what is happening (How do typical performers demonstrate the desired skills or knowledge? What do the operational indicators report as being true now?), and what gap exists between what should be and what is (What are the greatest skill or knowledge deficiencies?).

Information must be collected from a variety of sources: clients, potential participants in a training program, managers of those participants, and other interested parties (such as co-workers, customers, and suppliers). Sometimes, this information can be collected in a few days; other times, it may take weeks. The information is sometimes collected through interviews or questionnaires, sometimes through review of documents and observation of employees. However assessment happens, its ultimate goal is to differentiate, as specifically as possible, the desired state from what actually is occurring. (How to design and implement such an assessment is the focus of Chapter Six in this book.)

NU-KARPARTS: From information collected outside Nu-Karparts, it was learned that an effective model for handling customer complaints required customer service representatives (CSRs) to use such techniques as restating what customers have said (to confirm understanding) and acknowledging feelings expressed by customers. The clients believed that these were important techniques and wanted customer service representatives to demonstrate them.

At Nu-Karparts, the performance effectiveness assessment focused on identifying how CSRs typically performed at the time (the "is"). Did they demonstrate any behavior identified as important in the "should" model? Assessment results follow:

1. CSRs gathered information in a variety of ways from customers who had complaints. There was no standard method

or format. Therefore, the type of information collected was inconsistent and not always complete.

2. While most CSRs obtained such information as name of the customer, retail store number, and general nature of the complaint, few of the CSRs obtained more specific information, and only rarely did CSRs summarize what they had understood.
3. Of the customers who were interviewed as part of the performance effectiveness assessment, 75 percent indicated that when they had complaints, CSRs seemed defensive. CSRs expressed little empathy to customers; rather, they commonly assumed a defensive posture by indicating why problems had occurred or by commenting that they were not responsible.
4. Approximately 12 percent of the calls coming into a distribution center each month were complaints. In the past, approximately 1 percent or fewer of those complaints had ended up in a manager's office. For the past three months, however, between 4 percent and 6 percent of these complaints had been landing in a manager's office.

From these and other findings, it was determined that few CSRs had the skills needed to probe a customer for information regarding a complaint or to appear empathetic and nondefensive when discussing a complaint. It seemed as though a developmental need did exist.

Step 5: Conduct a Cause Analysis. Once a gap in performance has been identified, it is important to determine the cause(s) of such gaps. As Mager and Pipe (1970) have indicated, a true developmental need exists when a person is unable to perform, even if his or her life depends on it. We do not advocate using this concept in the literal sense to test for a developmental need; we do advocate investigating the apparent performance gap carefully, to be certain that lack of skill is the cause.

Other than employees' not knowing how, what could be the reason for lack of desired performance? Our research indicates several possible answers to this question: managers who do not model or set an example of how to perform; lack of clear incentive, or accountability, to perform as needed; and lack of authority, time, or equipment to perform.

How many times have you "thrown" training at a problem, only to find that the problem remains? For example, the client in a high-tech corporation with which we once worked was concerned because people producing disk drives were not following the procedures that were clearly identified in various manuals and taught in several training programs. Our client was ready to have the entire unit attend a training program but was savvy enough to ask that the situation be investigated first.

Our cause analysis indicated that the primary reason why operators were not performing as desired was their lack of tools. Tools required by the operators were often misplaced or not close by. When the correct tools were not handy, operators would use whatever tools or methods they needed to get the job done. This often resulted in shortcutting of procedures, as well as in problems for other people farther along the line. The client purchased $3,000 worth of tools and never conducted one day of training—and the problem disappeared. (Cause analysis is discussed in Chapter Seven.)

NU-KARPARTS: During the front-end assessment phase of the project, the HRD manager at Nu-Karparts included questions to determine why CSRs were not demonstrating desired behaviors when handling customer complaints. Some of these questions focused on the reward structure for a CSR. It quickly became evident that CSRs were held accountable for the number of orders taken in a day in a correct manner. Their "call span" (average length of call) was also monitored. CSRs who were considered to be meeting their job expectations had a high number of orders per day and a low call span. Effective handling of complaints was not a performance criterion. Moreover, the criteria that were important worked against taking time to handle a customer's complaint. If CSRs took the eight to ten minutes required to handle a complaint effectively, they would miss order calls, and their call span would increase.

Clearly, a lack of skills needed to be addressed, but training alone could not meet the business need of having complaint calls handled at the clerical level. Management needed to set up a new accountability system, one that would reward the handling of complaints as well as the number of orders taken.

Steps 6 and 7: Tabulate, Interpret, and Report Results to the Client. Once information has been collected, an HRD professional is in a position to really make a difference. Now is the opportunity to provide management with the results of the assessment efforts, and to do so in a manner that encourages management to take necessary action.

Too often, results from such assessment efforts are reported in a manner that tells management what the results were and what actions should be taken. This approach to feedback invites resistance on the part of the very people we want to influence, because they are not involved in identifying solutions; they are told what would be appropriate to do. Information should be provided for joint interpretation, and actions should also be jointly identified. Here is where the partnership of HRD and management really begins to pay off. (How to tabulate and report the results of front-end assessments to client managers is discussed in Chapter Eight.)

NU-KARPARTS: In a data feedback meeting with the three primary clients, the HRD manager distributed results from the assessment phase of this project. Together, the clients and the HRD manager drew conclusions from these results and identified what actions needed to be taken. Two flipcharts were used to record decisions that were made. One flipchart was for the HRD manager and indicated which training actions would be needed. The other chart was labeled *management actions*; it indicated what the clients would need to do if this project were to have a successful conclusion. As a result of this meeting, the HRD manager prepared to deliver a two-day training program on handling customer complaints. CSRs would be given ample opportunity to practice the process they would be learning. Meanwhile, management set about redesigning the accountability system to include accountability for effectively handling complaints and altered the call span average to allow for increased time in handling complaints.

Step 8: Design the Reaction and Learning Evaluation Systems. There are two ways to evaluate the actual learning experience: by obtaining information from participants about what they thought of the program (reaction evaluation) and by determining the degree to which people have learned the skills and knowledge presented in the program (learning evaluation). Our experience indicates that almost all HRD professionals provide end-of-course questionnaires, which are completed by participants and given to instructors. Our experience also indicates that, too frequently, these reaction evaluations are poorly designed and yield minimally helpful information. (In Chapter Nine, we provide several suggestions for how reaction evaluations can be made more effective.)

Learning evaluation is beginning to occur more frequently than ten years ago. Tests are one type of learning evaluation; they help instructors know the degree to which participants are learning the skills and knowledge presented in programs. Paper-and-pencil tests are commonly used for knowledge that is being learned; competency demonstrations of some type are used to determine skills acquisition. (In Chapter Ten, we offer several ideas about how to test for learning in your training programs.)

In either evaluation case—for reactions or for learning—the planning and designing of the evaluation should occur before the delivery of the training program. These evaluations should be designed concurrently with the training program itself.

NU-KARPARTS: Once a commitment had been made to deliver a training program on how to handle customer complaints, the HRD manager began designing the reaction evaluation. He used this opportunity to obtain information not only on what participants thought of the program but also on their intent to use what was learned back on the job. To assess the degree to which participants were learning the skills taught in the program, a decision was made to put the participants into practice simulations, which would be videotaped. The individual taking the role of CSR would view the tape with the instructor, to evaluate how effectively the desired skills were being demonstrated.

Step 9: Design Tracking Systems: Behavioral, Nonobservable,

and Operational Results. To determine what training program(s) will be offered to employees is to identify only the training activity that will occur. We must also have a clear view of the outcomes we expect from that activity. Outcomes are generally of three types: behavior or skills that people demonstrate on the job; nonobservable results, such as increased analytical ability in problem solving or desired changes in attitudes or values; and improved operational indicators.

Identifying these outcomes is, again, done with the clients, in a meeting. Often, these outcomes refer back to the symptoms that initiated the project in the first place. What business problem was being addressed? What business opportunity was to be maximized? Here, we must become very specific in what we identify, so that the item can be measured.

It is also important that such results be clearly identified and agreed to before the training begins. This not only ensures that training is correctly targeted and positioned but also provides the opportunity to collect pretraining, or baseline, information. Against such a baseline, posttraining information will be compared. (Chapters Eleven, Twelve, and Thirteen discuss these evaluations in depth.)

NU-KARPARTS: There was agreement that CSRs should be demonstrating such behavior as restating customers' complaints and acknowledging the feelings of customers. These could best be identified by obtaining information from CSRs, their supervisors, and a sampling of customers. Therefore, questionnaires would be sent to customers within twenty-four hours of a conversation with a CSR. Questionnaires would be completed by supervisors and CSRs just before training and again two months later.

The percentage of complaints escalating to management would also be a measurement of impact. Currently, the percentage of complaints escalating was between 4 percent and 6 percent of all complaints received. The actual amount varied from center to center. The goal set by the client was that this percentage would drop to 1 percent or less. This information would be monitored by review of documents already kept by Nu-Karparts.

Step 10: Conduct Training. We have completed nine steps before we begin to conduct any training program. In the Training-for-Impact approach, the program is positioned so that maximum impact to the organization is ensured. Such positioning requires time, but the dividends, in terms of results, are tremendous.

In this book, we will not be discussing the how-to's of delivering high-quality programs, but our omission of this subject in no way minimizes the requirement that this step be handled skillfully. Only if the learning experience is of high quality will people learn, and learning is the first requirement if results are to occur on the job.

NU-KARPARTS: A two-day program was delivered to the CSRs in each of the two distribution centers included in the pilot effort. This program was evaluated at the reaction and learning levels, as previously discussed. The reaction evaluations indicated that people valued the program and had high motivation to use what they had learned. The learning evaluation (completed by videotaping skill practices) indicated that 92 percent of the participants had successfully demonstrated skills. A few participants required some additional coaching, which was arranged for them once they returned to the job.

Step 11: Collect, Tabulate, and Interpret Evaluation and Tracking Data. If HRD professionals are to measure results from training, the process begins with the collection of baseline, pretraining information. With what frequency are learners using the desired skills or behavior (the "should," as we call it) before the training starts? What is the frequency of use some weeks or months after training has concluded? Have the values or attitudes of participants shifted in a desired direction? Are problems being resolved with more efficiency and effectiveness? These are the types of questions addressed in a tracking effort.

Moreover, if there are operational indicators to be measured, we need to determine the level of an indicator before training (baseline) and compare that to what the indicator evidences some months after training. To the degree that we can report skills being transferred to the job and operational indicators moving in the desired direction, we know that training has contributed to addressing a business need. We know that people are using what they were taught to obtain the results that we see. (In this book, how to design and draw conclusions from evaluation and tracking systems is discussed in Chapters Eleven, Twelve, and Thirteen. Chapter Eight will also prove helpful with this step.)

NU-KARPARTS: At Nu-Karparts, the results indicated that the business need had been met. As Figure 4 illustrates, the frequency with which CSRs were using the desired behaviors had increased, according to all sources of information. It was also clear that the number of complaints escalating to a manager's office had been reduced. Most complaints were now being handled by CSRs.

Step 12: Report to the Client. In this final step of the Training-for-Impact approach, results from all evaluation efforts are reported. Of particular importance to clients are results from tracking studies. Again, a process is used that involves the client in determining what the results mean and what actions (if any) are required.

NU-KARPARTS: Clients were more than satisfied with the results of this pilot effort. The director of distribution asked that the training program be provided to CSRs in all remaining distribution centers.

The Activity-Impact Continuum

Frequently when we discuss the Training-for-Impact approach, HRD professionals feel somewhat overwhelmed. We often hear the comment "It all makes sense, but how can I do all of that?" We would like to anticipate that response by indicating how we hope you would use this approach to training (see Figure 5).

Training programs characterized by all the items on the left side of the Figure 5 continuum are being implemented in the "pure" Training-for-Activity approach. By contrast, training programs implemented with all the characteristics listed on the right side of the continuum are in the "pure" Training-for-Impact approach. There are, however, many training programs that are

Figure 4. Results from Nu-Karparts Tracking Study.

	Before Training			After Training		
Behavior	CSR's Self-Report	Supervisors' Reports on CSRs	Customers' Reports on CSRs	CSR's Self-Report	Supervisors' Reports on CSRs	Customers' Reports on CSRs
1. CSRs will acknowledge the feelings of customers by labeling the feelings	3.21	2.96	2.14	4.45	4.26	4.23
2. CSRs will restate what a customer has said before rephrasing	2.93	2.62	2.54	4.16	3.98	4.03
Scale: 1 = behavior never used 2 = behavior used about 25% of time 3 = behavior used about 50% of time 4 = behavior used about 75% of time 5 = behavior used about 100% of time						
Organizational results						
Percent of complaints per month escalated to director-manager level of the organization		4%–6%			1%	

Note: In a typical tracking study, dozens of behaviors may be observed. Only two are selected here for illustration.

Figure 5. Activity-Impact Continuum.

Training for Activity	⟷	Training for Impact
Characterized by • no client • no business need • no assessment of performance effectiveness or of cause • no effort to prepare the work environment to support training • no measurement of results		Characterized by • partnership with client • link to business need • assessment of performance effectiveness and of cause • preparation of work environment to support training • measurement of results

characterized by some attributes from each side. We believe that the more a training implementation can support the characteristics of Training for Impact, the better; but it is not necessary (or possible) always to do everything. What is important is to move toward the Training-for-Impact end of the scale with as much frequency and skill as possible.

To assist you in selecting from what you read, so that your training implementations are moving toward the Training-for-Impact approach, suggestions are offered at the end of each chapter. For each summary, we have selected some of the major techniques or ideas described in the preceding chapter, and we encourage you to use one or two of them in future training projects. The more you use these ideas, the more you approximate the Training-for-Impact approach.

What will be clear (if it is not already) is that Training for Impact requires HRD professionals to view their organizational role as different from the role of professionals who use the Training-for-Activity approach. Training for Activity makes the HRD professional primarily accountable for the design and delivery of training courses; Training for Impact views the HRD professional as accountable for effective human performance. For that accountability to be realized, the professional must have skills in consulting with managers and influencing them in decisions that are relevant to human performance; diagnosing the organization and determining specific deficiencies in skills and knowledge, as well as the causes of such deficiencies (which may or may not be addressed through training); and measuring business results from training programs.

In our opinion, the effective, skillful HRD professional cannot function without skills in these three areas (or access to and use of people who have such skills). We will discuss the types of competencies required to implement the Training-for-Impact approach when we get to Chapter Fourteen. For now, let us begin discussing in depth the how-to's for each of the major components of our Training-for-Impact model (see Figure 3).

Part Two

Creating Strategic Partnerships with Management

Partnership—a relationship between two or more people, usually involving close cooperation and with each party having specified and joint rights and responsibilities: Such is our definition (somewhat supported by Webster) of this term. In HRD efforts, it is not possible to have organizational impact by yourself. HRD professionals must be partners to the key decision makers, or clients, who can contribute to the overall effort in many key ways. When such a partnership is skillfully developed, then the formula of 1 + 1 = 3 really holds true. In essence, each member of the partnership accomplishes more than either member could have alone.

In the next three chapters, we describe in depth how to identify both a business need and the owners of the business need (the people we call clients) as well as how to form partnerships with these people so that organizational impact from training programs is virtually ensured.

Three

Identifying Business Needs and Clients

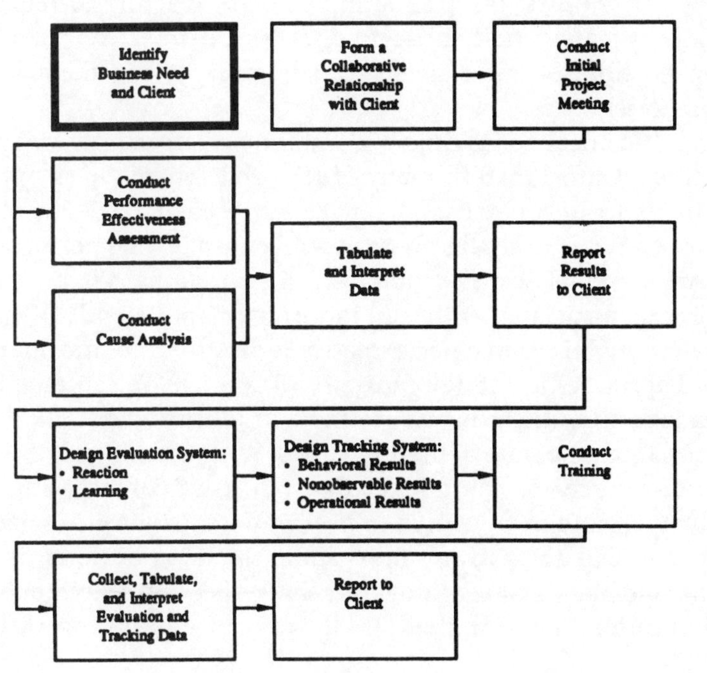

As HRD professionals, we learn of potential training needs in a variety of ways. Some of these take the form of requests. For example, a senior manager calls to say that all sales personnel need to learn how to close sales calls more effectively. Our boss may indicate that she wants all customer contact people to learn skills in the handling of complaints, or perhaps a new corporate appraisal system is about to be implemented, and the human resources department has indicated that all supervisors must learn how to use it.

Sometimes we identify a pattern of symptoms or problems that alerts us that a training need may be developing. For example, every time people attend the midlevel management program, we hear a request for training on influencing skills. Again, when working with people on one project, we learn of their lack of knowledge regarding a new product that was just launched, and we decide to bring this lack of knowledge to management's attention. Further, when we review productivity reports, we may see that output is declining, and so we decide to investigate.

In the first three situations, we are reacting to requests made by managers; in the second set, we are proactively identifying possible business needs and then exploring them more completely.

Business needs can be identified both reactively and proactively. Unfortunately, many HRD professionals miss opportunities to be proactive. To make sure that we do not allow opportunities to slip away, we should constantly be performing environmental scans of our own organizations. We can read journals associated with our industry to spot trends. We can review organizational performance indicators and information to determine how the organization is doing. We can take line managers to lunch or just see them at meetings and ask questions about the state of their business. We can volunteer to serve on task forces or committees that put us in contact with line managers and in a position to hear of potential business needs. We can read and ask questions about the organization's vision, strategic plan, new ventures, and challenges and search out the implications for training. Finally, we can question workshop participants at breaks and at lunch to find out what business challenges they are facing.

Acknowledging that business needs can be identified both reactively and proactively, we find they also come in two "flavors": business opportunities to be maximized and business problems to be solved.

Business opportunities are future-focused and deal with something about to happen. For instance, the organization may be opening a new agency, and people will need to be trained to operate the office and serve the public; or perhaps the organization is about to invest in high-tech equipment and will need trained operators and troubleshooters. The hiring of new employees is also an opportunity, since management will need them to be trained so they can perform effectively in as little time as practical.

Business problems, in contrast, are past-focused. Some quality or quantity of output problem has caught management's attention. Perhaps waste is too high, or output is too low. Perhaps the number of customer complaints has increased, or turnover has risen. Whatever the situation, management is examining the current trend and is feeling that a change is required. Management is interested in identifying the cause of the problem and finding a solution for it.

Managers often do not call us with a business problem. Rather, they call with a solution and request a specific training program. A frequent request is for time management; it seems to be the cure for many performance ills. This is when it is important to probe and find out what business need is driving the request. What performance problems have been identified? Is there an upcoming organizational change driving this training request? The HRD professional interested in using a Training-for-Impact approach must look beyond the request for training and uncover what business need is driving that request. (We discuss how to do this in Chapter Five.)

Once we know what the business need is, we can position training as an activity that will meet it. What do we mean by the term *position*? The following two situations will illustrate the difference between just implementing a training program and using training to meet a business need. Each of these situations actually happened. We will let you judge which one would more probably result in organizational impact.

SITUATION 1: A training director of a large corporation went to a national conference and viewed a program on influencing skills. She knew that influencing was being discussed a great deal as a skill required for success. She had heard of the vendor's reputation and believed this program to be thorough. Upon her return to her office, she encouraged her boss (the vice-president of human resources) to take a look at the program. A sales representative came to call and provided information on the program. Both the training director and the vice-president agreed that the program would develop influencing skills. They decided to bring it into the organization. The program was put into the training catalogue, and people could now register to attend it.

SITUATION 2: A training director in a different organization was contacted by some executives. It seems this organization had just spent two years and a great deal of money to reform its previous functional structure into lines of business. Each of the lines of business would be held accountable for its own profits. There would no longer be a central marketing function; rather, there would be marketing professionals in each line of business. This would also be true of other functions, such as manufacturing and distribution. These executives were now ready to put the new structure into operation and wondered what new skills would be required for people to perform successfully. Further analysis indicated that the ability to influence people was one of the skills that would be needed. People could no longer rely on the use of legitimate organizational authority to get things done. To be effective, managers and staff specialists would need to influence people over whom they had no direct authority. A decision was made to offer a program on influencing.

In Situation 1, the training director and her manager made a decision about what the organization needed in the way of skills. There was no clear business need driving the decision to offer the program. This is a Training-for-Activity approach and has low probability of providing organizational impact. In Situation 2, the training director worked with executives to maximize a business opportunity—specifically, to ensure that the new organizational structure would succeed. Situation 2 exemplifies the Training-for-Impact approach and has a good probability of yielding organizational results. Not only is there a client with a vested interest in the program, but those who attend it also understand the business purpose for the skills.

Even though you have successfully identified the business need behind a request for training, you should be aware of two risks. First, do not assume that the request for training is based on correctly identified training needs. Moving directly from a request to design and delivery can be dangerous. Front-end assessments are vital if you wish to avoid offering the wrong training to the wrong people. (How to obtain line management's support for such assessments, as well as how to conduct them, is discussed in Chapters Five, Six, and Seven of this book.) Second, do not assume that the individual who has contacted you about the training is the appropriate and only client for it. While our initial contact is usually a person important to the project, it would be unusual if this individual were our only client. Misidentifying the client in this manner can prove disastrous. The following example, which we encountered while one of us was working as the manager of training and development for a *Fortune* 500 firm, may help illustrate this.

The Case of the Misidentified Client

One day, two directors from the sales department of this organization contacted us and requested that a training program be developed for all district managers. In a meeting with these directors, it was learned that the training effort would focus on Equal Employment Opportunity issues and would have to be delivered when the district managers attended a sales meeting, scheduled in eight weeks.

During this initial meeting, we helped the directors see

the benefit of taking time to investigate the need more completely. What were the most common issues faced by managers in this area? What specific learning objectives should be agreed on for the program? What types of organizationally specific content could be incorporated so that the cases and exercises were job-relevant? A front-end assessment would address these types of questions. The directors agreed that gathering more information would be helpful, but they placed two conditions on this assessment effort. First, because the program had to be delivered within eight weeks, the data would have to be collected quickly. It was agreed that on-site interviews would be held with a sampling of appropriate people and that all information would be reported in three weeks. Second, while four groups of people potentially had information of relevance to this project, the directors asked that a sample from only three of these groups be interviewed. They questioned the quality of the data that could be obtained from this fourth group, and they saw some risks to involving those people.

These parameters were agreed to, and approximately forty people were interviewed within the agreed time span. The data were then analyzed, and a report was readied for the directors. Just before this meeting, we received a call from the vice-president of sales, the person to whom the two directors reported. He asked why no one from the fourth group of people had been interviewed. He said that without the buy-in and support of this group, the project would not be successful and could not be continued.

Immediately after that call, we interviewed a sample of people from this fourth group over the telephone, and we integrated their data into the final report. This report was made to a client team of three – the two directors and the vice-president of sales – and the project moved forward. Nevertheless, because we had assumed that our initial contacts were the clients, the project almost met a premature end. What we learned is that misidentifying the client can prove fatal. We cannot overemphasize the importance of determining the true client for the business need and the training project. Let us discuss how to identify the true client.

Identifying Your Client

A client for any training project that is being implemented to meet business needs and yield organizational results must meet two criteria.

1. The individual must have legitimate organizational authority to make a decision on implementing the training project in question. If displeased, this individual can stop the project in its tracks. If pleased, this person can extend and expand it.
2. The individual must have a need to be involved in and make decisions regarding the strategic implementation of this training project.

It is possible that more than one person will meet both of these criteria, and so a client team will be formed. We urge that client teams be limited to six or fewer people, because decisions must be reached through consensus, which is difficult with large groups of people. For ease of writing, however, we will refer to the client singularly.

It is essential that a client meet both criteria. Thus, when determining who has authority, you typically go to the top of the organization in which the training will be implemented. If the program is to build clinical skills in nurses, all of whom report to the department of nursing, then the client could be the top person in the nursing department. Should the project be offered throughout an organization to people from several different departments, however, the client could be the organization's chief operating officer or its most senior officer.

To determine who the client specifically is, we must also determine whether this person meets the second criterion: having a need to be involved in and make decisions regarding the strategic implementation of the project. Sometimes the answer is yes; sometimes the answer is no. When no is the response, we have not found our client. We must continue down the organizational chain until we reach the person who meets both criteria.

Client Characteristics

Over the years, we have found that internal clients tend to have similar characteristics. While titles and positions may change, most internal clients share in these descriptors.

1. *The client is usually two or more levels above the learners.* Typically, clients are in the middle to upper levels of management in an organization and carry the title of director, manager, or even vice-president. They are the people who have the legitimate authority to stop the project if it is not meeting their needs. They are also the people who can make such decisions as changing the reward system of the learners to support the skills to be taught, if such decisions are required. They can make strategic decisions that allow the training project to provide positive organizational results.

Why are learners not clients? Learners lack the organizational authority to make the strategic decisions necessary to any training project that will have organizational impact. Because they can control their own involvement and use of skills, their input must be solicited during front-end assessment. In reality, their role is more as customers than as clients.

What about the bosses of learners—are they clients? Here, the span of control and the legitimate organizational authority of the bosses are often too limited. They can make decisions regarding the involvement of their direct subordinates, but these participants are usually few in number compared to all who may attend a program. It is wise to involve bosses of learners in the project implementation, because they must be developed to coach and reinforce the skills being taught. Like learners, bosses rarely have the necessary authority to make organizational decisions (such as modifying the reward system) that may be required during the life of the project.

One implication of this characteristic is that HRD professionals often work with clients who are higher in the organizational structure than they are. What is being developed here is a business partnership: For the life of this project, the people involved are partners, equally concerned about accomplishing results and equally responsible for ensuring that they do.

2. *The client must approve significant actions associated with the training project.* Imagine that you have agreed to design and deliver a training program that will build decision-making skills in seventy-five supervisors. The initial commitment is to take supervisors off the job for sixteen hours of training.

Now that you are designing the program, you have determined that insufficient skill building will result if the program is limited to sixteen hours. In fact, twenty-four hours will be required if sufficient skill building is to occur. Whom would you need to influence—and who would have the authority to approve a decision—to have all seventy-five supervisors attend the program for the eight additional hours? This is an example of a significant decision, and this is how you begin to identify your client.

3. *The client is the "owner" of the business need that is driving the request for training, and the client has the most to gain or lose from this effort.* For clients to be willing to invest the time required, there must be something in it for them. The business need being addressed must offer the client an opportunity to solve a problem or maximize an opportunity. This way, the client has something to gain if the project goes well and, conversely, something to lose if the project founders.

As an HRD professional interested in Training for Impact, you must be certain that the training project is linked to a business need. If this link is not apparent, then you must work to establish it. Who in your organization has something to gain if customer complaints are reduced? Who really cares if products meet quality standards? Who is really interested in improving service to customers? Asking and answering these types of questions help identify the client of the project.

4. *While client teams can involve others, someone in the client group must be in the chain of command of the learners.* In Chapter Two, we presented the formula for training results:

Learning Experience × Work Environment = Business Results

The HRD professional has much control over the "learning experience" side of this equation—for example, determining the learning design and conducting the training. The client in the chain of command of the learners controls the "work environment" side of this equation. If an accountability system must be altered or if bosses of learners must be developed to coach and reinforce the new skills, only a client can ensure that those things will happen. If training is to have an impact on business needs, those who have control over the learning experience and those who can change the work environment must work together as partners.

Sometimes people outside the learners' chain of command should belong to the client team. If the training includes human resources issues, someone from the human resources function may need to be included; for technical training, the vendor or someone from engineering may be needed.

5. *The client receives all reports regarding the project.* It is interesting to note how often training reports go to the manager of the training function and stop there. What about those people who ultimately benefit from the training efforts? What reports are they given? Clients should be supplied with information pertinent to the training project, and then they should be offered the opportunity to make decisions in light of this information. (Reporting information to clients in a manner that prompts them to take action is described in Chapter Eight.)

These characteristics are designed as general (not absolute) rules. They should provide you with some guidance in determining your client, but there may be instances in which some of these characteristics will not apply. For instance, if you report to the vice-president of production, and all the learners are in production, your client will always be your direct manager. In a small company, it is possible that the direct managers of the learners will be your clients. What is crucial is to consider the two identification criteria as you determine who is your client. Does the person meet both criteria? If so, you are probably where you need to be.

The Situational Element

When you link training to business needs, each training effort may have a different client, because your client is the "owner" of the business need. For instance, the vice-president of sales may be your client for sales training. At the same time, the director of marketing may be your client for a project to provide his staff with skills in market research. Both may be your clients for a training effort that deals with the introduction of a new product line.

Clients often change during a project. Early in the life cycle of the project, a need may emerge for certain individuals to be closely associated with the project, yet once the decisions involving those people have been made, they may leave the project, and others may enter. Recall that using the two identification criteria—authority and a need to be involved in strategic decisions—results in a client team that evolves and changes as the nature of the strategic decisions changes. Generally, however, one or two people will remain in the project's client group throughout the life of the project.

Methods for Identifying True Clients

From working with hundreds of HRD professionals, we know that identifying and gaining agreement to work with the true client are not always easy. We are often contacted by someone who, while crucial to the project, is not the only individual with whom we should be partnered. In such situations, it is vital to think through who the client is and then formulate a strategy to work face to face with that person.

Certain methods have proved useful both in identifying and in obtaining permission to work with true clients. Some of these methods are direct: You openly request the opportunity to work with someone who is not now a member of the client team. Other methods are indirect: you gather information about potential clients or increase the visibility of the project. Consider the people with whom you are currently working to determine which method would be right for your situation.

Direct Methods

1. Ask your contact if there are any other people who should be involved in meetings associated with this project.

2. Ask your contact if a specific individual (name that person) should be involved in meetings for this project. Note the benefits of including that person.
3. Indicate your concern at not including the necessary individual(s) in meetings regarding this project.
4. Listen for a name that is being mentioned often by your contact as someone with opinions regarding this project. Consider the organizational level of this person. Ask if that person should be included in project meetings.
5. If there has been a time when a project ran into difficulty because a certain individual was not involved, remind your contact of that shared history. Encourage your contact to have this person more directly involved in the project now.

Indirect Methods

1. Ask questions that will determine whether there is any other individual to whom your contact is reporting information about this project. If there is, discuss the advantages of involving this person more directly.
2. Select a significant meeting associated with the project, and encourage your contact to invite the true client. Often, in attending such a meeting, the true client becomes vested in the project and decides to remain active.
3. If your contact needs the approval of another person on major project decisions, discuss with your contact the feasibility of inviting that person to be a member of the client team.
4. After each meeting regarding the project, write a memo summarizing the meeting's outcomes and the actions that are planned. Send a copy to the true client. Should that individual review these memos, it is likely that the client will come to understand the types of decisions being made and will develop an interest in contributing to those decisions.

Often, HRD professionals are not associated with appropriate clients because line managers have formed expectations about what training is and how it will be implemented. Managers may assume that training means putting together a program and conducting a workshop. This is the Training-for-Activity approach.

When you investigate a training situation from the Training-for-Impact approach, you start to ask questions that may not have been raised before. For example, you pose questions about the business need that drives the request for training, and you determine which business outcomes are expected as a result of training. These are questions that true clients have an interest in addressing. They will want their opinions heard. Getting clients interested in how training can help to meet business needs is essential if you wish to use a Training-for-Impact approach. Thus, from the start, you approach the situation not as a training request but as a request to meet a business need.

Clientless Situations

One of the tough questions you should always ask when faced with a potential new training project is "Who is the client for this project?" If you honestly answer this question, there will be times when you determine that no one is the client. There is no one individual or group of individuals in the chain of command of the learners who cares whether outcomes occur or who will have something to gain from it.

Projects listed in training catalogues are often clientless and exemplify this situation. Training catalogues are often published once or twice a year. They list many corporate training programs for which individuals may nominate themselves or that their supervisors may suggest that they attend. While the programs are often designed to build skills that participants can apply on their current jobs, the programs are frequently detached from any clear business need. They are offered for one or more of the following reasons: Everyone agrees that they are needed; they have been offered for several years, with people attending, and so they must be important; according to current literature, the topic is of importance to business; and similar businesses offer the courses.

What is missing is any link to clear business outcomes that could be derived from the skills and knowledge taught. Without such links, how can there be a client? Who would see any benefit in spending time making strategic implementation decisions about a training program that does not provide clear benefits to the business? Who has anything to gain or lose from the training efforts?

We do not mean to say that all catalogue courses are doomed to low—or no—results. We do believe, however, that when you are facing a clientless situation, you should consider one of the following actions.

1. Work to formulate a client team. Whom can you approach, and what benefits can you offer for having someone work with you in this manner?
2. Reassess the business need for this program. Is the need still present, or has it changed over the life of the program? With some modification, can the program be tied more directly to a current business problem or opportunity?
3. Consider eliminating the program. Would people really miss it if it disappeared from the catalogue?

Clientless programs are inherent in the Training-for-Activity approach. If you want to implement a Training-for-Impact approach, one that ensures that measurable results for the organization will occur, then having a client will be a requirement.

Identifying a business need and the client who "owns" that need is only the first step in the initial phase of a Training-for-Impact approach. You must now become a consultant and work with the client in a manner that maximizes the contribution of each person (client and HRD professional) involved in the project. A relationship must be forged with the client so that mutual influence and support can be achieved. (We will discuss the how-to's of effective HRD-client partnerships in Chapter Four.)

Summary

The following techniques move training toward impact:

Activity **Impact**

- Environmentally scan your organization to uncover potential business needs and challenges.
- Look for business opportunities as well as business problems to link to training.
- Use these two criteria to determine whether you are dealing with the true client: (1) Does the person have the authority to make decisions regarding this project? (2) Does the person have a need to be involved in decisions regarding the implementation of the project?
- Check your current course offerings to determine which ones may be clientless. Develop a plan to formulate client relationships with members of management who benefit from such programs.

Four

Forming a Collaborative Relationship with Clients

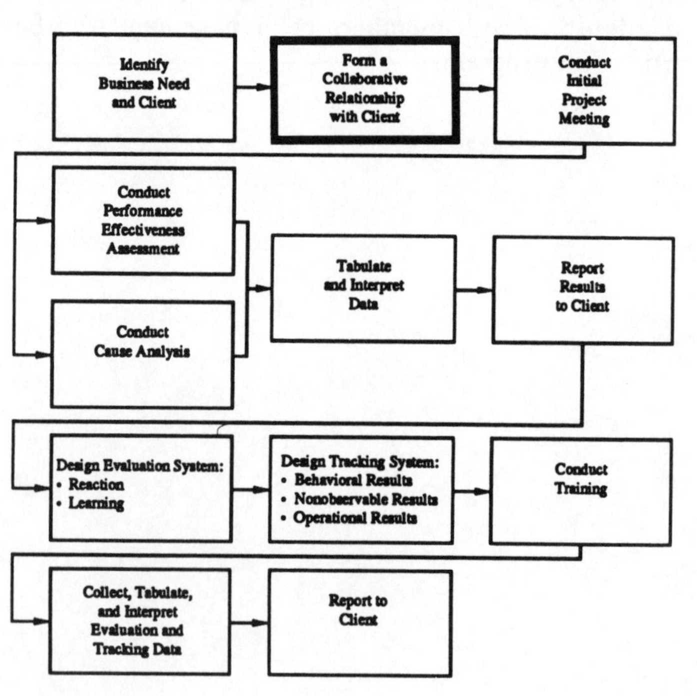

In positioning a training project so that it is linked to a business need, the HRD professional must form a consulting relationship with the client. This approach to training means that working with the client is more like a marriage than a date.

Much of the literature in the HRD field indicates that there are people who do training and there are people who do consulting. It is as though those processes are separate. In our opinion, they are totally interdependent and connected. We define consulting as a synergistic process by which the expertise of each party is maximized through the dynamics of working together. Successful consulting is a 1 + 1 = 3, where two parties working together can accomplish more than each could individually. How can HRD professionals strategically implement training efforts that result in organizational impact without consulting with the very people who have the most to gain or lose from those efforts? HRD professionals do not have the organizational authority to make changes in the work environment. Instead, they must work collaboratively with their clients. This also is part of the consulting process.

Finally, the HRD professional will need to ask the right questions in the right ways throughout the life cycle of the project. Asking questions is a competency required for the consulting process. When you put it all together—the need to influence, to ask high-yield questions, to maximize the expertise of both the HRD professional and the line manager—consulting must occur during the life of the training project. Your skills as a consultant will be as important to the success of the project as your skills as a trainer. Your training skills will ensure that the learning experience is good; your skills as a consultant will ensure that the work environment will support the new skills.

This chapter focuses on the skills required to consult successfully with your clients during a Training-for-Impact endeavor. Before we begin to discuss the styles, we encourage you to complete the style inventory displayed in Exhibit 1 at the end of this chapter. This inventory will assist you in identifying how you now consult with your line management. Once you have completed the inventory, we will meet you back here and begin describing the various consulting styles possible. We will also show you how you can interpret your own score.

Consulting Styles

We owe a debt of gratitude to Block (1981), whose work has assisted us in thinking through all that is required if an HRD professional is to effectively consult with clients when linking training to business needs. What follows is a summation of Block's work, with some additions of our own.

There are three major consulting styles that an HRD professional can use: the expert style, the pair-of-hands style, and the collaborator style.

Expert Style. The following conversation depicts the first approach.

Client-Manager: My area of responsibility has many project teams. What I've noticed is that the team meetings are long and unproductive, and I find that many team members lose their commitment to the project over time. What do you suggest to correct these problems?

HRD Professional: It sounds as if your project team leaders lack skills in meeting management, as well as the skills needed to build strong team commitment. I know just the training program for those team leaders. . . .

The HRD professional has put on the hat of the expert, identifying the cause of the problem (lack of skill on the part of project team leaders) and the solution (training of the team leaders).

This consulting style has several advantages.

1. The HRD professional retains a great deal of control. The HRD professional decides what needs to be done, how, and when. When HRD professionals are experienced in the topic being offered, their experience-based decisions can move the project in the right direction.

2. It feels good to be seen as an expert by client-managers, and there is certainly no harm in having one's self-esteem enhanced.
3. The time needed to implement training can be reduced. There is no need for several meetings with managers to make decisions. The HRD professional can make those decisions, and so time is saved.

There are also disadvantages associated with this style.

1. There is risk of low or no support from managers for decisions they were not involved in making. As an expert, the HRD professional recommends actions to management. It is not unusual for managers to verbally agree to actions but have no emotional investment in those actions. Over time, the degree of management support often declines. Client-managers may react to the expert's recommendations by saying, "Yes, but. . . ." How many times have you seen recommendations presented and then ending up in a drawer, never to be acted on?
2. Making an inaccurate diagnosis becomes more probable. As good as the HRD professional may be, he or she is still approaching the performance and organizational issues from an HRD perspective, not from the perspective of the line manager. Therefore, there is too great a chance that the HRD professional may inaccurately interpret a situation or overlook an important factor and thus make a wrong decision about the project.
3. The client-manager accepts no responsibility for results from the training effort. This may be the greatest risk associated with the expert consulting style. Because the client-manager is inactive throughout the project and is looking to the HRD professional to make the decisions, the client-manager often feels little ownership of the project. Should the project not produce the desired results, the HRD professional is in a vulnerable position, easily blamed for the failure. The role of the client-manager in this scenario is often that of an evaluator and judge.

Pair-of-Hands Style. The expert style can be contrasted with that of the pair-of-hands consultant through a review of this conversation.

Client-Manager: I'm having a problem here. My supervisors don't manage their time well, largely because they are not delegating very often. They continue to do too much of the work themselves and get bogged down in details. I know that you have that two-day course on delegation. I'd like you to run it for my supervisors the week after next.

HRD Professional: I'll be glad to. Either I or a member of the staff will call to make final arrangements.

In this situation, the client-manager has determined what the problem is (supervisors do not delegate often enough) and what the solution should be (put them into a training program on delegation). The HRD professional becomes an implementer of those decisions and is a "pair of hands" to the client.

There are advantages to this role.

1. The HRD professional is relieved of decision-making responsibility. The client-manager has taken over the decision making, and so the HRD professional does not need to.
2. The HRD professional appears to be responsive and supportive of management decisions. Conducting the program requested by the client-manager, the HRD professional is viewed as being responsive and supportive.
3. The time needed to implement training is reduced. Again, because the decision making is handled by one person, the response time is reduced.

There are also disadvantages to the pair-of-hands style.

1. The situation may be inaccurately diagnosed. Offering a training program based on the analysis of a client-manager can be quite dangerous. There is a greater chance that supervisors attending the program on delegation will say, "I

already know how to do this" or "Why are you teaching me these skills? There is no way I can delegate with the production problems we have in our department."

2. The probability of the training's being implemented without a link to a business need is high. Rarely does a client-manager phone and say, "Here is my business need." Rather, the request is more likely to be "Please deliver a course." To the degree that the HRD professional responds to that request, training becomes the end result. When the program has been delivered, the contract is complete. This is a Training-for-Activity approach. There is no attempt by the HRD professional to link the training to a business need.
3. The parameters placed on the training may be unrealistic. By agreeing to provide a training program without at least making an effort to better assess the situation, the HRD professional implicitly endorses the belief that sending poor performers to a workshop will turn them into good performers. The client-manager may want skills developed but wants fifty people in each class; or the client-manager establishes time constraints ("You can have my people for only one day") that prevent adequate skills from being developed during the training. The pair-of-hands role encourages that type of client-manager behavior.
4. The HRD professional is in a position to be blamed when results do not occur. Once again, the client-manager has not accepted accountability for results. The client in this example did take on the responsibility of assessing the need and determining what kind of training was needed. At that point, the HRD professional scheduled and conducted the training and in so doing accepted accountability for the project. Should the training effort not provide the desired results, the client-manager is in a position to blame the HRD professional for conducting ineffective training.

Collaborator Style. In this approach, the HRD professional and the client-manager are viewed as equal partners in diagnosing the problem and determining the solution. Consider this scenario.

Client-Manager: The reject rate on line 24 is increasing each week. It is now .5 percent above standard. Do you think training could help?

HRD Professional: What do you think is the cause of the problem? Could the equipment be defective in some manner . . . the raw materials of poor quality? Or do you think it is the operators? Could they be having some difficulty?

Client-Manager: I'm not certain, although I doubt that the equipment is defective. I would have heard about that. Could you look into it for me and see what you find? I'd like us to decide what we should be doing to correct the problem.

HRD Professional: I'd like to look into it. Let's get together and see what we can find out about the problem.

In this situation, the client-manager seeks the HRD professional's assistance as an equal, to determine both the cause and the possible solutions to a performance problem. There is no initial expectation that a training program will be the answer. Each person is bringing professional knowledge and expertise to the situation to maximize the probability of a correct diagnosis and solution.

There are several advantages to this style.

1. There is joint accountability for results. In the collaborator style, both individuals indicate through words and behavior that they will take responsibility for project results. Both the learning experience and the work environment are being managed by a person interested in getting results. Decisions about the project are jointly made, and actions are carried out by the person responsible for that area.
2. The HRD professional and the client-manager learn from each other. During the life of the training project, much influencing takes place in both directions. The HRD professional learns about the business objectives and challenges of the unit, and the client-manager learns about what must be done if results from a training effort are to materialize.

Such learning is generic in the sense that each person retains that increased knowledge, to be used when future projects come along.

3. The probability of accurate diagnosis is increased. Because input from both the HRD professional (representing expertise in people development) and the client-manager (representing expertise in the environment of the business) is used, there is an increased probability that accurate diagnosis will occur and that appropriate decisions will be made.
4. The probability that training will be linked to a business need is high. Working in the collaborator style, the HRD professional asks several questions of the client-manager to further clarify and verify the need for training. During this process, information is shared about business needs, problems, and opportunities. The training can then be positioned to address the business need. Thus, the scope of the project will shift away from training as an activity and toward training as a vehicle for accomplishing business results.
5. There is an increased probability that management's reinforcement for the training effort will occur. Now that the client-manager is actively involved in making decisions regarding any training effort, there is a good probability that the manager will want to reinforce those decisions. Certainly, the manager's involvement in the project will communicate a message to people who attend the program: that this specific training effort is important.

Of course, there are also disadvantages to this style of consulting.

1. Client-managers who want HRD professionals to act as experts may see the collaborator role as nonresponsive. As a collaborator, the HRD professional typically seeks input from others and includes others in the making of decisions. Even though the decisions may be better, this approach requires more time and delays responses. The client-

manager may view the delayed response time as a result of nonresponsiveness.

2. Client-managers who want HRD professionals to act as pairs of hands will view their efforts to become collaborators as insubordination. The client-manager may challenge the HRD professional who is seeking additional input to decisions already made: "Are you questioning my judgment?"
3. This role increases the staff time needed to complete the project. The collaborator style is to consulting what the participative approach is to management: It requires more time, because the input of all key players is sought. It entails meetings, collection of information, and negotiation of differences. There is no way to enter a training project under the collaborator style and show up in one week with a training program.

Interpreting Your Score

Before we proceed with our discussion on these styles, it may be beneficial to review your own score on the style inventory. The (a) statements in this inventory depict the expert style, the (b) statements reflect the pair-of-hands style, and the (c) statements represent the collaborator style. By looking at the total point values you have for each of these categories, you can determine what percentage of time you now spend using each of the three styles.

If your responses are similar to those on the more than 2,500 completed inventories we have seen, your expert-style score is the highest value, your collaborator-style score is next highest, and your pair-of-hands–style score is the lowest. As a profession, we have developed a body of expertise. Many of the people in HRD today have advanced degrees, and we are viewed by our management as the experts in human resources development. Our style reflects how we behave, not how much we know. We can be experts in HRD but still work collaboratively with management. Our challenge is to use our expertise in a collaborative manner. We must form partnerships with line management, so that we can be seen both as a viable resource for solving business problems and maximizing opportunities and as a vital resource for the development of people.

Implications for Linking Training to Business Needs

We believe that, in any one year, HRD professionals will need to work in each of the three consulting styles already described. We know that is true for us. There are times each year when we are asked to deliver a particular program for a group of people. The decision has already been made that certain individuals need this program. We know we can deliver it well, and we agree to do so. We are acting as a pair of hands to our clients in these cases. They have identified the problem and determined the solution; we implement the training. We expect that some learning will occur, and we also hope for some results, but we do not know whether results actually materialize. We do not delude ourselves that ours is anything other than a pair-of-hands role.

There are times when we find ourselves in the expert role during a project. For example, there was a client for whom we were designing a customized training program for the organization's middle-level managers. In order to ensure that the program would be on target, we did the front-end assessment of needs. Typically, our style for reporting the information to a client is to provide the results of our assessment and then determine with the client what those results mean (this collaborative style of data feedback is described in Chapter Eight). This client, however, insisted that we tell him not only what the results were but also what they meant and what should be done as a result. To meet his expectations, we used an expert approach to data feedback.

Our point in reviewing these three styles is not to indicate that the collaborator style is the only one worth using; we are saying that if you want to link your training efforts to a business need, and if you want to ensure that the work environment will support the skills you are about to build, and if you want to do all that is possible to ensure that the training will yield organizational results, then you must work as an equal partner with your clients, in a collaborative style. If working as an expert or a pair of hands is the only option available, then do the best job possible, but realize that the probability of dealing with and resolving a business need would be greater if you were working collaboratively.

One additional point: If your personal score on the style inventory indicates that most of your time is spent as an expert or a pair of hands, you may want to consider how to change. Efforts toward spending the majority of your time collaboratively with management would probably yield results over the next few years. With the insight you now have regarding your own consulting style, let us look more completely at the collaborator style.

An In-Depth Look

In many ways, the collaborator style of consulting requires greater expertise than the expert style. In either role, HRD professionals must have knowledge about both the HRD profession and the organizations in which they are working. As a collaborator, however, the HRD professional must also have skills to influence others over whom there is no direct authority and to consult with others about what they must do to achieve results from the training project.

What concerns people who consider using the collaborator style is that the professional must be willing to release some control over HRD decisions. This release means that some decisions may be made in a different manner than the HRD professional may desire. To the degree that the HRD consultant is skillful in influencing and developing others, these decisions can be mutually beneficial, but there is no doubt that collaboration means letting go of some control.

Being collaborative does not mean, however, that every decision with the client is made in a fifty-fifty manner. There will be some decisions for which the HRD professional will have more responsibility (for example, program design decisions). There will be decisions in which the client's input will have greater weight (who should attend the program, for example). What is true about the collaborator style is that, with respect to all decisions made during the life of the project, there is input from both parties and a sharing of decision-making authority. Consequently, there are better decisions.

It may seem obvious that the collaborator style is preferable if training efforts are to have organizational impact. What is less obvious is how to move into the collaborator style when management wants the HRD professional to use one of the other two styles. As you start to work with your clients, it is important to do three things.

1. Determine which style you are using now. Look to your own behavior to be your guide for making this decision. If you are often expected to follow directives, you are probably acting as a pair of hands. If you are in the position of telling managers what should be done, you are probably working as an expert. You need to know which style you are using before you can develop a good strategy for moving away from it.
2. Determine whether the style you are now using is appropriate to the situation. As we indicated, there are times when the pair-of-hands style is the best option. For example, when the requesting manager has promised that a training program will be conducted in two weeks, it is important to that manager that training take place on time. Responding to that request as a pair of hands by providing the best program would be a wise course of action. There are also times when the expert style is your best option. If the client-manager is unwilling to accept any responsibility for the project and firmly indicates a desire to have little involvement with it, then accepting the role of expert is the best alternative.
3. If you determine that a move into the collaborator style is possible and worth attempting, then consider using the techniques that follow. Remember, it takes two people agreeing to a style for it to become operative. Thus, when you

work in the pair-of-hands or the expert style, you essentially agree to do so.

From Pair of Hands to Collaborator

1. Request a meeting with the client-manager. In this meeting, ask several predeveloped questions designed to raise the awareness that to implement the training now could be premature. Possible questions are "What are the causes of. . .?" or "Does this happen all the time, or only infrequently?" The more often your client must respond to questions with "I don't know" or "I'm uncertain," the better. You can then comment on that insufficient information and indicate the value of collecting more data before making a final decision regarding any training program. You are also moving toward becoming a part of the decision-making process.
2. Comment on a recent situation of which both you and your client are aware and in which a training program was developed for a misidentified need, so that problems arose during the project. Indicate your concern about moving ahead too quickly and without adequate information.
3. Help the client-manager articulate expected outcomes for the project. What business need, problem, or opportunity does the client want to address? To the degree that you can assist the client in clarifying such wants, build on that common vision. Indicate that those outcomes are achievable but that it is crucial to obtain adequate information to ensure that the training will be on track. If your client indicates that the request is for training activity only, and not for business results, continue using the pair-of-hands style and provide the training program.

Moving from Expert to Collaborator

1. Do not bite when your client says, in word or deed, "You're the expert—tell me what should be done here." Instead, indicate that while you do have expertise and a point of

view, it is crucial to get the input from this client and others who live and work every day in the area targeted for training. Stress that multiple sources of data will result in an accurate diagnosis of the causes of the problem. Stress that you need the client-manager to review the data and to decide with you on the training need.

2. In presenting your client with information about the problem, do not tell your client what that information means and what should be done in light of it. Rather, present the data and then ask your client what she or he thinks they mean. This interactive approach to data feedback (discussed more completely in Chapter Eight) is crucial in the early stages of a project if you wish to avoid using the expert style.
3. Rather than arriving at a meeting with a proposal for what should be done, come with a series of questions to ask your client. These should be awareness-raising questions: "What factors, other than training, are affecting. . .?" (In Chapter Five, we discuss the use of awareness questions in greater detail.) The outcomes of your posing these questions should be an acknowledgment of your expertise and a joint interest in moving forward collaboratively to resolve the tough issues raised during the meeting.
4. Use a give-and-get approach to move toward collaboration. If the client has requested information about a training program, be sure to investigate it even if you doubt that the program will be helpful. In this manner, you are giving, and you then have the right to ask for things in return (such as time to investigate other programs that may produce better options). This give-and-get approach can be the first step toward collaborative work.

Where are we in the process of linking training to business needs? We have a situation that may require training. We have identified the person (or people) with whom we will need to work—our client. We have determined that we must form a collaborative relationship with that client. The next step in this process is the initial project meeting. This important meeting is pivotal in determining the thrust of the project—Training for Impact or Training for Activity.

Summary

The following techniques move training toward impact:

Activity **Impact**

- Diagnose the style that you are using for each major project.
- Determine whether that style is the best one for the situation.
- If the answer is no, develop a strategy for influencing the client-manager; that is, develop a list of awareness-raising questions and plan how you will express these issues to your client.
- Meet with the client-manager to reach agreement on how the two of you will work together during the project.

Exhibit 1. Style Inventory.

Instructions for Completing the Style Inventory

1. This inventory describes ten situations that commonly occur during implementation of training projects. For each one, you are provided three options from which to select.
2. Read each question, and focus on how you now work with your line management in these situations.
3. The term *line management* refers to any line managers with whom you might work during a training project. They may or may not be clients as we have defined that term, but they are in the chain of command of the people whom you train.
4. For each situation, you have ten points that you must allocate among the three options provided. For example, if option (a) describes how you now work about 60 percent of the time, you should allocate six points to it; if option (b) describes how you work 30 percent of the time, it should be given three points. Option (c) would then have to be given one point, because the points must total ten for all three options.
5. You may distribute these ten points in any manner; a combination of 10-0-0 would be acceptable. Allocate the points to represent how you now work with line management on training projects, rather than how you would like to work.
6. If you read of a situation that you have never experienced, disregard it and move on.
7. Once you have responded to all relevant situations, total the point values in each column at the bottom of the page. Then turn to the scoring instructions.

Style Inventory

	A	*B*	*C*
1. When I work with line management on training and development problems, what generally happens is: a. Management looks to me to develop solutions. b. Management has its own solutions and expects me to follow its directions. c. Management and I work together to develop solutions.			
2. In determining the type of training that is needed, what generally happens is: a. I indicate to line management that a specific type of training is needed. b. Line management determines the training program that is needed and tells me. c. Line management and I jointly make decisions about the type of training needed.			

Exhibit 1. Style Inventory, Cont'd.

	A	B	C
3. In determining the content for a training program: a. I generally determine the content of the training program. b. Management knows what content it wants in a training program and tells me. c. The content is determined through discussions between management and myself.			
4. In working with line management to develop and implement a training program: a. Disagreements usually do not occur, because my expertise in training and development is recognized. b. Disagreements usually do not occur, because line management knows what it wants. c. Disagreements are expected and are resolved by discussion between line management and myself.			
5. After it has been determined that a training program is needed, what generally happens is: a. I proceed to design and implement the training program. b. Management tells me what it wants in the program and how long the program should be. c. Design and implementation decisions are made through discussion and agreement between line management and myself.			
6. When I am diagnosing training needs, what generally happens is: a. I collect data and tell the line manager what the training objectives should be. b. The line manager tells me what the training objectives should be. c. We work together to analyze the situation and determine the training objectives.			
7. When a training program is being implemented, what generally happens is: a. I manage the implementation process alone. b. The line manager decides how to implement the program and I carry out his or her plan. c. The line manager and I meet regularly to discuss how the implementation is going and determine the actions to be taken.			
8. When skill transfer appears not to be occurring, what generally happens is: a. I identify the problems and then take action to solve them. b. Management identifies the problems and takes action to solve them. c. Line management and I identify the problems and determine actions to solve them.			

Exhibit 1. Style Inventory, Cont'd.

	A	*B*	*C*
9. When evaluating the effectiveness of a training program: a. I decide on the type of evaluation and do it myself. b. Line management decides what it wants evaluated, and I carry out the evaluation. c. Line management and I jointly agree on what items should be evaluated, and I carry out the actions.			
10. When I work with line management on a training program, what generally happens is: a. Collaboration is minimal because my expertise warrants that I determine what needs to be done. b. Collaboration is minimal because line management determines what needs to be done. c. There is collaboration between line management and myself in determining what needs to be done.			
Total	___	___	___

Scoring Instructions

1. Total each column.

Summary Box

	A	*B*	*C*
Total			

2. Graph your total scores by following these steps.
   a. Select the point value in the Summary Graph column A (below) that most nearly represents your total in the Summary Box column A.
   b. Draw a horizontal line at this point and shade in the column below this line. This represents your score for the Expert consulting style.
   c. Repeat steps (a) and (b) for your total in columns B and C.

Summary Graph

A *Expert Style Points*	*B* *Pair-of-Hands Style Points*	*C* *Collaborator Style Points*
100	100	100
90	90	90
80	80	80
70	70	70
60	60	60
50	50	50
40	40	40
30	30	30
20	20	20
10	10	10

Five

Conducting Initial Project Meetings

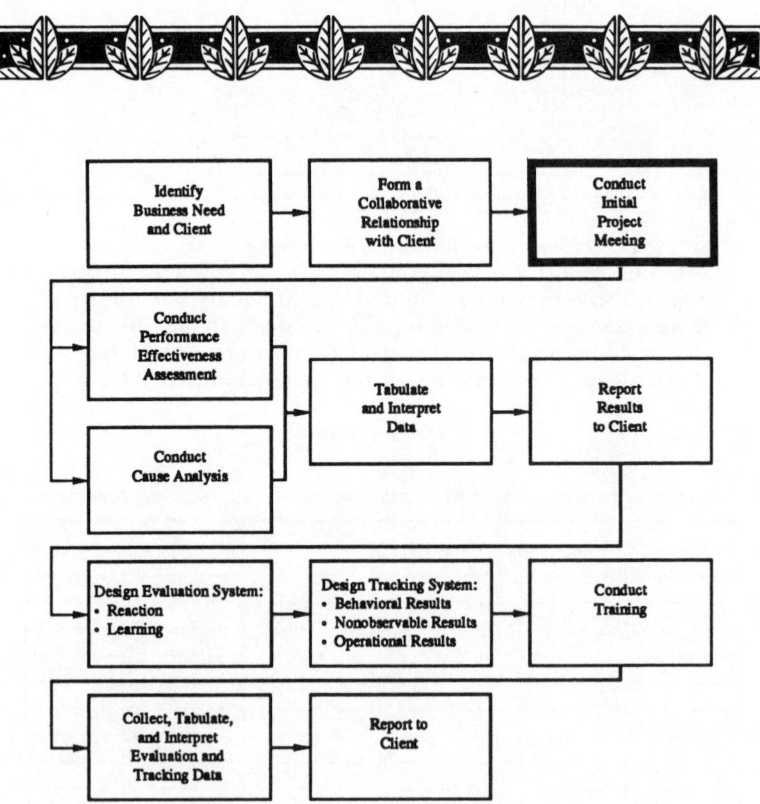

The Case of Lou Karlin

Maxxon, Inc., is a company that provides computer services to several hundred organizations in North America. Lou Karlin is the director of human resources development; Jack Plunkett is vice-president of operations. Jack is responsible for the largest division in the company, a division that includes more than five thousand people.

In a phone conversation with Jack, Lou learned of a training need in the operations area. Because of the high technology involved in the firm and the rapid rate of change that is a part of that technology, Jack has determined that it will be beneficial to set up task forces to look at specific problems. He has found that the variety of talents and disciplines brought to such a task force increase the results coming from it.

The problem is that in the last several months at least four of these task forces have been spinning their wheels; they do not appear to be accomplishing much. Jack would like to change this and has contacted Lou for assistance. The two have agreed to meet to discuss the situation more fully.

Lou knew he needed to prepare for this meeting, and so he scanned two books on subjects related to the situation—one on project management and the other on team effectiveness. He also clarified in his own mind the purposes of his meeting with Jack: to identify Jack's expectations for the project and to set up a mechanism for doing a needs assessment. He also hoped to develop an action plan for the project.

The Meeting. In the initial client meeting, Jack indicated that he wanted task force leaders and members to develop the ability to carry out task force missions. He felt that these groups lost time in getting organized. He believed they would be more efficient if everyone on the task force knew how to do cause analysis, problem analysis, data collection, decision making, and project planning. Because so many of these skills were taught in programs offered internally through Lou's department, Jack proposed that the appropriate course selections be adapted and put into a special workshop for task force members.

Lou indicated that while this could be done, the program would probably be enhanced if special case studies and examples of relevance to the learners were included. He also stated that the program would benefit from front-end analysis, which would identify the specific skills and knowledge that task force members would find beneficial. Jack doubted the need for this step, feeling that he had appropriately identified the needs. Further, he was unwilling to wait for this analysis to be completed, wanting the program to be offered as soon as possible.

In light of Jack's persistence, Lou indicated that he could see the value of progressing in this manner and that he would be pleased to provide the program being suggested. Lou said he would get back to Jack the next day to finalize a date when the program would begin.

Eight Weeks Later. Eight weeks from the date of the initial conversation, the workshop was conducted. Jack provided a forceful presentation at the beginning of the workshop, indicating why task forces were important to the department and why their effectiveness needed to be increased. Then Jack left, and the workshop began.

Lou noticed that the energy of the group appeared to wane as the workshop continued. About halfway through the program, several people in it asked Lou why topics like clarifying the task force mission, clarifying the roles of members, and developing commitment of members to the task force objectives were not included in the curriculum. Rather than skill development on the analytical processes to use in task forces, these participants needed help in managing the interpersonal aspects of such groups. They had already learned problem- and cause-analysis skills in previous workshops.

On the third day of the workshop, four of the participants were not present. In checking with them later, Lou found that they said the program was covering material they already knew. The reaction questionnaires from the workshop indicated a satisfaction rating of only 5.5 on a scale of 1.0 to 10.0. The biggest complaints were that the workshop did not deal with the primary needs of the participants and that much of the material had been previously learned.

Lou was very disappointed in this reaction. Much time, effort, and cost had gone into the design and delivery of it. In a meeting with Jack, Lou provided a summary of the reaction questionnaires and of his own observations. Jack indicated that he had already received many complaints of the workshop's being a waste of time. He wondered out loud how Lou could have designed a workshop so contrary to his people's needs.

What Went Wrong? This fictitious scenario occurs many times for people in the HRD profession. Wanting to be viewed as responsive to management, HRD professionals often agree to do whatever the client requests, in whatever time frame is indicated. Then, unfair as it may seem, these same professionals pay the price of reduced credibility when the desired outcomes are not accomplished. It is like getting punished for being helpful.

Such was the case for Lou. In essence, he agreed to be a pair of hands to his client by accepting both the client's diagnosis of the problem and his identification of a solution. Difficult as it might have been with a forceful client like Jack, Lou did not develop or attempt to implement a strategy to help Jack see the benefit of assessing learning needs more completely to ensure that Jack's desired business needs were met. Lou also did not fully identify the desired outcomes. He moved forward to meet a target articulated only as to have the task forces work more efficiently. It is difficult to address such a vague goal successfully.

The project veered off course in the initial face-to-face meeting between Lou and Jack. That meeting set the tone and direction for both the project and the working relationship of Jack and Lou. The importance of an initial project meeting to the success of any training effort cannot be overemphasized. Let us look now at how to handle such meetings skillfully.

Initial Project Meetings: Purposes and Techniques

Initial project meetings associated with a training project have one main objective: to formulate a contract or an agreement that both the HRD professional and the client-manager can support. This is really a social contract, not a legal document. As Block (1981, p. 42) describes it, "A contract is simply an explicit agreement of what the consultant and client expect from each other and how they're going to work together. It is usually verbal, sometimes in writing. . . . It is designed not so much for enforcement, but for clear communication about what is going to happen on a project." To negotiate this type of agreement with your client-managers requires the use of the collaborator style (see Chapter Four). It is one that both you and they must support; both sets of needs must be addressed in it.

Negotiating this contract can be the most difficult part of the Training-for-Impact process. This will be especially true the first time that you, in your HRD role, attempt to negotiate. As difficult as it may appear, however, this is the time to negotiate for a contract that will provide a successful experience for both you and the client. It is less difficult to negotiate for needed resources and implementation plans at this point. Once the project is under way, it becomes almost impossible to change the game plan. As Lou Karlin learned, the price paid by HRD professionals who support whatever the clients want can be very high.

To derive a mutually agreed-on contract, several types of information are required.

Background Information. What business need has prompted the initial request for this training project? What should be happening technically, behaviorally, operationally, and attitudinally? What is actually happening in each of these areas? What are the causes for any gaps? What specific information does the client have that indicates a skills or knowledge deficiency? In what areas of the company, and for what functional groups, should the desired program be offered? What time frame does the client have in mind? What business goal or objective of the client's will this project be supporting? Who, besides the individual with whom you are meeting, has a stake in this project?

Information on Deliverables and Outcomes. What specific outcomes does the client seek as a result of this project? What techniques, skills, knowledge, or behavior does the client expect to see demonstrated on the job after the program's conclusion?

What, if any, operational results does the client wish to see (for example, reduced customer complaints or increased output)? Are there any nonobservable outcomes, such as improved analytical skills or change in values, desired by the client? Are there any secondary deliverables desired by the client, such as providing people with a chance to develop networks during training?

Information on Activities to Accomplish Outcomes. What specific plan of action will be used to accomplish the outcomes for the project? Who will be responsible for which activities? What are the target dates for each major phase of the project and for the project in general?

Additional Information. Which people must be brought into the project as content experts, decision makers, and instructors?

Throughout these initial meetings, it is imperative that the HRD professional set an example by demonstrating collaborative behavior. This is a give-and-get style of consulting, and so it means continually eliciting from clients what they want, as well as indicating what you need (such as time, people, money, and information) if you are to meet those desires. It is important to avoid both telling the client what is required and being told by the client what is going to happen. It also means that time must be allocated for this negotiating process; it cannot occur in a ten-minute phone call.

You may have noticed our plural reference to initial project meetings. That is a purposeful plural, because only rarely can a training contract or agreement that uses the impact approach be negotiated in one meeting; usually it will require several. It is also common to find that additional key players are identified during the first meeting who become involved in future project meetings. Thus, you move from having one client to having a client team. You begin by working with one or two people. Over time, you add a few others, who are stakeholders in the project. We have found that such teams are frequently formed over the life of a training project. Generally, such teams comprise up to six people.

Initial project meetings must be thoughtfully planned by the HRD professional. Learning as much as possible about the client ahead of time (for example, management style and high-concern issues) is important. Formulating good questions to ask the client is also essential. If a client wants to jump into action, questions should be developed to help the client see that such action may be premature. If a client's desires are vague, questions should be developed to assist the client in articulating what is needed. This initial meeting is not one to be conducted casually or with a seat-of-the-pants technique.

Critical Steps

We have found that successful initial project meetings on training projects incorporate certain steps and techniques. They are listed here to serve as a guide. Again, all steps may not be completed in one meeting, but when the training project is fully contracted, all steps undoubtedly will have taken place.

Confirm and Agree on the Purpose of the Meeting. As with any good meeting, the purpose for this one must be established. Its purpose should be stated at the time the meeting is arranged and should be reiterated as the meeting actually begins. Generally, the purpose will include fuller understanding of the client's business need and desired outcomes. Statement of the purpose also provides an opportunity to sketch out the project's plan. Finally, the time of the meeting should be reconfirmed. The following is a list of typical purposes for such meetings:

- To identify and gain an agreement to meet with all true clients for the project
- To frame the context for this particular training effort into that of the business need that is driving the request for training
- To begin to identify the business results desired by the client for the project
- To position the HRD professional in the role of collaborative consultant to the internal client
- To gain agreement on the need for front-end assessment and to identify the general purposes of such assessment

- To begin to articulate the roles of the consultant and the client for the project
- To lead the client away from thinking that a training program is the only action needed

Summarize Your Understanding of the Situation. In this step, you summarize what you understand about the situation or the request for training. This information may be a result of any initial conversation between you and the client, or it may come from any initial research you have done before the initial meeting.

Seek Additional Information to Identify the Possible Business Need. This is the step that really pays off, if you have done your homework. If you ask the right questions in a skillful manner, your client's awareness is raised on several levels. Is there really a training need? Is there a business need driving the request for training? If so, what is it? Is there sufficient information available for you to be certain that the training need is correctly and specifically identified? Is the work environment of the prospective learners ready to support the new skills? Have the desired program outcomes been fully articulated? How will you and the client know that the project has been successful? Are all the necessary key players involved?

The technique here is to ask questions that help the client identify the need for front-end assessment work and determine other strategic steps that will be needed. It is important to avoid telling the client what is required: That is the expert approach to consulting, and it brings with it an increased risk that the client will not be supportive. The more questions asked for which the client's response is "I'm uncertain" or "I don't know," the better. Later in the meeting, reflect on those areas for which no information is currently available, and point out the risk of moving forward without it.

Identify the Client's Expected Outcomes for the Project. It is not unusual for a client to think of outcomes only in vague terms, such as to improve morale or get better communication between groups. It is your responsibility to assist the client in becoming more specific. What will employees do or not do to show improved morale? What will people be doing or not doing to show that communication has improved? Reflect on the symptoms of a business problem or a request to maximize a business opportunity when you are seeking information on outcomes. Questions that help clients verbally paint their visions of what success will look like are important to ask. This is what the client has to gain from working collaboratively with you.

Indicate What Actions Are Required by the Client and Yourself to Accomplish These Outcomes. You may have noticed that, up to this point in the process, you are doing most of the seeking, and the client is doing most of the talking. Now those roles shift. Here is where you indicate what will be needed to accomplish the outcomes identified by the client. It is also important to acknowledge the risks of moving ahead without certain information already identified as lacking. Common requirements that may be discussed at this time include access to certain information already available in the organization but not currently available to you; collection of information that is now not available at all; additional people to be involved as clients or to assist in other ways; consideration of budgetary issues, such as who will pay for what; and time to meet all these requirements.

Should front-end assessment be necessary, an additional point to cover concerns the specific decisions that will be made on the basis of collected information. Such decisions become the purposes of assessment. More information regarding the establishment of such purposes will be discussed in Chapter Six; for now, it is important to note that they are identified during the initial project meetings.

Agree on Actions to be Taken and Next Steps. This is the time when the collaborative relationship is firmly cemented. Here is where it is understood which specific actions you will be taking and which will be the client's responsibilities. Each partner should leave the meeting with a "to do" list.

The HRD trainer-consultant's responsibilities include:

- Arranging for and facilitating meetings associated with the training project

- Designing, implementing, tabulating, and reporting on any front-end assessment effort
- Designing or purchasing and delivering any training efforts associated with the training project
- Managing all logistical and administrative requirements associated with the project
- Managing the process to measure organizational impact from the program
- Managing all activities associated with the "learning experience" aspect of results

The client-manager's responsibilities include:

- Communicating the business need for the training project to all employees and to management
- Providing HRD professionals with access to necessary people and information
- Ensuring that the entire client team (if there is one) is available for and present at all project meetings
- Allocating time for project meetings and generally being accessible to the HRD professional
- Kicking off any training efforts associated with the project (or asking that another member of the client team do so)
- Taking needed actions when it is evident that the work environment will not support new skills
- Managing all activities associated with the "work environment" aspect of results

Summarize the Agreement. As the project and its parameters are agreed to, you should summarize your understanding of it. We encourage the summarizing of the agreement in a memo to all members of the client team. A Training-for-Impact project typically occurs over a period of months, and so this memo can serve as a useful baseline against which to compare the project's progress. A sample of such a memo is shown in Exhibit 2.

Exhibit 2. Sample Memorandum.

To: Client-Manager(s)
From: HRD Professional
Topic: Summary of Initial Meeting on Project

This memo summarizes my understanding of the agreements we made in our meeting last week regarding the current difficulties in customer contact and the actions each of us will be taking as a result.

Actions I Will Be Taking

1. I will be contacting supervisors in customer contact and arranging for time to interview them concerning their current problems.
2. I will be calling three colleagues in other companies to determine what types of training they are doing in this area.
3. After my meetings with the supervisors, I will draft a questionnaire to be distributed to the clerks. This draft will be forwarded to you for review before I distribute it.

Actions You Will Be Taking

1. You will be informing the supervisors that they should expect my call regarding some interviews.
2. You will be forwarding to me some of the operational data that indicated problems in the unit.

As I understand it, we will plan to meet once again on (*date*). Should any of the items enumerated here contradict your understanding, please give me a call. I am looking forward to working with you on this situation. I am certain that together we can turn it around.

Things That Can Go Wrong

Not every meeting proceeds smoothly through each of the steps we have described. Let us look at some of the things that can go wrong and at what you should do in those situations.

When You Are Unable to Reach Agreement. You and your client may be unable to reach agreement on what is needed or on how needs should be met. The client may want the project done within two months, but you require sixteen weeks. You may believe that the training program should be a skill-building workshop of three days, while the client wants only a one-day, theory-based workshop. You believe front-end assessment is needed, but your client does not want to take the time. When disagreement is an isolated incident, the best approach is to acknowledge the difference of opinion and ask the client for suggestions on how to proceed. For example, you might say, "It looks as if we have a deadlock here. What do you suggest?" Often, a client will make a suggestion that you can build on to keep your discussion moving forward.

When you encounter disagreement as a trend, however, a slightly different approach is required. You will want to comment on the resistance by indicating to the manager what you have observed, asking for reasons. For example, you might say, "I notice that you rejected the last three suggestions I made. Can you tell me what is bothering you about the project?" Then just wait in silence, and let your client respond.

There will be times when the issues that block agreement are so great that you and your client cannot resolve them at this time. If this is the case, acknowledge the situation and say that you feel it would be best to summarize areas of agreement and disagreement. Then call a recess, to last until each of you has had a chance to think about the project and about possible ways of reaching agreement to move ahead.

If agreement is not possible at all, it may be time to implement the requested project as an activity, one for which measurable outcomes are unlikely. At least you will have made every effort to conduct the project differently.

When the Client Is Not the Decision Maker. Often, as you begin the initial meeting, it will become apparent that your contact does not have the responsibility or authority to make the types of decisions required. In fact, the decision maker may be your contact's boss or someone else in the operating chain of command. If this is the case, acknowledge that the additional person should be approached and discuss with your contact ways to get that person involved in the project. (See Chapter Three for ideas on how to discover the true client.)

When the Client Wants You to Be an Expert or a Pair of Hands. Even when you indicate to the client that you want and need to be a collaborator, the client may still deal with you as an expert or a "pair of hands." When this happens, you need to decide, first, whether you can have a successful project if you are in one of these roles and, second, whether the role is agreeable to you.

If you answer yes to both questions, then you may elect to operate within that framework, even though it is not your first choice. If you answer no to either question, however, then you need to move yourself into the collaborator role. In Chapter Four, we described ways of moving from an expert or pair-of-hands role into the collaborator role. Those are the types of strategies you should engage now.

How Well Did the Initial Meeting Go?

After the initial project meeting, you should assess it in three ways: Did you accomplish the purposes of the meeting? Did you handle the meeting effectively? Have you and the client agreed on actions that move the project forward in the impact approach? A rigorous self-appraisal will assist you in fully developing your collaborative skills. The following checklist may prove helpful.

1. Which of the identified meeting purposes were fully accomplished, partially accomplished, or not accomplished?
2. For purposes only partially accomplished or not accomplished at all, was any plan developed to assist in moving the decision process forward?
3. What are the strengths of your agreement with your client?
4. What are the weak areas in your agreement with your client? Have you considered what can be done to minimize the risks inherent in the weak areas?
5. How committed is your client to this agreement?
6. What must you do in your next meeting with your client to keep the project moving in the right direction?
7. Assess the style of all the other persons who were present. Who was an expert? Who was a collaborator? Who was a pair of hands?
8. Assess your own style.
9. What positive things did each client do in these meetings?

10. What negative or dysfunctional things were done by each client? How did you manage those situations?
11. What positive things did you do during these meetings?
12. What negative or dysfunctional things did you do? What learning did you gain from those experiences?
13. Are there specific actions that each of you is taking as a result of the initial meeting?
14. Have plans for these been written down and distributed?

As you can see, the initial project meeting is crucial to the success of any training project that will be tied to business needs and will result in measurable impact to the organization. As an HRD professional, you need to facilitate these meetings in a manner that enables your clients to view you as a professional, capable and partnered with them on an equal basis for the purposes of the project. Initial project meetings set the tone for all that follows.

Plan these meetings thoroughly. Have a colleague whose opinion you value review your plan with you. Remember that time spent now on negotiating "win-win" agreements is time well spent. It is certainly preferable to time spent on developing excuses when a project derails because of a poor beginning.

The Case of Lou Karlin Revisited

In light of the various techniques and strategies presented in this chapter, it might be interesting to revisit Lou Karlin after his initial phone conversation with Jack Plunkett. Let us see how he could have handled the initial meeting more effectively.

Preparation. Before the meeting with Jack, Lou developed the outcomes he expected from the meeting, as well as a list of questions that he hoped to discuss. Lou wanted to identify the specific problems of the task forces, as well as the impact of those problems on the business, as Jack saw it. He wanted to help Jack understand that it was too soon to determine specifically whether any training program was needed. He also wanted to determine what information he and Jack had and still needed.

Finally, Lou wanted to agree with Jack on an action plan to move forward with collecting any needed information.

Lou also prepared a list of questions to ask Jack so that he might understand more completely the situation Jack was facing.

1. How long have you been using task forces as a way of getting things done?
2. How many different task forces operate at any one time?
3. How are task forces structured? Is there a leader, and how many other members might there be?
4. How is the leader selected?
5. What is a typical assignment for a task force?
6. Over what period of time do task forces meet?
7. What is not happening that you want to have happen? What is happening that you would like to have stopped?
8. How do you know about these problems?
9. What is the impact of these problems on your business?
10. Was there ever a time when these things were not happening? When did the problems start to happen?
11. Are all task forces experiencing these problems, or only a few?
12. Do you know the causes of these problems? Do people not know how to do what you want? Could there be other reasons?
13. Have you communicated with the task force leaders and members about what you have observed? What information have they provided?

Lou also developed questions to help himself identify what Jack wanted to accomplish as a result of the work to be completed.

1. Regardless of what actions are taken, what do you want to see happen that will make this project a success?
2. What do you not want to have happen?
3. What needs to happen so that the project will be successful according to the team leaders and members?

4. How would you suggest the project be measured so that any results achieved can be identified?

The Meeting. With this preparation, Lou went to Jack's office. Lou began the meeting by saying that he had reviewed some information regarding the task forces but also had some questions about the project. From Jack's answers, some interesting information emerged. Jack had begun using task forces about a year before. At the time, he had personally chosen two people to lead the task forces. These two individuals had been quite successful at accomplishing the necessary tasks in the time available. On the basis of that success, Jack had determined that task forces were the way to go and had set up several more. It was the second set of task forces that was having problems. The leaders of these groups had been selected primarily because of their content knowledge about the tasks the groups would be addressing.

Lou found that Jack lacked specific information on what was going wrong. He could only note that assigned tasks were not being accomplished in the time allotted. The groups seemed to get bogged down and go nowhere. Jack was also vague about the causes of the problems. Of the four task forces currently operating, one appeared to be functioning well; the other three did not. Jack did not know what was making the difference.

Lou said that it would be important to determine exactly what was causing the problems. What was the difference between them and the task force that was working well? Jack agreed that it would be important to find out, but he wanted that information to be collected quickly. This problem was serious now, and it needed to be corrected as soon as possible.

It was agreed that Lou would contact the four leaders of the task forces and interview each one. He would also interview one member of each task force. He felt that he could conduct those eight interviews within the next week. At that time, he would relay to Jack the information he had found, and together they would decide what the next steps should be.

Now you have a client who is indicating an interest in moving forward—not with a training program, but with an assessment of the business need to determine whether a training program is appropriate. This is the moment of opportunity. We will look next at more specific kinds of information that you need to collect before a training project if that project is to have organizational impact.

Summary

The following techniques move training toward impact:

Activity **Impact**

- When a line manager calls with a request for training, make an appointment to meet and discuss the project. Prepare for that meeting by developing questions to determine more completely what the manager believes should be happening, as well as to understand what is happening.
- From the moment you meet with a manager on a project, set an example as a collaborator. Indicate the need to obtain information, and be willing to provide some yourself.
- Even though the manager may only give you a few days to do front-end work, take that opportunity and maximize it. Collecting some information is preferable to collecting none, and it may help to influence your client-manager that more information is needed.

Part Three

Diagnosing Organizational Needs and Making Training Decisions

When considering the implementation of a training program for which organizational impact is expected, front-end assessment work is not optional—it becomes mandatory. This is because there is a great deal of information required and low probability that all that information is known to the decision makers at the start of the project.

What should people know and do to be successful? What skills and knowledge are they demonstrating now? Is that ability level consistent throughout the organization, or does it vary by department? What is causing any deviation between desired skills and current demonstration of skills? The answers to these questions are required before you can move forward with a training effort designed for organizational impact. And finally, the skill with which the collected information is reported becomes a key "make-or-break" point in this effort. If it is done well, a great deal of managerial support results; done poorly, the project can be derailed.

In the next three chapters, we discuss the steps required to skillfully assess performance needs and organizational obstacles to performance. How to report such information to clients is discussed in Chapter Eight.

Six

Assessing Performance Effectiveness

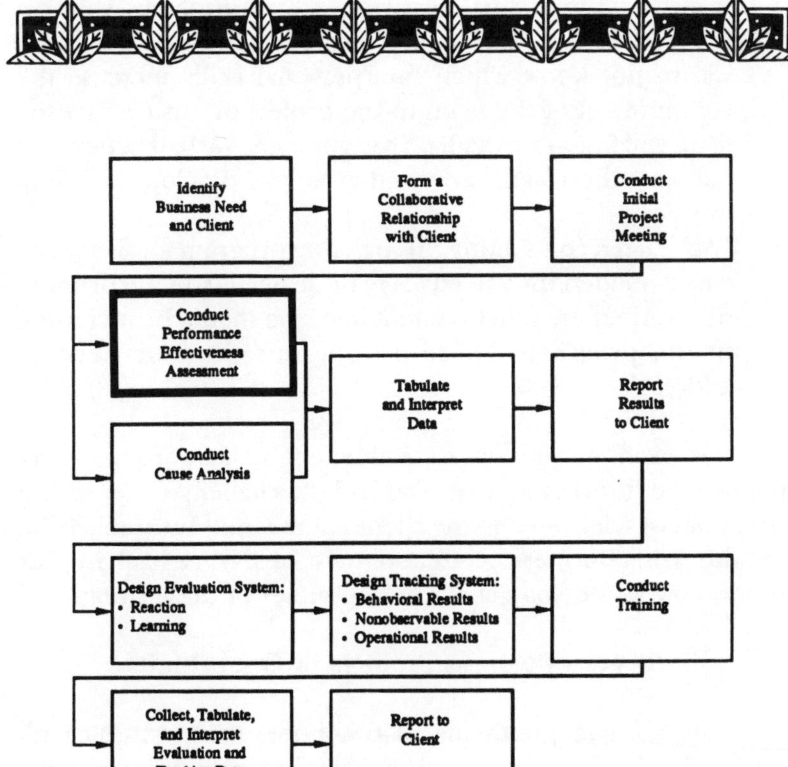

Once you have had your initial client meeting, and once the client has agreed to some front-end assessment, you will find yourself in a "good news–bad news" scenario. The good news is that you have the opportunity to assess the situation, confident that any training program provided will affect the business. The bad news is that you must deliver on the commitments made and the expectations raised in your initial meeting. You must be prepared, with skill and timeliness, to respond to the client's decision to move ahead.

For example, consider some of these actual comments we have heard when the client gave the green light at the initial project meeting to move forward with front-end assessment.

1. "Okay, so we know we want to develop our project managers in the skills required to successfully manage project teams from an interpersonal perspective. Unfortunately, while we know what analytical skills a project manager should use, we do not know which interpersonal skills increase the commitment of the team to the project or ensure that the team will follow through on assignments. We had better find out what those skills are, so that we can develop them in a workshop."
2. "We've been conducting this training program for five years, based on identified needs. Are these needs still the primary ones? Are there other content items we should be including in the program? Those are the questions we need to address."

In each instance, we were able to move forward to collect the needed information. We also had the challenge of ensuring that what was delivered to the client was meaningful and helpful in addressing business needs and questions. Once back in your office, how would you get started on either of these situations?

Is There a Business Problem or Opportunity?

Recall a major theme of this book: that training with impact results only from training that is linked to some business

Table 1. Problem-and-Opportunity Matrix.

	Current Problem	*Future Opportunity*
End-Result Data	Customer complaints rising Sales below goals Output below standards Turnover too high	New product/service about to be introduced; must generate $500,000 in revenues this fiscal year Purchase of word-processing equipment will increase output by 16 percent
Behavioral Data	Salespeople not identifying customer needs quickly or effectively Supervisors not demonstrating participative management techniques Clerks appear defensive to customers with complaints	New skills required of technicians so that they can operate/service new piece of equipment Skills and knowledge required of salespeople so that they can sell new service

need. This link captures the attention and interest of your client-manager and helps ensure that the client will work with you as a partner to get results. Therefore, one of the first things you need to do after returning from the project meeting is to review all your notes. What data indicate that there is a business problem? What data indicate that there is a business opportunity? Is any apparent business need driving the request for training?

We use a two-by-two matrix to assist us in sorting out what we know from what we do not know. Table 1 depicts such a matrix. The vertical axis indicates the type of information you may have collected: *end result data*, which are typically quantifiable and are derived from operational reports; and *behavioral data*, which are usually qualitative and are derived from observations or conversations with others. The horizontal axis indicates problems in their respective time frames: *current business problems*, which are happening now (this means that there is a deviation from what should be happening, and these problems are generally sources of pain for your clients); and *future business opportunities*, which are about to appear and should be maximized to their fullest potential.

Current Business Problems. Has the client identified a current business problem and used end-result data to describe the situation? As Table 1 notes, this would mean that the client has indicated that something is not happening as it should, and the client has provided you with quantifiable, operational data to make his or her point. Decreases in sales revenue and increases in customer complaints are examples of such situations. While clients may not actually give you the numbers, the information they provide can be quantified. Therefore, you can determine that sales revenues have dropped by 10 percent or that customer complaints have increased by 6 percent.

If your client has provided you with information by using such phrases as "Supervisors aren't participative enough," then you are receiving information about a business problem in behavioral terms. In this case, it would be beneficial to probe more deeply by asking the client what the impact of a nonparticipative style is on the business. Do good ideas go unnoticed? Are people unmotivated to help out during production crunches? The more you learn about how the behavioral problem is affecting the client's business, the better.

Future Business Opportunities. Sometimes clients focus on a future event that they wish to be successful. Perhaps the company is about to offer a new product or service. There may have been goals set for how much revenue this product or service should generate in the first year. If you receive such information, you are learning of a business opportunity in end-result terms.

Perhaps the client has indicated instead that word-processing equipment has been purchased for the entire department, and he or she wants the operators to use it to its fullest potential. Now you are learning about behavior that must be developed in order to maximize the business opportunity of "going high-tech" with administrative work. Again, if your client has provided you with this type of information, it would be good to delve deeper and learn what the impact on the operation will be because of this equipment. How much more work will be accomplished in a day? Will fewer people be required? Will the quality of the work improve in some manner?

By assessing and categorizing the information collected from your client, you will know whether you have identified a business purpose for the training project and what that business purpose is. If you have left the meeting without an identified business purpose for the training project, it will be necessary to have another meeting. Moving forward with a training project that lacks any link to a business problem or opportunity is returning to the Training-for-Activity approach.

Consider the following situations. In situation 1, the client-manager says, "I would like to have all professionals in my area learn how to negotiate for resources with both internal and external customers. We have many people who need these skills. I know the skills will increase performance effectiveness." In situation 2, the client-manager says, "Recently, there have been some problems drawn to my attention. It seems that some of our staff engineers and technical people are entering into negotiations with internal and external customers but are not thinking of the big picture in these negotiations. In one instance, the engineer agreed to a request by a customer, and it cost this company $50,000. In another case, the technician couldn't successfully negotiate for some internal resources, and we missed a deadline to a customer. It seems many of my staff do not know how to identify objectives for a negotiation and are quick to acquiesce to whatever the other guy wants."

In situation 2, the business problem that needs to be addressed is clear: Your client has something to gain if this occurs and something to lose if it does not. This means that there is a reason for your client to work collaboratively with you to achieve this common business goal. Situation 1 lacks any identified business purpose, other than a vague desire to increase effectiveness. Moving forward in such a context without helping the client articulate the business purpose of the training more specifically means that the program runs a high risk of becoming just another course in the training catalogue.

When you revisit your client to obtain more information in this area, you might ask the following questions.

1. Why do people require the training you have suggested? How will it specifically benefit them on the job?

2. What would happen to the business operation if people did not receive the training?
3. What is or is not occurring in your business operation to make you believe there is a need for training?

Should your client be unable to provide this type of information, collecting it will be one of the purposes for your front-end assessment. If you are serious about wanting to be considered a partner with management in the accomplishment of organization goals, then all training must be linked to the business in some manner. If that link has not been articulated by your client, it becomes your responsibility either to identify the link or to influence the client not to have a training effort. If you put your data into a matrix similar to that illustrated in Table 1, it will be clear what information is lacking and still needs to be collected.

What Type of Assessment Is Needed?

Let us assume that you have been given the go-ahead by your client to investigate a situation in more depth. Getting started is often the most difficult part, because you must identify where to begin. The first step is to identify what business need is driving the training situation you are facing. If that need is not clear, then one purpose for the assessment is to identify that business link.

The second decision is to identify what type of assessment you will need to conduct. We believe there are two major types of assessments: performance effectiveness assessment and cause analysis. We will discuss cause analysis in Chapter Seven. Here, we will discuss the purposes of a performance effectiveness assessment.

In a performance effectiveness assessment, you should collect information to determine gaps between desired and actual performance as well as identify the relationship between desired operational results and the skills or knowledge required to accomplish them. Obviously, you will want to avoid designing and delivering a training program to improve low productivity

Figure 6. Link Between Operational Results and Skills and Knowledge.

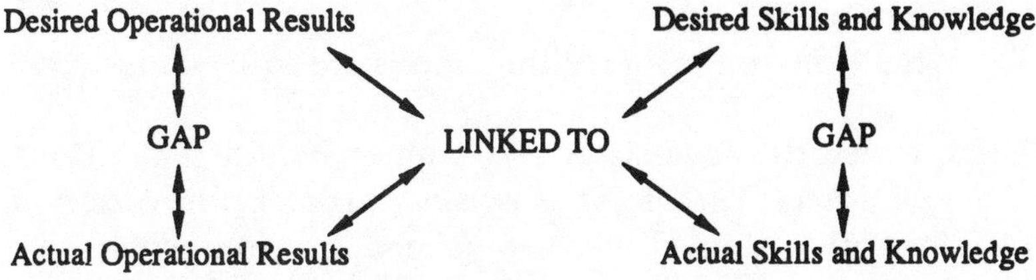

if the primary cause of the problem is the poor quality of raw ingredients or equipment. For a training program to be considered part of the solution to a business problem, the connection between desired operational results and required skills and knowledge must be clearly defined. Figure 6 depicts this relationship.

Thus, there are three purposes of performance effectiveness assessment. You want to know or confirm the "should," the "is," and the causal relationship between skills and knowledge, on the one hand, and the operational results, on the other.

If you already know what people should do, what they are doing, and the relationship of that performance to operational results, then you do not require a performance effectiveness assessment. It is rare, however, for HRD professionals to be handed all this information. Therefore, collecting some of it will be necessary.

Seven Decisions

Once you have determined your need to design a performance effectiveness assessment, you must make seven decisions so that the designed assessment system yields valid and credible information.

1. What are the purposes of the assessment?
2. Who will review data and make related decisions?
3. What sources of information will be needed?
4. How will the data be compared?
5. How many people should be included in the assessment?

6. What is the preferred data-collection method for you and the client?
7. What skill and resource limitations are to be considered?

Let us review the issues associated with each of these decisions.

Decision 1: Purposes of Assessment. To determine what type of information you will need to collect and from whom, it is important first to determine the specific objectives for your performance effectiveness assessment. As we noted earlier, there are three general purposes for such an assessment: to identify gaps between desired and actual operational results in specific, quantifiable terms; to identify gaps between desired and actual skills and knowledge in specific (often behavioral) terms; and to determine what link, if any, exists between desired skills and knowledge and desired operational results.

When you are ready to conduct an assessment, there will be specific, unique purposes for your study, which need to be articulated. By identifying specific purposes, you increase the odds that your assessment will be targeted to and focused on the unique needs of your client. Defining purposes also helps ensure that your assessment will be done in an efficient manner; after all, you are seeking certain information, not doing a broad-based organizational study. Specific objectives regarding end-result data (which may be relevant, if you need more information) may be to identify when the deviation from desired results began to occur, to determine the trend of the deviation, and to determine whether the deviation is constant for every part of the organization or only present in certain parts.

If your focus will be on the identification of gaps in skills and knowledge, then specific objectives for your assessment may include determining what competencies lead to success, determining what typical incumbents are doing in the situation, learning whether skills and knowledge gaps are similar in all parts of the organization or present only in certain areas, and determining the frequency with which incumbents are expected to display the desired skills and knowledge.

The purposes of your performance effectiveness assessment will need to be identified and written down. Your client should support these. These very purposes start to identify the type of information that will be required. For example, if you want to know what successful incumbents do, you will need to seek out such individuals and ask specific questions about their behavior in the situations being analyzed.

Decision 2: Who Will Review Data and Make Related Decisions. The only reason to collect information is so that you and others can make informed decisions about the project or situation. Therefore, in determining what kind of information you will seek out in your assessment, you need to consider who will be reviewing the information. While your client is undoubtedly one of these people, there may also be others. For example, your own manager or subject-matter experts may be among those making decisions from the collected information.

What is important to determine now, as you begin to design your performance effectiveness assessment, is what information will be both meaningful and credible to these people. You want to know their preferences for the type of data to be collected (end-result, behavioral, knowledge), sources of data to be solicited (types of people or types of performance documents), and methods of collecting the information (questionnaires, interviews, and so forth).

You will want to avoid having your key decision makers reject whatever results are obtained from your assessment because they do not value the type of information gathered or the manner in which it was collected. A client may say, when results from an assessment are being reviewed, "Why didn't you ask section managers what they thought?" This can be a most disheartening experience. It is unlikely that good decisions will be made from the assessment's results, because the client has shown no faith in the information itself.

Decision 3: Sources of Information. Once you know the purposes of your assessment and the data preferences of your decision makers, you must consider the various sources of information available to you. Collection of information usually draws on the following five sources.

1. *Clients.* These are the people identified in Chapter Three. Clients can be sources of information for both actual and desired skills and knowledge and end results.

2. *Potential learners.* These are the people who would attend any training program resulting from this assessment. They certainly have a perspective on current skills, knowledge, and end results. They may or may not be sources of information on what will be required for success in the future.
3. *Managers of potential learners.* These are the direct superiors of the people who would attend any training program. Managers have information about current levels of performance, as well as about desired levels.
4. *Other interested parties.* These are people outside the learner-manager relationship. They include direct subordinates of learners, colleagues of potential learners, and customers of the learners. Anyone should be considered who is in a position either to observe the potential learners and their current levels of skills, knowledge, and end results or to have organizational information about what is desired in these areas.
5. *Organizational records.* These include such documents as waste reports, incident reports, and absenteeism and turnover reports. Performance appraisal documents may also be consulted, since they can provide good data on current performance.

The purposes of your specific assessment will help you identify which of these five sources you should consider. The following list offers a guide for decisions.

To find out . . .	*Collect information from . . .*
Current end results	Organizational data, operating reports, clients, managers, potential learners
Desired end results	Clients, managers, potential learners
Current skills and knowledge	Potential learners, managers, other interested parties, sometimes clients
Desired skills and knowledge	Clients, managers, potential learners, research reported in the literature

Links between skills and knowledge and end results	All sources within the organization; research reported in the literature

Two considerations should guide your decisions regarding sources of information. First, select people as sources of information about actual skill and knowledge levels only if they are in a position to directly observe potential learners. Do not ask people to tell you what they think is happening or what someone else has told them is occurring. For example, if you want to determine how performance appraisals are currently conducted, you potentially have two primary sources of information: the potential learners and their subordinates. Unless managers sit in on such conversations, managers can only report on behavior that they think is occurring. This is not reliable information. Second, you should always select a minimum of two sources of information for each major objective to be addressed in your assessment. Multisource data are the most reliable, for they provide multiple perspectives on the same situation.

Decision 4: Data Comparisons. In determining your method of collecting data, you should consider how the data you collect will be divided up and compared. For instance, will you want to know what operations managers believe are the skills required for success and then compare those responses to what managers in marketing or research say? Will it be important to compare the views of people in the company for more than five years and those of people in the company for fewer than five years? These are the types of questions that must be considered early in the design of a performance effectiveness assessment.

In general, we have found that data are most commonly divided in any of the following ways: by functional groups within an organization, by managerial level, by length of service in the organization, by geographical location, by area of technical expertise, and by types of people managed.

HRD professionals often make the error of overcomparing data. This error is realized only after all the data have been tabulated and are about to be reviewed and interpreted. Every time you want to compare the data, you will need to complete an analysis. Therefore, if you wish to do five comparisons, the data will need to be analyzed five different times. That makes for a lot of information to review.

Another consideration is that each comparison of your data will have implications for both the cost and the time required to collect the needed information. In this type of front-end assessment, you are looking for patterns of response. Before a pattern can emerge, several people must be questioned. Therefore, each subgroup to be compared will require interviews from several people, a procedure that increases both the cost and the time of assessment.

Our rule is to ask ourselves and our clients, "If we learn that the needs are different for these different groups, will we create a separate program or take an action?" If the answer is no, then there is no need to compare the data in that manner. If you would be willing to take an action, however, and if you think that there may be some differences in responses from the various groups in question, then it is wise to compare your information. Everything done in the design of a performance effectiveness assessment should be planned to help yourself and others make decisions and take action. "It would be nice to know if . . ." is not a reason to compare information.

To illustrate this point, let us look at a recent assessment we were asked to complete for a client. The client's organization wanted to determine the training needs of its midlevel managers. Three options were considered.

In the first and simplest option, the client would determine training needs according to the input of a sample of managers from the entire organization. No comparison of information would be made. It is generally true that in determining "should" and "is" information, two of the best sources are incumbents and their bosses. Therefore, the sources of information would be a sample of incumbent managers and their bosses.

With respect to the second option, there was reason to think that managers of supervisors and managers would have different training needs from those of managers of individual professional contributors (people who had no one reporting to them). If so, the client was prepared to develop two different training programs. To design this type of performance effectiveness assessment, the sources would need to include a group of managers of managers, a group of bosses of these people, a group of managers of individual contributors, and a group of bosses of these people. Thus, four groups of people would become sources of information in the second option.

In the third option, the client also believed that the three major departments in the company might have different training needs and requirements. If we were to collect information to determine whether that assumption was accurate, sources would have to include a group of managers of managers from three departments, a group of bosses of these managers from three departments, a group of managers of individual contributors from three departments, and a group of bosses of these managers from three departments. Therefore, a total of twelve groups of people would be required. As we moved from the first option to the third in this case, we went from needing two groups of people for data collection to needing twelve. For this client, it was determined that the second option was most appropriate. While willing to have different training programs for managers of managers and managers of individual contributors, the client was not willing to have different programs for managers from each area of the company. Without the willingness to take action, the third option would have been a wasted effort. Keep data comparison simple.

Decision 5: Number of People in Source Groups. Remember that this type of assessment is attempting to describe a situation. You will require enough people in your assessment to ensure that patterns will emerge and that the situation will be described. If you interview only three people, it is unlikely that you can count on a pattern to appear. What if the total population in your target groups is too large to be included? How many people should you select in that situation?

One option is to consult a table in any basic statistics book. If you do, you will find that, for a total population of 300, you would need to collect information from 168 randomly selected people to prove or disprove certain hypotheses to a level of .05 significance. (What that means is that you can be 95 percent certain that the results you receive from the sample will reflect the entire population; there is a 5 percent chance that the sample's results will be different from what is actually true for all.)

In performance effectiveness assessments, however, we are not proving or disproving hypotheses. We are trying to describe a situation—as it should be, as it is, or both ways. Therefore, we need to include enough people so that a pattern can be seen. We use criteria such as the following to decide how many people to include in our data-collection efforts.

1. How many people are in the total group to be assessed? Generally, the larger the total population, the more people you need to include in the assessment itself.
2. What are the characteristics of the total population? If there are people all over the country, then your assessment requires some individuals from each major location. If the total population is composed of people from various departments within the company, then some people from each department should be included.
3. What should you do to be politically and organizationally sensitive? What will be the repercussions if some people are not included in the study? If you cannot exclude people, then you will probably need to consider questionnaires as one of your data-collection methods. If you require maximum visibility with minimum time, then you may want to consider focus-group interviews.
4. What will your client support, in terms of numbers of people to be included? If your client wants only four or five people to be interviewed, then you will need to influence your client to increase that number. There may be a limit that the client would consider appropriate, and this is reasonable. It is important to be sensitive to this type of request.

Over the years, we have found it helpful if we can obtain data from a minimum of twelve people for each comparison group we will be assessing. With twelve people, patterns and trends in responses can be identified. If there are fewer than twelve people in the total group, we want to include them all.

Decision 6: Data-Collection Methods. Organizations often have preferences for particular methods of data collection. A client may also have a clear bias against an assessment method. On several occasions when we were retained to design assessments for client organizations, we were told, "We don't want to use questionnaires – no one ever returns them" or "Interviews are not possible, because they take too much time." As you consider the methods you will use, it is important to clarify the opinions of your clients and of others associated with the project.

The geographical locations of your sources of information will also have implications for the methods used to collect information. If people are concentrated in one location, all survey approaches become possible. When people are dispersed, however, questionnaires become the method of choice, because of their lower cost. A second option might be telephone interviews.

Decision 7: Resource Limitations. There are five survey methods typically used by HRD professionals to collect data on performance effectiveness: one-to-one interviews (in person or over the phone), focus-group interviews, questionnaires, behavioral observation, and analysis of organizational documents and data. Each of these methods has implications for the resources required to complete the assessment. Interviews and observation are labor-intensive processes, but any one of these methods requires skill. You should consider your own situation and assess which method you are best able to support. Perhaps the following information will be helpful as you make decisions regarding data-collection methods.

For one-to-one and focus-group interviews, consider the following questions.

1. Are there enough professionals available to conduct the number of interviews required?
2. Are these professionals skilled in interviewing techniques? If not, is there time for them to develop skills?
3. If you are using focus-group interviews, can the interviews be audiotaped with good equipment, so that all background noise is omitted and the voices of interviewees are clear?

4. Do you and others on the interview team know how to do a content analysis on the data you collect? Interview data are usually open-ended, which means that the process of analyzing them is time-consuming and requires skill. (This process will be described in some detail in Chapter Eight.)

If you are considering the use of questionnaires, ask the following questions.

1. Do you have enough information to build a good questionnaire? Questionnaires should contain primarily closed questions (allowing for ease of tabulation), which means that you must know enough about the situation to create the right questions with the most probable answers.
2. Do you have access to a computer? Tabulating responses by hand is a tedious, labor-intensive, and boring process.

For help in determing when to use interviews and when to use questionnaires, please refer to Table 2.

With behavioral observation as a method of data collection, the following questions should be considered.

1. Are there enough people available to do the observations?
2. Are these observers skilled in observation techniques?
3. Are they or can they be developed to guarantee interrater reliability (so that one person codes a behavior exactly as another person does)?

When considering the use of organizational data, ask the following questions.

1. Are the data usefully organized, or will time need to be spent on reshuffling the data?
2. Are the data available for the time period you require and in a time frame that will be helpful? Or are the data old or not available until after a time when they would be useful to you?

Table 2. Advantages and Disadvantages of Data-Collection Methods.

Advantages	*Disadvantages*
Questionnaires	
More people can be included in study, to meet considerations of time and cost.	It is difficult to create good questions and requires a high degree of knowledge regarding the situation to do so; potential answers must also be created.
Respondents can be in several locations and still be included in the study.	You cannot ensure that individual receiving the questionnaire will be the one responding to it.
Confidentiality is more protected.	Response rate may be poor.
Each question is consistently presented to the respondent.	Instrument must be piloted to ensure clarity, which requires additional time.
Results are easy to tabulate (if closed questions are used).	Respondent may not understand the survey (even though it was piloted), and a certain percentage of returned surveys may need to be discarded due to responding errors (such as marking two answers to the same question).
Cost per instrument is less than with other data-collection methods (Zemke and Kramlinger, 1982, indicate cost as approximately $10 per person; with inflation, that probably means the per-questionnaire costs have risen to $13 or $14 in 1989 dollars, making questionnaires still less expensive than interviews).	
Interviews	
Respondents have opportunity to give information openly and freely.	They are labor-intensive, requiring more time to include enough respondents.
If question is unclear, interviewer can restate.	If more than one person conducts interviews, each person must present each question in a similar manner.
If response is unclear, interviewer can probe for clarity.	Confidentiality of respondents cannot be ensured.
They are easier to create than questionnaires, because only questions need to be created (not potential answers).	Cost per interview is higher than cost per questionnaire (according to Zemke and Kramlinger, 1982, cost was $30 to $75 per interview in 1982; in 1989 dollars, such costs are probably $40 to $100 per interview).
They provide increased control over high response rate.	Tabulation is time-consuming (must be done manually); if more than one individual analyzes data, interrater reliability must be ensured.
As new information is obtained, interview process can be adapted so that additional information, other than what was initially considered, can be collected.	

Rarely is there only one right way to structure your data-collection effort; a combination of methods is often a good approach. It is important to consider all the issues raised in this chapter and then make choices in light of your constraints, resources, and needs.

Putting It All Together: The True Story of a Performance Effectiveness Assessment

We recently worked with a corporation that has approximately 120,000 employees in its worldwide organization. The director of corporate management development was interested in determining what competencies first- and second-level managers would need to be successful in the 1990s. By determining this information now, the HRD department could proactively prepare for the design of training programs that might not currently be available. This information could also be used to identify selection criteria for people who would be promoted into first- and second-level management positions in the coming years. Finally, the information could be used to modify the performance appraisal system so that competencies being evaluated would reflect the changing needs of the organization.

This assessment was to focus on the skill and knowledge gaps between what would be required in only a few years and what existed today. The business need for doing this emanated from senior management's desire to prepare people to meet the challenges of a more global and competitive marketplace. If managers were ready for the next decade before it arrived, the company would be more assured of maintaining its position in the marketplace, despite growing competition.

The following summary indicates how each of the seven major decisions described in this chapter was addressed, resulting in the methodology design that was used.

Decision 1: Purposes. As a result of this assessment, clients would know what skills and knowledge would be required of successful first- and second-level managers in the 1990s; to what degree first- and second-level managers were demonstrating the needed competencies now; and what intraorganizational and environmental challenges first- and second-level managers were most likely to face in the 1990s.

Decision 2: Who Will Review Data. The director of corporate management development, together with the human resources (HR) managers for several of the major lines of business within the organization, would be the primary reviewers of the information. They would be responsible for making decisions from the data. Senior management would be informed of this study's results but would not be a part of the decision-making client group. Decision-making responsibility and authority would rest with senior HR management.

Decision 3: Sources of Information. Because we needed to identify both desired (future) performance and present performance, it was decided that managers of incumbents would be the most reliable sources of information. To determine what the future would look like, research was conducted outside the corporation. Futurists, the literature, and industry-specific projections were sources of information.

Decision 4: Data Comparisons. There was reason to believe that the training needs of first-level supervisors would be somewhat different from those of second-level supervisors. In the first instance, a supervisor is overseeing the work of operators and performers; in the second, the supervisor is overseeing the performance of other supervisors. Therefore, it was determined that two groups of people would be required for the study: managers of first-level supervisors and managers of second-level managers. There was also reason to believe that the needs of people might be different according to the major area of business in which they worked. The organization was divided into four functional areas, with information collected from appropriate people in each area. Thus, eight sources of information were required for this assessment effort.

Decision 5: Number of People in Source Groups. The total population in these groups numbered in the thousands. Most people were in one major city. It was determined that approximately seventy-five managers would be included in this study, because patterns of opinion would reveal themselves with a group this size.

Figure 7. Competency Assessment Study Design.

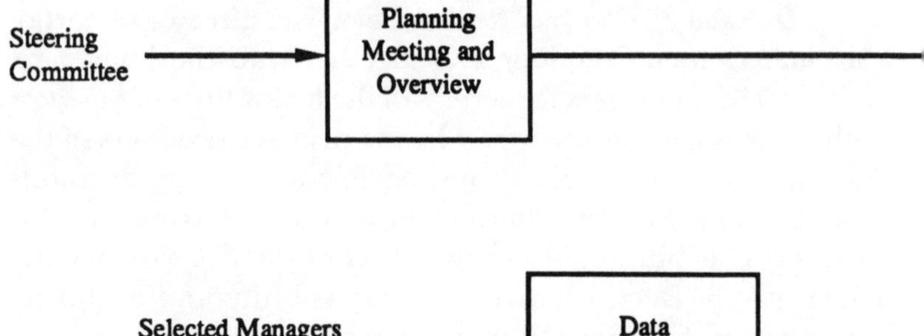

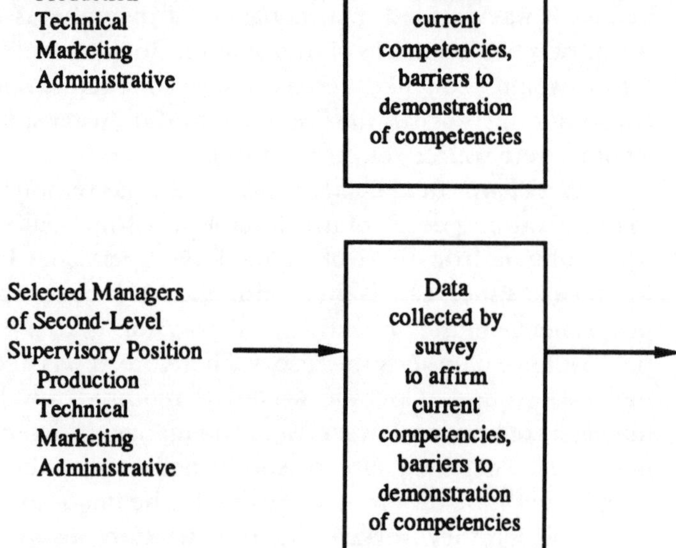

Phase 1
Identification of current
competencies and abilities

Figure 7. Competency Assessment Study Design, Cont'd.

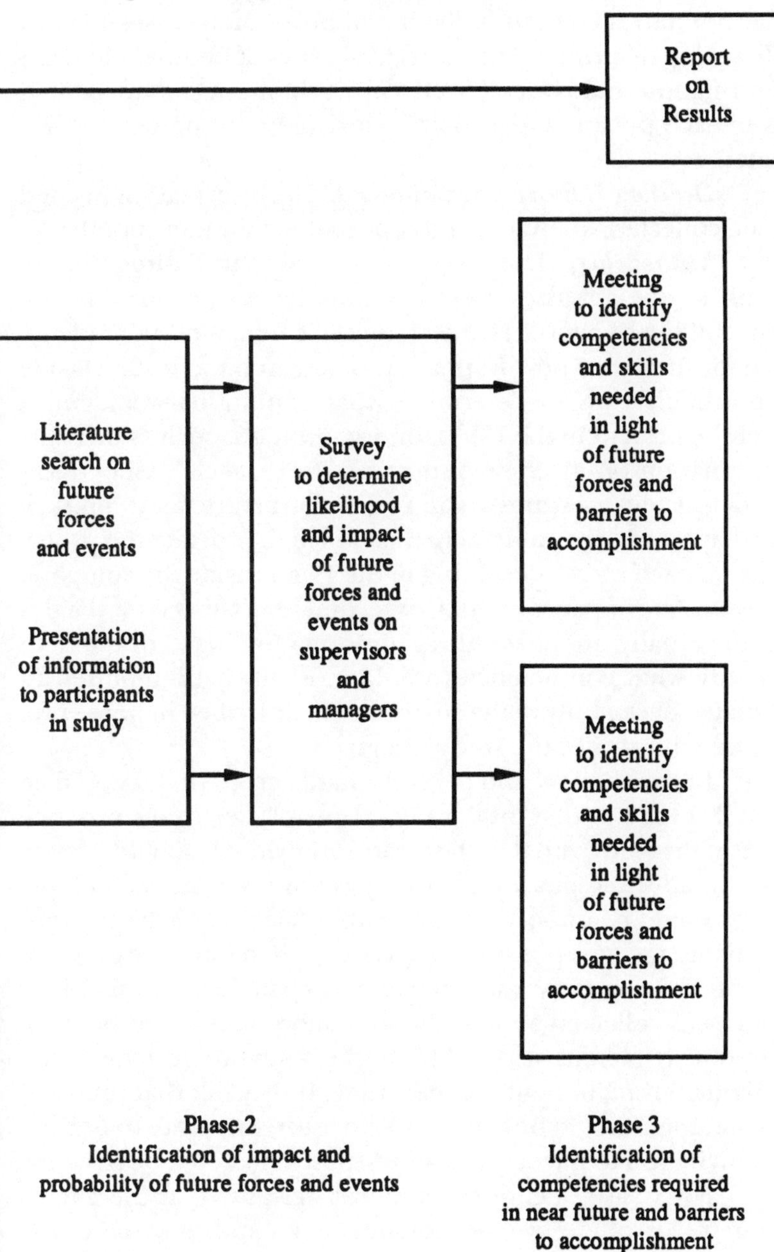

Phase 2
Identification of impact and
probability of future forces and events

Phase 3
Identification of
competencies required
in near future and barriers
to accomplishment

Decision 6: Data-Collection Methods. It was requested that questionnaires be used in the initial phase of the assessment, a phase that determined the current abilities of people. Thus, the information could be collected with a minimum amount of time from each person. Other than that request, no preference was stated.

Decision 7: Resource Limitations. The information needed to be collected, analyzed, and reported within four months.

Methodology. The project was divided into three phases. In phase one, an assessment was completed to determine current abilities of people against required competencies, as identified for their jobs now. In phase two, research was done outside the organization to determine what conditions would most likely be present in the 1990s for organizations such as this one. Information on diversity of the work force, social issues, technological advances, and organizational structure was examined. Participants in the study were then asked to indicate the probability of each event's occurring in the 1990s inside the company, as well as the impact on a first- or second-level supervisor if it did occur. Finally, in phase three, information was collected to identify what competencies would most likely be required to manage successfully in the environment described in phase two. Figure 7 illustrates the study design.

Both the client and the consultant agreed that it would be best if there was one total group of people selected to participate in the study and that these same individuals should participate in all three phases. Learning would occur at each phase, and it would be important that people carry that learning with them into the next phase of the process. Therefore, one group of seventy-five people was selected to particpate in the study. Their data were collected so that the four subgroups could be compared. Participants were told that the study would require approximately eight hours of their time. If they felt that this time commitment would be impossible to meet, they were to decline the invitation to participate, and a substitute would be selected.

For phase one, questionnaires were used, at the client's request. For phase two, outside interviews and research of the literature were conducted. This information was then formulated into a presentation, which participants in the study were asked to attend. In this three-hour presentation, they learned what experts outside the organization thought the future would be like. A questionnaire was then created and distributed to the participants in the study. The results of this questionnaire indicated which events people inside the company believed would most probably occur and what impact such events would have on a supervisor. In phase three, focus-group interviews were conducted. Each group was composed of people from one of the functional areas and addressed either the first- or second-level management position. Therefore, eight focus groups were interviewed, and participants discussed the implications of the future scenario for competency requirements of managers.

Thus, three methods of data collection were used in this study: questionnaires, interviews, and focus-group interviews. The number of people selected was sufficient to reveal clear patterns of data and provided the client with a basis from which to make the decisions that constituted the purposes of the study.

Summary

The following techniques move training toward impact:

Activity **Impact**

- When beginning a training project, evaluate what information you have regarding business needs, required skills and knowledge, and actual skills and knowledge. If you lack some of this information, collect it, even if you must do so in less than ideal circumstances.
- Always write down the purposes of an assessment before you begin collecting information. Know why you are collecting the information and what decisions you plan to make from it.
- Collect information from multiple sources of data.
- Know what information your client will find meaningful and credible before beginning any assessment effort.

Seven

Analyzing Causes of Performance Gaps

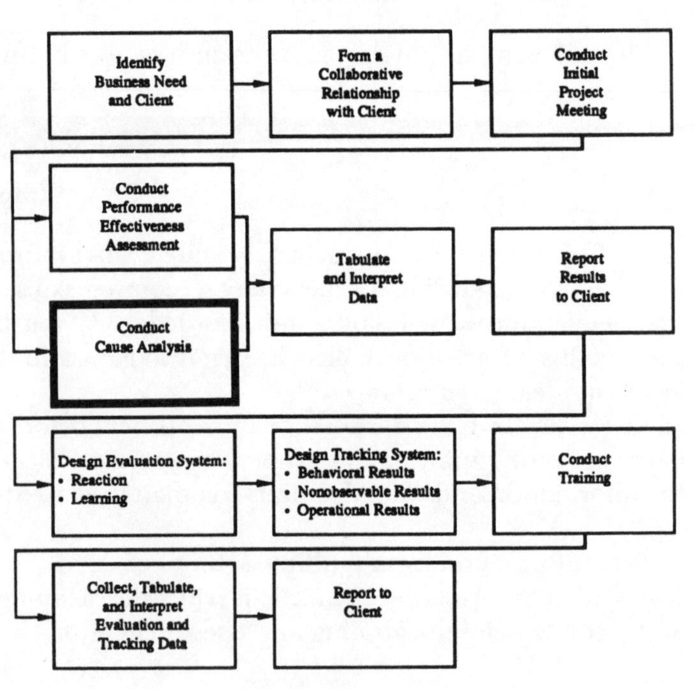

When there is a performance deficiency that is creating a business problem for your client, it is important to understand why that deficiency exists. If the situation is future-oriented (for example, a business opportunity), then it becomes critical to determine what might prevent the skills that you are about to develop from being transferred to the job. A cause analysis provides us with the data to respond to either of these two questions: What is causing an end-result and/or on-the-job performance deficiency? What might prevent newly learned skills from being transferred to the job?

Before we look at how to conduct a cause analysis, let us revisit a concept discussed in Chapter Two. In that chapter, we defined the "results formula" to be:

Learning Experience × Work Environment = Business Results

In this formula, "business results" means on-the-job skill transfer and/or end-result improvement.

A cause analysis must examine all possible causes of performance deficiencies, including current and future causes. This means that we need to gather data to determine whether a deficiency is due to people's not knowing how to perform, the work environment's inhibiting performance, or a combination of both factors.

It has been our experience that the vast majority of performance deficiencies addressed by HRD professionals are caused by a combination of factors. People may not have the skills to perform, but there are also environmental reasons that make it difficult or impossible to perform. As Rummler (1983) has said, "You pit a good performer against a bad system and the system wins every time."

A situation we experienced a few years ago is typical. An insurance company wanted its claims representatives to demonstrate active listening and the use of empathy when they discussed medical claims problems with policyholders. The cause analysis showed that the representatives were not skillful in the use of active listening and the expression of empathy, and that they were operating according to a performance standard that required calls to be concluded in three minutes. These representatives felt that they did not have time to use the skills of active listening and empathy. To bring about the desired change, claims representatives would participate in training to develop the skills of active listening and the use of empathy, and management would modify the performance standard so that claims representatives could spend more time on the phone with policyholders who had claims problems.

When conducting a front-end assessment, be alert to the client who unilaterally determines the causes of any performance deficiencies. The risk here is that the client may have incorrectly diagnosed the cause of the deficiencies or determined only some of the causes. This situation can be avoided if you make sure the client understands the unique purposes of this assessment, as well as its benefits, and acknowledge the client's observations regarding causes but also indicate the need to determine whether there are other causes. In this way, you ensure that the business need of the client is addressed and that the real causes will be identified.

Major Causes of Performance Deficiencies

For twelve years, we have been collecting data about the major causes of performance deficiencies encountered by HRD managers. These causes fall rather conveniently into three major categories: causes due to the learner, causes due to the manager (boss) of the learner, and causes due to the organization.

Causes Due to the Learner. This category focuses on causes that are a function of the learner. In other words, the learner is the source of the barrier to achieving results. Certainly, this category includes lack of the skills or knowledge required to perform effectively on the job. The learner's lack of confidence to use new skills on the job would also be in this category. In addition, it includes learners' disagreement with the values or concepts that are the underpinning of a new training program or management thrust. An example of just this situation occurred at Agway Inc., when one of the authors was identifying the needs of supervisors in three distribution centers. Supervisors were managing employees who had previously worked in smaller, older warehouses, which had been phased out. Performance effectiveness assessments indicated that the supervisors would be more effective if they used specific interpersonal skills with their subordinates. These skills included maintaining or enhancing the self-esteem of subordinates, listening and responding with empathy, and asking for subordinates' ideas or help. The cause analysis indicated that supervisors were not demonstrating these behaviors because they did not possess these skills and did not value using these skills with employees. Both of these causes were a function of learners and could be remedied only by direct interventions with learners.

Causes Due to the Learner's Manager. This category involves causes that are a function of the learner's manager and includes the need for the boss to be a positive model, using skills that are the same or congruent with those that subordinates are learning and are expected to use on the job. This category also includes the need for the boss to coach learners in the use of new skills, to reinforce learners when they use new skills, and to clarify when learners are expected to use the new skills on the job. Research conducted by Rackham (1979) at Xerox Corporation indicates that 87 percent of newly learned skills can be lost when there is no follow-up coaching by the boss after training.

Again, at Agway Inc., the cause analysis indicated that distribution center managers were not positive models and did not effectively coach and reinforce their subordinates in the use of new interpersonal skills. Therefore, these managers needed clarification of their roles as models, coaches, and reinforcers. They also needed to develop these skills.

Causes Due to the Organization. This category includes causes that are a function of the organization: causes originating from organizational structure, systems, values, and norms. Organizational rewards or punishments for using new skills would be in this category. It also includes any interference by the organization with learners' applying their new skills on the job. Because organizational causes are in the work environment, they require the attention of your client.

We encountered these types of barriers in a situation that

we examined recently. Drivers who covered routes and delivered products to the same customers each week were trained in how to ask the customers about additional needs. These delivery people were then to fill out a form with information about the customers' needs. Nevertheless, the organization provided the drivers with no feedback on how many of the completed forms resulted in customers' being contacted and, eventually, in customers' using additional services. After about five weeks, almost no forms were being turned in. Lack of organizational feedback resulted in the new skills' being extinguished.

Cause Analysis: An In-Depth Look

Before you begin a cause analysis, it is important to determine the link between on-the-job behavior and end results. This step should have occurred during the performance effectiveness assessment. If we have determined that on-the-job use of certain kinds of behavior will lead to identified business results, then our challenge becomes to identify why such behavior is not being applied. As we know, one reason may be the employees' lack of the necessary skills or knowledge, but there may be other reasons.

One benefit of identifying the causal relationship is that the value of determining the real cause of the deficiency becomes apparent to the client. Perhaps the following example, adapted from several experiences we have had, will illustrate the point.

A performance effectiveness assessment focused on the sales force of an industrial supplies firm uncovered deficiencies in both on-the-job behavior and sales results. The performance effectiveness assessment determined that salespeople were not sufficiently skilled in asking high-yield questions to uncover customers' needs, relating products' features to customers' needs, expressing the benefits of those features for satisfying customers' needs, and eliciting and dealing openly with customers' objections. The performance effectiveness assessment also determined that salespeople in other, similar organizations who did use these selling skills had annual sales of $350,000. In this

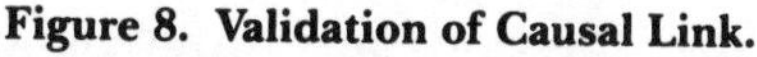

Figure 8. Validation of Causal Link.

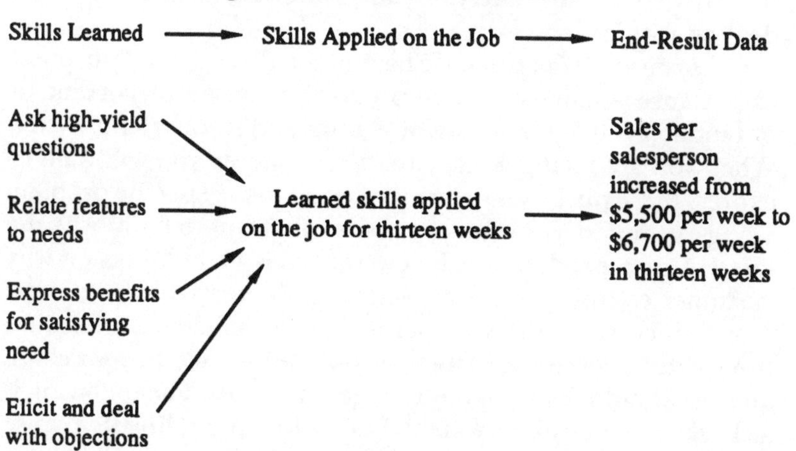

organization, the average annual sales figure per salesperson was $275,000.

An examination of behavioral and end-result data within this organization and other, similar organizations enabled the HRD director and the client to establish a causal link—namely, that when sales people use the skills just described, their annual sales reached approximately $350,000.

This causal link was validated in a pilot program in one district, where the salespeople and their district managers were trained in the new skills. Sales revenues and use of the new skills were tracked, both before and after training. The results are illustrated in Figure 8.

What is the implication of this causal link? Because there is a link between on-the-job behavior and sales results, a solution that ensures that salespeople will use the new skills on the job will also ensure improvement in end-results data. There is a clear benefit to the client in identifying and addressing causes.

Decisions in Conducting a Cause Analysis

The decisions made during cause analysis are the same as those made during performance effectiveness assessment, but the answers to the questions are different, because you are dealing with different data.

Decision 1: Purposes. We have noted the "generic" purposes of a Cause Analysis: to determine the causes of current or potential on-the-job behavioral and end-result deficiencies. When you are facing a real situation, however, you will want to express these purposes in terms relevant to the specific problem being examined. For example, you might want to know why the sales of one product are below the sales of another, or why customer complaints are escalating in the service department.

Since the causes of performance deficiencies fall into three categories, the specific questions addressed in your cause analysis should focus on these three categories. The following is a checklist of questions you might consider including in a cause analysis.

Category 1: Causes Due to the Learner

1. Could the learners satisfactorily demonstrate the desired behavior if their lives depended on it? Of course, if the answer to this question is yes, then the learners do not have a deficiency in skills and knowledge. If the answer is no, then the learners do have a deficiency in skills and knowledge (Mager and Pipe, 1970).
2. Are the learners' personal values and concepts compatible with the values and concepts underpinning the new skills and behaviors?
3. Do the learners have sufficient confidence to use the skills in an effective manner on the job?
4. Do the learners perceive a payoff to themselves for using the new skills on the job?
5. Do the learners understand that they are expected to use the new skills on the job? Do they understand the specific end results they are expected to achieve?
6. Can the learners identify when they are effective in using the new skills on the job?

Category 2: Causes Due to the Managers (Bosses) of the Learners

1. Are the managers positive models of the new behavior? Is the managers' behavior the same as or congruent with the behavior being learned by subordinates?

2. Do the managers coach their subordinates on how to use the new behavior on the job?
3. Do the managers reinforce those who do use the desired behavior on the job?
4. Do the managers clearly communicate their expectations regarding learners' use of the new behavior on the job and the corresponding improvement in results?

Category 3: Causes Due to the Organization

1. What is the balance of consequences for using or not using the new skills on the job? Is it rewarding or punishing to use the new skills on the job? Does it make any difference if the new skills are used on the job? Is failure to use the new skills on the job rewarding, punishing, or immaterial?
2. Are there task-interference factors that get in the way of using the new skills on the job? These task-interference factors may include lack of time, lack of information, higher-priority assignments, and lack of support from other units.
3. Is there organizational feedback that provides learners with information about the impact on the organization when learners use the new skills on the job? For example, do the learners know that, when they use the new skills, quality is improved, costs are reduced, and customers are happier?

Which questions to include depends on the situation you are facing. For example, if there is no doubt that managers of the learners are effectively coaching them in the use of the new skills, then you should not spend time addressing that area in your study. If it is clear that the reward system supports skills, it does not need to be investigated. Select areas to investigate that have some probability of being causes of performance deficiencies. Of course, when you have no reliable prior knowledge of causes, you should investigate all the questions listed here.

Table 3 lists the most frequently occurring barriers to skill transfer. These frequencies are based on our research collected over the past ten years. We collected data from 359 training managers from a cross section of organizations. They were asked to indicate the primary causes of lack of skill transfer from training programs that they had offered. They were asked to include only instances in which skills had been learned but on-the-job application was less than expected.

Decision 2: Who Will Review Data and Make Related Decisions. The primary decision makers for the type of information you collect should be your client group and others (including yourself) in the HRD function. The criteria used to determine who is a client are the same as noted previously: Your client is the highest-level person with decision-making authority on the project and a need to be actively involved in its strategic decisions.

What is important to you as you begin to develop your cause analysis is that you collect information that will be both meaningful and credible to these decision makers. You want to avoid a situation in which the client says, "I just don't believe those data. I don't think that what you got is an accurate picture." Your question to your client should be: "Which data do you need and want so that you can make the necessary business decisions?"

Decision 3: Sources of Information. Now that you have determined your purposes, you must decide on your sources of information. In Chapter Six, we described five general sources of information: clients, potential learners, managers of potential learners (bosses), other interested parties, and organizational data. We should consider using each of these sources for each potential cause that we wish to investigate. A key concept is to keep in mind that the most reliable data are always to be found in the source closest to the situation you are investigating. Therefore, if you want to know whether bosses of learners are effectively coaching and reinforcing their employees, your primary sources will be the bosses and their direct subordinates. If you want to know what kinds of interference are preventing learners from practicing skills, you will need to ask those learners.

It is also important to recall the need for at least two different sources of information for each major question being addressed. The reliability of your information increases as you add sources. This is particularly true when you are collecting

Table 3. Barriers to Skill Transfer: Definitions and Frequencies.

	Frequency of Occurrence[a]
Conditions of the Learners	
Do not see payoff for using the skills: The learners feel that the disadvantages outweigh the advantages of using the skills.	48%
Do not have sufficient confidence to use skills: The learners feel a lack of confidence to use the skills successfully on the job. This may be the result of not developing sufficient confidence in the classroom or of having failed in a first attempt to use the skills on the job.	42%
Do not know when they are effectively using skills: The learners do not have sufficient behavioral guidelines to be able to evaluate whether their on-the-job skills are effective.	33%
Fail when using the skills: The learners tried to use the skills on the job but were unable to achieve the success that they felt they should achieve.	29%
Disagree with the values and concepts of the program: The learners feel that the values and concepts being taught in the program are contrary to their personal values and their concepts of people and organizations.	25%
Do not have an immediate application for the skills: The learners do not see immediate on-the-job applications of the skills they have learned.	22%
Conditions of the Immediate Managers	
Do not reinforce learners' use of the skills: Managers do not provide reinforcement to learners when there is evidence that they have used the skills.	92%
Are not positive models: Managers are perceived as not using or supporting the skills learned.	88%
Do not coach learners in use of the skills: Managers do not coach learners in how to handle specific on-the-job situations, even when learners solicit their advice.	85%
Conditions of the Organization	
Task interference: Many barriers—including lack of time, physical environment, procedures and policies, and lack of authority—inhibit learners as they attempt to use the skills.	68%
Lack of feedback to the learner: The learners receive little or no feedback about the organizational impact of their use of the skills.	60%
Negative balance of consequences: The use of the skills by learners results in a punishing effect.	23%

[a] These percentages indicate the frequency with which this barrier was noted as a cause of the lack of skill transfer. Training managers generally indicated multiple causes when transfer did not occur.

behavioral data from people who are not skilled observers of behavior. Multiple sources of data will reduce the chances that your data will provide inaccurate information.

Decision 4: Data Comparisons. Generally, you will need to respond to the same considerations noted in Chapter Six. In addition, you should observe the following points in your cause analysis.

1. Always collect your data in a manner that enables you to compare them in the same way you did for the performance effectiveness assessment, except when you and your client definitely agree that a specific comparison is no longer required.
2. For questions that deal with environmental barriers, compare the data so that the people responsible for specific groups of employees can see the data that pertain to their units. For example, you may want to divide data from the manufacturing group into major departments (such as fabrication, subassembly, and final assembly). In this manner, the managers of those departments can view data relevant to their own functions and make the appropriate decisions. Remember, however, that each time you wish to compare data, data collection, tabulation, and reporting become more costly and time-consuming.

Decision 5: Number of People in Source Groups. We discussed this decision in depth in Chapter Six. The same issues pertain to cause analysis. As we indicated, you use statistics to describe a situation or a group, rather than to prove or disprove a hypothesis. You need enough people so that patterns and trends will be clear. We suggest a minimum of twelve people for each group or subgroup in your analysis.

Decision 6: Data-Collection Methods. Organizations—or, more correctly, people in organizations—often have preferences for or aversions to specific data-collection methods. Our experience has been that aversions are usually stronger than preferences. They are often due to bad experiences with certain methods. Therefore, as much as possible, we try to use methods preferred by client groups and other organizational members. Nevertheless, we must give a few cautions.

Sometimes key people in an organization confuse the cause analysis with an opinion or attitude survey, probably because opinion surveys often deal with environmental factors, as do cause analyses. Therefore, key managers make decisions regarding methods on the basis of good or bad experiences they have had with opinion surveys. It is important to clarify the difference between a cause analysis and an opinion survey—the purpose of each and how the data of each are used. We often explain that the data from a cause analysis are used by a small group (the client group) to make very specific decisions regarding specific desired on-the-job behavior and end results. Generally, the data from opinion surveys are examined by a larger number of people, and the decisions are broader in scope.

Sometimes key managers want the individual who is designing the organization's opinion or attitude survey to design, tabulate, and record the cause analysis data. Our experience has been that, because of the great difference in perspective between an opinion survey and a cause analysis, turning the cause analysis over to the individual who creates opinion surveys has the potential of bringing the entire project to a screeching halt and giving you an ulcer. Make sure that you control data collection.

Sometimes there is a conflict between what your client group does not want and what you must have to collect reliable data. In these situations, we suggest that you raise this issue with your client group after you have had a chance to think it through thoroughly and that you provide specific examples of why your approach will present the most reliable data. In the same discussion, clarify concerns about using your approach, and outline steps that can be taken to alleviate those concerns. For example, if your clients are biased against a questionnaire because of a previous bad experience, and yet you realize that the sheer numbers of people to be surveyed require a questionnaire, make your case in favor of the questionnaire, and discuss ways to minimize your client's concerns. It may be that previous questionnaires were not returned. If this is the case, then discuss strategies for increasing the return rate of questionnaires. Our experience has been that return rates of 80 percent are realistic, if an appropriate strategy is used.

Decision 7: Resource Limitations. In Chapter Six, we discussed the factors to consider with respect to this issue. The same factors pertain to the cause analysis. One additional factor is the amount of your own experience with environmental factors. Many times, gathering data on these factors requires a high degree of expertise. Therefore, we suggest that you review your methodology and your data-collection instruments with someone who has had experience in this area. In this way, you can learn from their mistakes and avoid the embarrassment of explaining to your client group that your cause analysis data are meaningless or confusing.

How Do Performance Effectiveness Assessment and Cause Analysis Work Together?

It may seem as though performance effectiveness assessment and cause analysis are always used in sequence: First you determine the performance deficiencies, and then you discover the causes of any gaps that have been identified. There are times when conducting these assessments in sequence is the only option, but there are also times when they can be conducted concurrently.

If you are looking at a situation where little is known from the start, you will undoubtedly need to perform your assessment in phases. The first phase of the project begins to narrow down what must be investigated. This phase often involves identifying what people should be doing on the basis of the challenges facing the organization or the performance problems that are causing concern. The next phase of the assessment identifies where typical performers are with respect to this model, as well as why they perform at this level.

We have been involved, however, in situations where performance-deficiency data and cause data were collected concurrently—for example, when there was a sufficient base of information available so that the areas being investigated were narrowed down, or when it was the best option available because of time constraints. Collecting some information concurrently is better than collecting none at all. Here is a recent example: An organization had a program in its catalogue of courses that new managers attended. Because of the size of this company, there were approximately one thousand new managers each year coming to this five-day workshop. The workshop had been designed five years before, on the basis of needs identified at that time. Our clients wanted to determine whether those needs were still the priority items, or whether other developmental areas should be included in the program. We were starting from a base of information, and we knew the area we would be focusing on: the interpersonal and analytical competencies required for the success of new first-level managers in this corporation. Because of time constraints, we needed to collect all the data in one phase. We did this in the following manner, using two groups.

In the first group, successful incumbents and their managers were asked to determine the relative importance of a list of competencies for first-level managers now. Their responses would provide us with the "should" information.

In the second group, typical incumbents and their managers indicated current ability of these incumbents against this same list of competencies. This provided us with the "is" information and, therefore, with information on the gaps. In addition, the second group indicated the frequency of certain environmental barriers that would make it difficult to demonstrate the listed competencies. Analysis of all data indicated the most critical competencies required for success and provided us with data about how typical performers currently demonstrated the competencies. It also gave us information about the impact of the work environment on the managers who would be expected to demonstrate those competencies. We were able to obtain all the data the client needed to make sound decisions with only one phase of data collection. Now the training program could be redesigned to include the competencies that were identified as having the greatest gaps and for which the environment was ready to support skills. This ensured that the organization would receive the greatest return on its training investment.

Aspects of the work environment that inhibited successful performance could be addressed through influencing key managers who were in a position to take action regarding those barriers. Figure 9 illustrates the decisions to be made in determining which of these two assessments are required, or if both are.

How It Works

Let us look at an actual situation in which we worked with an organization to study the needs of managers at a time when business forces were driving the organization away from its traditional lines of business and into new lines where the organization had little experience. This *Fortune* 500 corporation had traditionally produced and sold industrial chemicals and gases. When the front-end analysis was done in 1987, the company was not only moving into new markets but also knew it needed to change its management practices if it was to be successful.

An interesting characteristic of this study was that the performance effectiveness assessment and the cause analysis were conducted concurrently. In other words, one study would be used to identify performance deficiencies and their causes. This study was also intended to be future-oriented. While many managers currently performed at satisfactory levels, the prediction was that their current skills and knowledge would not be sufficient to enable them to perform effectively in the future.

Decision 1: Purposes. The purpose of the performance effectiveness assessment was to identify the competencies that managers would need in the future so that they would be successful in an ever changing marketplace and workplace. The term *competency* was used to mean the combination of skills and knowledge that a manager would need for success in a specific area.

The purpose of the cause analysis was to identify any environmental barriers that would inhibit managers from successfully using the required competencies on the job. The focus during the cause analysis would be on the identification of

Figure 9. Determining Required Front-End Assessments.

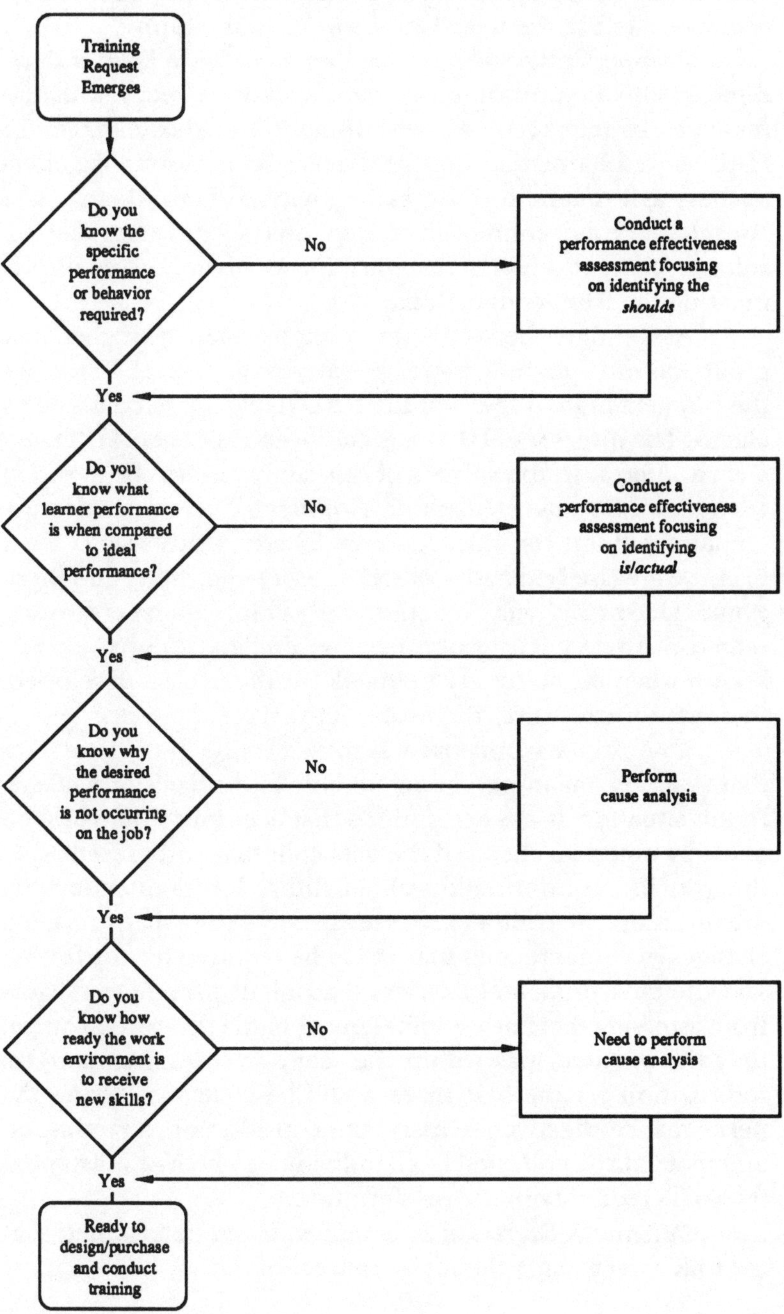

current environmental barriers that had to be changed if managers were to use the new competencies in the future.

Decision 2: Who Will Review Data and Make Related Decisions. In this organization, we were working directly with the manager of management development and the manager of HRD as we planned and implemented the performance effectiveness assessment and the cause analysis. Thus, there was a consultant group, composed of both internal and external consultants, charged with the responsibility of planning and implementing the front-end analysis.

At the time the study was being planned, a single client group was not apparent; there appeared to be several. Certainly, the two next-highest levels of the HRD department qualified as clients. The director of HRD and the vice-president of HRD had a keen interest in the success of this study and in the eventual curriculum for management development. There were also potential clients in the line, however. These clients would most likely be the chief executive officer, the vice-chairman, and three group vice-presidents. Whether the senior managers represented a single client group or several client groups was not known when the study was planned. (As the project developed, these senior executives did evolve into critical players.)

One primary purpose was to determine the type of data that would be meaningful and credible to the decision makers. In this situation, it was determined that decisions would best be made by potential clients, if the data collected and presented to them included information about future forces affecting the organization, the competencies needed by future managers, the changes in competencies that would be required for the future, and the environmental barriers that might prevent managers from applying their new competencies in the future. Of course, only the last item was within the scope of the cause analysis; information for the first three would be collected during the performance effectiveness assessment. In addition, it was important that data be collected from individuals who had substantial internal credibility in the organization.

Decision 3: Sources of Information. It was determined that the following groups should be sources of data.

1. Fifteen senior executives: They could provide information about the future forces affecting the organization and about the new competencies that would be required of managers in the future.
2. Successful, experienced managers: They could provide information about competencies needed by future managers, because these individuals were already viewed as managing in a manner seen as desirable for the future.
3. Immediate bosses of successful managers: This group could provide another viewpoint on what successful managers were doing. Bosses often provide an objectivity about incumbents' activities that incumbents are not able to provide.
4. Typical managers: They could provide information about the competencies currently being used by the typical managers in the organization. In an effort to avoid including new managers with limited experience in the interviewing process, a criterion was established that a participating manager must have at least twelve months of experience.
5. Immediate bosses of typical managers: They also could provide objective information about the competencies of typical managers.

Decision 4: Data Comparisons. It was decided that the data would be compared in four different ways, using four groups: successful incumbents and bosses, who would provide information about competencies required of managers in the future; typical incumbents and their bosses, who would provide information about current competencies; bonus-level managers, who were primarily the managers of supervisors and other managers; and non–bonus-level managers, who generally were managers of individual contributors.

Decision 5: Number of People in Source Groups. There were approximately two hundred bonus-level managers and six hundred non–bonus-level managers. About one hundred non–bonus-level managers had been in their jobs for less than a year, and so the target group actually consisted of some five hundred non–bonus-level managers. All these managers were at the same location, and so geography was not an issue.

In examining the number of managers to be used as sources of data, we determined that from 10 to 20 percent should be used as sources, primarily because we wanted the study to be visible to the maximum number of managers; we wanted a large number of respondents, so that patterns in the data would be more easily discernible; and the time frame of the study, as well as the client's desire to avoid using questionnaires, would prevent our reaching more than 20 percent of the total number of managers.

Of course, in addition to these managers, all fifteen senior managers were to be interviewed, because they could provide a variety of viewpoints regarding future business needs; they could provide a variety of viewpoints regarding the needs of managers, particularly in certain specialized areas; and we wanted the study to be very visible to them.

Decision 6: Data-Collection Methods. In this organization, there was a bias against questionnaires, because they were perceived as providing data of low credibility and because of concern about a low response rate. In addition, there was a bias in favor of interviews or focus groups, which were perceived to provide high visibility for the study. Therefore, we decided to use one-to-one interviews with the fifteen senior managers and focus groups with the remaining managers.

The decision to use one-to-one interviews with the fifteen senior managers was based on concern for the senior managers' time (a one-to-one interview required less of the interviewee's time than a focus group would) and concern that the senior managers would have a diversity of viewpoints (we wanted to capture every viewpoint).

The decision to use focus groups for the managers was based primarily on the need to be visible to as many managers as possible, the need to gather data from as many managers as possible within the shortest time, and the need to use the interviewers efficiently.

Decision 7: Resource Limitations. The internal HRD professionals, stretched by prior commitments, were using external

Table 4. Sources of Data for Front-End Assessment.

	Competencies Required in the Future			*Competencies Being Utilized Now*	
Level of Manager	*Senior Management*	*Successful Managers*	*Bosses of Successful Managers*	*Typical Managers*	*Bosses of Typical Managers*
Bonus-level manager	Fifteen one-to-one interviews	1–2 focus groups[a]	1 focus group	2–3 focus groups	1 focus group
Non–bonus-level manager		1–2 focus groups	1 focus group	2–3 focus groups	1 focus group

[a] Each focus group would consist of from six to ten managers.

consultants for this front-end assessment. There was an interest in having one HRD staff member work closely with us, so that development of that person would take place. It was anticipated that the learning from this project would enable that HRD professional to manage and implement a similar study in the future, independently of consultants. Table 4 illustrates the design used for this assessment.

What Was Discovered? The performance effectiveness assessment identified sixteen competencies clustered in three general areas: managing and leading others, analyzing situations and making judgments, and forming networks and intraorganizational alliances.

The cause analysis revealed environmental barriers that would make it difficult for managers to demonstrate needed competencies. First, managers valued hanging on to project work as part of their own job security. This value became a barrier to delegation and to the development of people. Managers also valued a "roll up your shirt sleeves" management style versus delegation of substantial responsibilities to subordinates. This value was also a barrier to delegation.

Second, bosses of managers were more likely to coach their subordinates on technical skills than on behavioral or interpersonal skills. This lack of coaching by bosses would become a barrier to the on-the-job application of many of the competencies within all three clusters.

Third, there was a strong belief that a new idea that proved unsuccessful would bring negative repercussions ("punishment") to the manager advocating the innovation. This belief became a barrier to innovation and risk taking. The organization also expected each manager to have in-depth data about each project. Therefore, managers tended to keep important projects for themselves and not to delegate. Moreover, managers were primarily rewarded for their technical expertise, rather than for their managerial competence.

The data from the cause analysis allowed the clients to make strategic decisions regarding both the competencies requiring development and the environment required to support those competencies. A three-year curriculum was developed. Competencies whose use would be supported by the work environment were included in the first-year programs—for example, communicating a vision, planning, coaching, giving feedback, and developing people. For competencies that the work environment would not support, senior management would be involved in making decisions about changes in the work environment. These changes would be implemented at the same time that the competencies were being offered in the training program. Examples of these competencies were innovation, risk taking, and team building.

Determining the Potential for Skill Transfer

There are times when a training director is asked to implement and conduct a training program that has been selected without the benefit of a needs analysis. This request often comes about because line managers have seen something that leads them to believe that training in a particular topic would be useful.

We experienced this some years ago, when the president of a regional lawn-and-garden chain received complaints from four members of the board of directors about poor housekeeping in stores. Upon receiving these complaints, the president stopped unannounced into two stores and found that the housekeeping in those stores was indeed unsatisfactory. The president then contacted the vice-president of retail operations and asked her to find a training program on merchandising and store appearance and to have every store employee attend the program. The vice-president of retail operations was aware of a training program conducted by a competing chain. She contacted that chain for the name of the vendor supplying that program. After reviewing the program, she decided to purchase it and implement it as a one-day workshop for all retail employees, a total of 5,400 workers. She then informed the retail training manager that he was to implement this training for all store employees.

The training manager was aware that, just two years before, a similar program had been offered to all store employees. In fact, he had conducted many of the workshops himself. At the time, he had heard that the stores were understaffed during the spring rush—the time when the housekeeping complaints had reached the president. During the spring rush, the employees worked as hard as they could just to meet the needs of the customers; they had little time to improve the stores' appearance or to do extra merchandising.

The training manager was concerned that this training, to be offered during the late summer and early fall, would not address the real need. He felt that most employees and all managers knew how to maintain clean stores and how to merchandise products properly. While the workshop might put some emphasis on the need for improved housekeeping and merchandising, it would be a costly approach, because there was not a deficiency in those kinds of skills or knowledge. Instead, the situation could be addressed more effectively by management actions. The causes were task interference and negative balance of consequences. Staffing shortages put employees in the position of handling customers first and working on housekeeping and merchandising only during slow periods. During the spring, there were no slow periods.

The training manager was in a dilemma. By being responsive and providing the program, he risked lowering his credibility, because people would be coming to a program for which they saw little need. It was also probable that the same housekeeping problems would remain after the program's conclusion. Senior management would probably blame the training manager for those continued problems.

The training manager decided that the best strategy would be to approach the vice-president of retail operations and tell his concerns about the potential for successful resolution of this business problem through a training effort. Through this conversation, the vice-president came to understand that training alone would probably not be the answer. With her as an ally, the training manager was then able to influence the president to adopt an alternative plan. Criteria for satisfactory housekeeping and effective merchandising were agreed to; these had not been documented before. Short overview programs were offered to familiarize district managers and store managers with those criteria. In addition, retail outlets that needed additional staffing were able to hire temporary help during the seasonal rush.

In situations of this type, it is important that the HRD professional make an effort to dissuade decision makers from implementing a training program and persuade them to collect data that will identify the true cause of a business problem. With such information, plans can be made to remove the cause. These plans may or may not include training efforts. The HRD professional must be willing to take some risk by explaining why moving ahead with a training program will not be successful. As a wise man once said, "You will never hear yes if you are afraid of hearing no."

Once we have the necessary data from our cause analysis, we must prepare a report for our clients. We want to do this in a manner that will enable them to make informed decisions about both developmental needs and environmental factors. In a feedback meeting, we provide our clients with information about what is needed to change the system and the people in it so that business goals can be met. Chapter Eight describes the process of readying for and facilitating a feedback meeting.

Summary

The following techniques move training toward impact:

Activity **Impact**

- Conduct a cause analysis to determine causes of current performance deficiencies and barriers that will inhibit the use of new skills on the job.
- Make all seven decisions of the cause analysis, even if you have time and data-collection restraints.
- Clarify the purposes of the cause analysis, and clarify who will make what decisions before collecting data.
- Become familiar with and look for evidence of barriers to skill transfer.

Eight

Tabulating, Interpreting, and Reporting Results to Clients

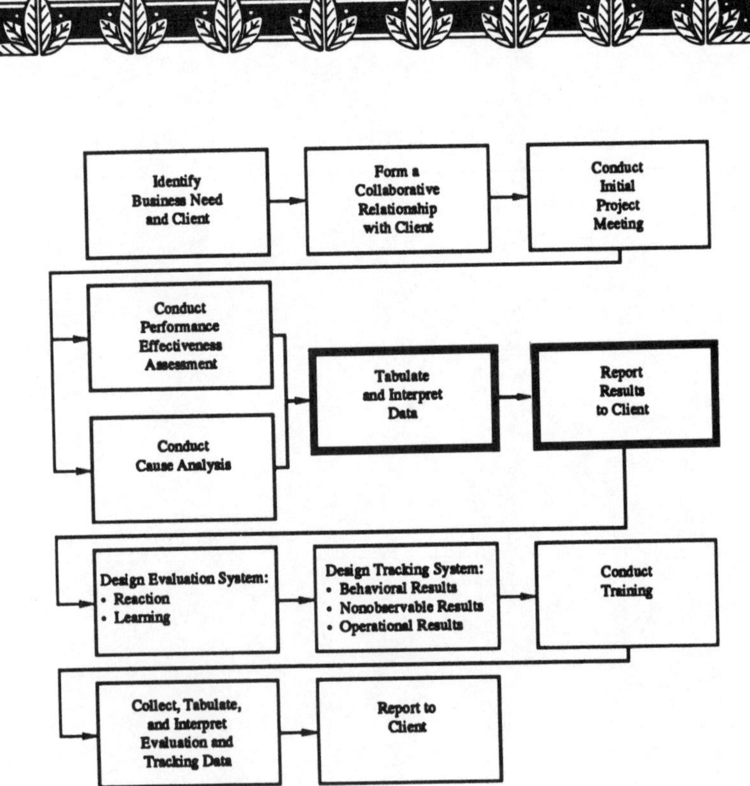

Picture this scene: You are sitting at your desk, staring at piles of returned questionnaires and completed interview guides. There may even be a few audiotapes from completed focus-group interviews. How do you turn all that paper (which often can be measured in feet) into hard, quantified data, so that you and others can make the appropriate business decisions from it?

Unfortunately, many people, after spending significant time to collect data, do not realize the full benefits from this effort, because of ineffective tabulation and reporting of the results. If the information is poorly presented, and if subtle patterns in the data are never identified, then you have lost the opportunity to maximize the return on this investment of time and effort.

The implication of poor data tabulation and reporting for a training project is that you may lose the opportunity to refocus a training project from a Training-for-Activity effort into a Training-for-Impact effort. From the data you have collected, and from the manner in which you present the data to your clients, you gain the opportunity to take the results-oriented approach to training implementation that this book is describing.

In a meeting where data results are presented, you and your clients will be making strategic decisions based on the information that is presented: What groups of people should be taught what sets of skills? What environmental conditions need to be addressed so that the skills taught will be transferred to the job? What business outcomes are we seeking from this effort to make it a good investment of time and resources?

We believe that agreeing on actions to be taken is the litmus test for determining the success of any data-collection effort. After all the information is collected and reported, if no actions are taken and no decisions are made, then the entire process will have been a waste of time.

Turning raw data (those stacks of surveys sitting on your desk) into hard data (from which decisions will be made) requires five steps: tabulation, formatting, interpretation, preparation, and reporting of the data.

Tabulation of Data

This first step is a critical one, although it can also be tedious. Tabulation of data means the process of actually "pulling off" from the surveys and interviews what people have indicated and starting to categorize that information so that it can be reviewed and understood. It means finding out how many people said yes to various questions and discovering the means and standard deviations for all responses. How the data will be tabulated was actually determined when the questionnaires and interviews were created—or it should have been. Perhaps a true, although disastrous, story will make the point.

We once met a training director who told of a personal experience he had had the previous year. It seems that he and two employees decided it would be helpful to conduct an assessment of the developmental needs of managers in a firm. They created a questionnaire, which was sent to more than one thousand people. Unfortunately, this questionnaire contained only open-ended questions (violating one of the points made in Chapter Six). They obtained a large response, with more than seven hundred questionnaires returned. At that point, they realized that they had no time to analyze the information. They were looking at the arduous task of analyzing twelve questions, as answered by more than seven hundred people. Such an analysis would have required several weeks, time they did not have, and so they destroyed all the surveys and moved forward without analyzing them.

The first point is to ensure that you have considered how the collected information will be tabulated before you begin your data-collecting process. Essentially, three options are available: for open-ended data, manual tabulation by completion of a content analysis; for closed data, tabulation either by a computer or by hand.

Whichever method is used, the ultimate goal is to reduce the data from their raw state into some type of quantified format, without changing the meaning of the data. If one hundred questionnaires are returned, tabulation would let you know exactly how many people responded yes or no to each question (when such choices were offered to respondents). Interpretation of data cannot begin until the data are tabulated and reduced.

Analysis of Open-Ended Data. Content analysis is the process used to tabulate open-ended data. It is what would be done to data from interviews or focus-group interviews or from any open-ended question on a questionnaire. When people have been given the freedom to respond to a question in any manner, content analysis will be used to tabulate the responses.

The process is relatively straightforward (if a bit tedious). Read the response from one individual to a question. Create a category label that captures the main point of that response and indicate (with a "tick mark") that one person noted that response. Read the next response to the same question. If the response is qualitatively different, create a new category label (and put down one "tick mark"). If the response reflects the same thought as the original label, indicate a second mark for it. Continue with this process until all responses to that particular question have been coded.

Table 5 provides some tips and techniques for doing content analysis. Recall that the ultimate goal is to tabulate data so that they are categorized and quantified as much as possible, with no interpretation. In content analysis, some interpretation may be needed, because you will be condensing several sentences into a label of few words, but such interpretation through condensation should be minimal.

Exercise: Customer Data from a Savings and Loan. Here are some actual statements made by customers of a savings and loan with which we worked. An effort was made to determine how the customers perceived the interpersonal and selling skills of branch personnel. How would you tabulate and categorize these statements? Once you have completed your analysis, compare it with what we actually reported.

In response to the question "What comments would you like to make regarding this branch and the service provided you?" some customers replied in the following ways:

- I think it is really great that you have special accounts for college students. It helps out a lot.

Table 5. Tips and Techniques for Content Analysis of Data.

1. Try to have the same person code all responses to the same question. This ensures that the interpretation applied to each statement will be consistent within each question.
2. Do not guess what respondents meant. If responses do not make sense to you, then eliminate the data.
3. Attempt to create data categories that are mutually exclusive, so that a response goes into one or another category but not into both.
4. At times, a respondent will answer a question with several statements. Be certain to code each statement into a category.
5. When in doubt about the category in which to place a statement, ask for a colleague's opinion.
6. Keep a record of any comments that would make good quotations in the final report. Do not hope to go back and find them later.
7. Some interpretation will be essential to compress data into manageable categories. The goal is to keep such interpretation to a minimum.
8. Occasional comments will not fit the codes. For example, such comments as "A-OK" or "Very good" lack any content substance and are often not recorded at all.
9. There will usually be a few "leftover" statements that cannot be put into any category. They will form an "other" category, into which miscellaneous statements will be placed.

Note: Data are usually obtained from one-to-one interviews, focus-group interviews, and open-ended questions on questionnaires.

- Tellers should not be answering phones. It is rude to the customers at their windows, and the tellers lose their train of thought.
- The branch manager has interrupted me while I was doing business in the branch to tell her employees that she needed them, there was a phone call, and so on. Even if I am exchanging pleasantries with an employee and our business is done, I am still a customer. The manager makes me feel like I don't count as a "real" customer.
- Interest rates are too low; there is too much of a spread between deposits and loans.
- I waited too long to open a new account.
- I was very impressed with the knowledge of the platform person.
- I am very satisfied with service. The bank employee was pleasant and helpful. The branch was busy, but she tried hard to let people know they hadn't been forgotten.

- I was impressed with the lovely surroundings in your branch.
- I found that the new-accounts person answered questions in a robotic manner.
- The service was very good, and the bank employee was very cooperative and nice.
- I like the personal touch to your service.

Our analysis was as follows:

Positive Aspects of Service
Special accounts available = 1
Personnel knowledgeable about service = 1
Pleasant service/personal service = 3
Branch decoration = 1

Complaints/Concerns Regarding Service
Tellers interrupted during customer transaction
  by phone = 1
  by other employee = 1
Bank interest too low = 1
Waiting time too long for service = 1
Impersonal manner of bank personnel = 1

If you need to tabulate data from audiotapes of focus-group interviews, the process is very similar, except that you are listening to a statement, rather than reading one. It means a lot of stopping and starting of the tape. We have found that tabulation of a focus-group interview requires twice the time it takes to conduct the interview. Therefore, if the interview was ninety minutes long, the tabulation of that interview will require up to three hours to complete. The time required to tabulate data from an interview guide will vary, of course, with the length of the interview. Again, our rule is that a one-hour interview will require about fifteen to twenty minutes to tabulate, once initial categories have been developed.

Whether you are tabulating information from interview guides or from focus-group interviews, be sure that you note salient statements and quotes from your respondents as you go along. The opportunity that open-ended data provide for making numbers "come alive" through verbatim quotations is tremendous. It is the difference between saying that 90 percent of respondents believed that risk taking was not encouraged in the company and making the same statement but adding, "This belief was expressed succinctly by one respondent, who said, 'In this organization, the punishment for failure after risk taking far outweighs any reward for success.'" Management remembers these statements, which often elicit understanding at an emotional level. When you find such statements, record them immediately. It is very frustrating to hunt through all your interview guides for that one statement you remember reading but now cannot recall where.

Analysis of Closed Data. To tabulate closed questions, determine exactly how many people responded to each option for each question. If, for example, a Likert scale from 1 to 5 was used for a question, then this tabulation would determine how many people responded to 1 on the scale, to 2 on the scale, and so forth.

Operational data are also tabulated in this manner. Perhaps there are sales figures that must be analyzed by month. Tabulation is done to determine how much of each product was sold by each region in each month. The process is fairly cut and dried. It requires someone to count the sales and perhaps place them in the appropriate intervals or created categories. For example, you may record the sales revenues below $50,000, between $51,000 and $100,000, and so on.

Closed data can be analyzed either manually or with the aid of a computer. The manual method is truly a headache. We are reminded of a situation one of the authors dealt with while managing the training function at a bank. A needs assessment on supervisory skills training had been conducted. Three hundred supervisors completed a twenty-four-item questionnaire. The response rate was approximately 85 percent, and so there were a few hundred questionnaires to tabulate. Since no computer was available, a temporary secretarial agency was asked to send someone to tabulate the data. A young woman arrived, eager to begin her day. She was instructed in how to mark off how many people had responded to each option for each item. As the day proceeded, her spirits drooped. By day's end, this woman indicated that even though there was more work to be done, she would not return; a fresh recruit would be needed for the next day. This process repeated itself. It took three women a total of three days to complete the analysis.

A much-preferred option would be to have closed data tabulated on a computer. If you use this option, you must consider the layout of the questionnaire from the start. You will want to devise a questionnaire that is easy for someone to input into the computer. Here are some tips we have learned over the years for providing ease of input.

1. Use numerical, rather than alphabetical, responses. A computer generally has a number pad on the keyboard, which allows for faster input. As much as possible, avoid mixing numerical and alphabetical responses.
2. Do not print the questionnaire on back-to-back pages. It takes more clerical time to turn both the page and the document than to turn the page only.
3. If questionnaires are to be returned from a variety of sources (managers, supervisors, employees), reproduce them for each source on different colors of paper. This ensures that the sources will be kept separate during input.

Some of these tips may seem like small savings in time, but recall that there may be hundreds of surveys to input. Therefore, the accumulated time savings could be hours.

If you are interested in having a computer tabulate your data, several software packages are available for purchase. Here are a few designed for installation in a personal computer and used frequently for the type of statistics generated by needs-assessment information:

A.S.K.
Albrecht and Associates
P.O. Box 99097
San Diego, CA 92109
619/272-3776

THE SURVEY SYSTEM
Creative Research Systems
1649 Del Oro
Petaluma, CA 94952
707/765-1001

SPSS/PC, Inc.
Suite 3000
444 North Michigan Avenue
Chicago, IL 60611
312/329-3500

SYNTHESIS
Bauer & Associates, Inc.
210 East Huron
Ann Arbor, MI 48104
313/668-1303

STATPAC
Walonick Associates
6500 Nicollet Avenue South
Minneapolis, MN 55423
612/866-9022

"Statistics 101." Now we know how many people said yes or no to a question, and we may have some statistical means and standard deviations. If this information comes to you from a computer, it is in the form of a computer printout. If the information has been tabulated in the form of a content analysis, it often consists of handwritten notes on multiple sheets of paper. Neither of these forms is suitable for presentation to your client. The challenge is to determine how the data will be statistically presented so that you and your clients will be able to see the picture described by the numbers. Two questions to consider in this decision-making process: Which statistics will be meaningful to the client and allow the client to easily understand the picture painted by the data results? Which statistics will most accurately reflect the raw results?

To meet the demands of the first question, we most often report information to clients descriptively, using such simple statistics as means, standard deviations, percentages, and frequency distributions. Most line managers are comfortable with and knowledgeable about these kinds of statistics; in contrast, many line managers, as well as many HRD professionals, are uncomfortable with other kinds. It is important to report results in a manner that does not intimidate or confuse your client. Remember, during the feedback meeting, your role will be to help the client understand the meaning of the information and to influence decisions that may be made as a result. Therefore, you need to be on an equal footing with your clients. Reporting data in a statistical framework that makes sense to you but not to your clients destroys the equality that collaboration requires.

The second question is also important. The old adage "Figures don't lie, but liars figure" applies here. Let us assume that you had four responses to a question, one *true* and three *false*. It would be technically correct to report that 25 percent of the respondents answered *true* and 75 percent answered *false*, but is that accurate? Such a statistic, in this instance, overinflates the results. On the basis of such a low response rate, it is doubtful that any substantive decision could be made. If we provide the client only with the percentages, we may mislead the client and misrepresent the data.

Table 6 indicates the most common descriptive statistics we use when we report information to our clients. A good rule, however, is that when you have a low number of responses (ten or fewer), you should report those as actual frequencies, rather than as means or percentages. (If you need more information on statistics, we encourage you to consult the many texts available on this subject.)

Formatting of Data

At this point, you have condensed the raw data. While the data are now easier to begin to use and interpret, you are still not ready for that process. Consider the fact that what is in front of you could be a computer printout noting the means and standard deviations for each of the seventy-six items on your questionnaire. Somehow, all those numbers must be placed into a graphic or visual format, so that patterns among the numbers become obvious. To determine what that format should be, you must return to some of the questions you asked at the start of the project: What decisions do you want to make from the information? From what sources did you collect information? How many different ways will the data be compared? In addition, you will want to consider from what topics or categories information was collected. For example, did one question category deal with what successful incumbents do to manage others, while another category focused on what these same successful incumbents do

Table 6. Statistical Display of Data.

Method	*Definition*	*Considerations*
Mean	Sum of all responses to a particular question, which are then divided by the number of responses given.	If a few responses are at the extremes, the mean may give an artificial picture of the data. *Example:* Three responses are 10, one is 100, mean is 32.5.
Median	The point on the scale above which 50 percent of the responses lie and below which 50 percent of the responses lie.	Less sensitive to the presence of extreme scores.
Mode	The score that occurs with the greatest frequency.	There can be more than one mode for a set of data (called *bimodal*).
Standard deviation	Indicates how spread out the data are from the mean. Used only in association with means.	Generally, it is desirable to have small standard deviations, which indicate that the mean is an accurate reflection of most of the people in the response group. Large standard deviations indicate that there is wide variance in how people within a group are responding to a question.
Percentage	Determines the relative frequency of a response within a set of responses.	Should be avoided when the raw number of responses is low. *Example:* There were two responses, and the results indicate that 50 percent of the responses were at a certain level.
Frequency distribution	Reporting of the raw number of responses to a particular question.	Often displayed in bar graphs or histograms.
Range	Reporting of the difference between the response of the lowest value and that of the highest value.	*Example:* If responses to a question were 5, 3, 5, 6, 4, and 5, then the range was 3. This is the difference between the low value (3) and the high value (6).
Rank order	Ranking of a series of items (provided by the interviewer or on the questionnaire) in some order	The coder determines the basis for ranking (what the respondent does most frequently to least frequently, values most to least, and so on). The coder needs to indicate clearly what the numbered ranks mean (whether 1 means the *best* or *worst*).

when interacting with people they do not manage? In this case, you will probably want to format the data so that each category is presented separately.

Determining how to format your data so that you and others can review them is not easy; it represents a conceptual challenge. We have found it helpful to close the door, hold the calls, and think about what would work best. Should a bar graph be created to illustrate how different groups of people responded to the same question? Would a table be better, with the means of each group's responses to a question noted side by side? Certainly, you must consider how your client prefers to have information presented.

In reporting results from front-end assessments, it is often important to illustrate any differences between what individuals indicate should be true and what is actually true in the organization now. We worked with an organization where this type of information was collected through questionnaires. The overall purposes of the assessment were to determine what competencies would be required for the success of first-level managers in the future and to determine how typical managers performed against those competencies at present. By comparing results for the two purposes, the client could determine where the greatest skill deficiencies (or gaps) existed, gaining the opportunity to set priorities among the training programs that might be required.

To collect information, managers were asked to indicate either the criticality of particular kinds of behavior and competencies in the future or their personal ability to demonstrate the behavior and competencies at the current time. All data were computer tabulated; two of the statistical results were overall means for each of the twenty-three competencies, indicating the criticality of competencies and current ability of managers to demonstrate them. Rather than just listing these means, we displayed them in bar graphs, as illustrated by Figure 10. Clearly, there is a larger performance gap in facilitating change than in writing skills. If this training function is going to provide courses where the need is greatest, it is clear which competency needs to be addressed.

Figure 10. Data Reported in a Bar Graph.

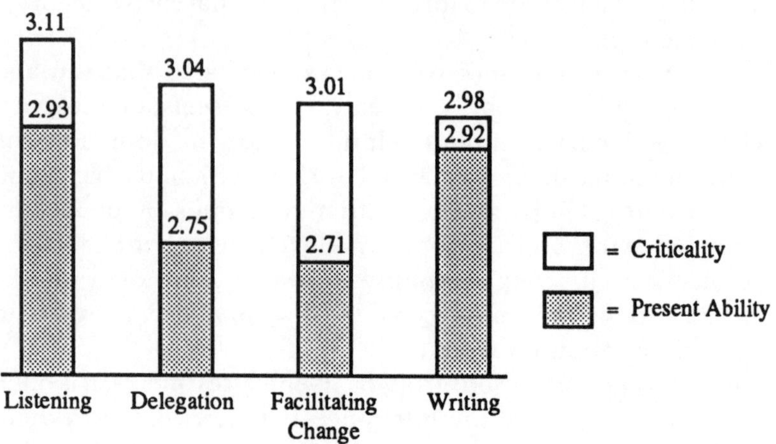

In another organization, where information was obtained through interviews, data were collected on current ability to demonstrate various management competencies. This information was collected for managers from different business groups within the organization. The client wanted to know whether there were any significant differences in current ability that should be considered in the development of courses. While the values collected for each item could have been displayed in a table, the data were displayed graphically, as shown in Figure 11. This graph made it easy for the client to determine which competencies required more development and the degree to which the two groups of managers were similar in their needs.

A large telecommunications corporation wanted to determine the value of a certain program to both attendees and managers. There were five major agenda topics in the program, which required one week to conduct. Each agenda item was investigated through interviews. There were some closed questions asked of those interviewed, including a question to identify which of the five agenda items had been of greatest benefit. The number of people indicating which agenda items were most beneficial could have been given in simple percentages, but compare that format with the one shown in Figure 12. In the bar

Figure 11. Identification of Competency Gaps.

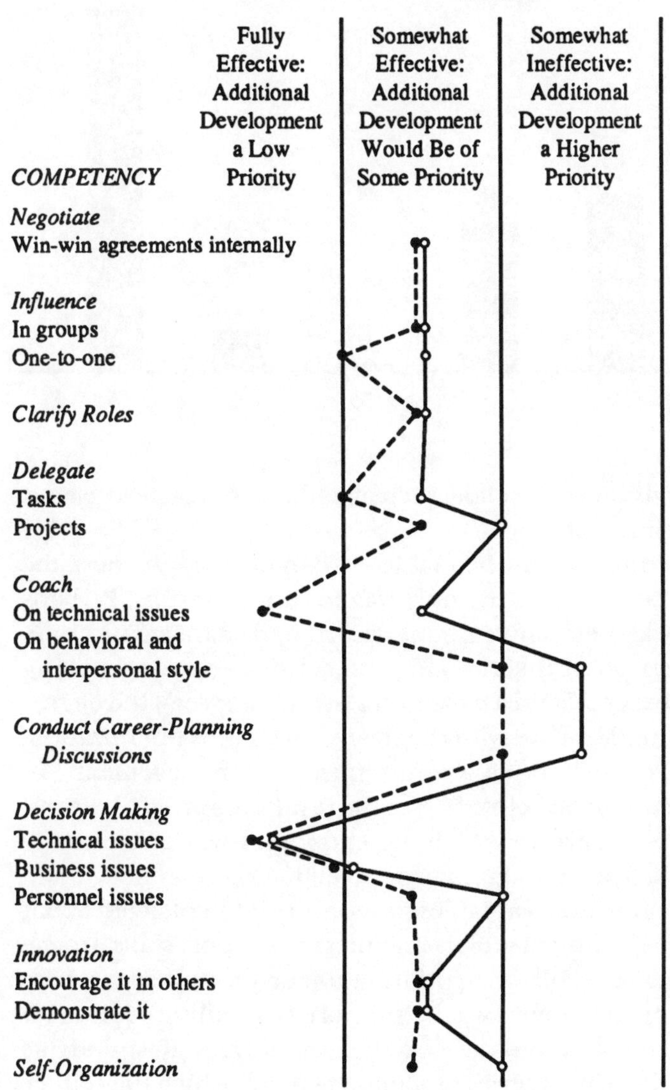

Figure 12. Sample Bar Graph.

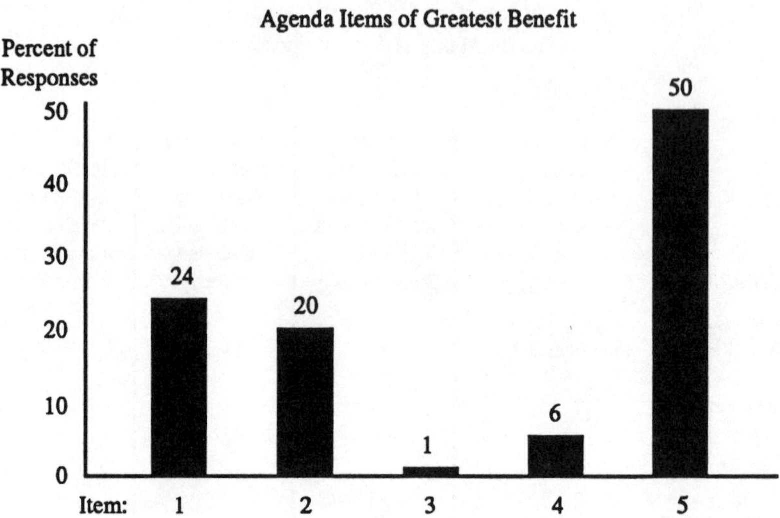

graph, the difference in how each agenda item was perceived is certainly apparent.

There are times when tables of numbers are the best, the most accurate, or even the only way to display results. Perhaps you have asked employees, supervisors, and managers to indicate on a six-point Likert scale (with a 1 on the scale meaning "strongly disagree" and a 6 meaning "strongly agree") the degree of agreement they have with the statement "In this organization, individual contributions are recognized by management." In this case, it might be helpful to see the results reported as means: The degree of agreement among employees was 2.79; among supervisors, 3.55; among managers, 4.90.

We have also used tables to report results collected about the work environment and its readiness to support skills. In one instance, we were collecting information on the degree to which the work environment would support the skills required of managers to coach and develop their employees. Respondents were provided with a series of statements, with which they either agreed or disagreed. When we reported these results to the client, we depicted them in the following manner:

Statement: There may be limited accountability and/or rewards organizationally for spending time to develop direct reports.
Percentage of individuals agreeing with this statement:

Total population: 37

Group 1 only: 40

Group 2 only: 28

Statement: Doing the job is of higher priority to me than managing others to do the job.
Percentage of individuals agreeing with this statement:

Total population: 41

Group 1 only: 38

Group 2 only: 50

These results indicated that training alone would not ensure that managers would be good developers of others; the organizational accountability system also needed to be modified.

Interpretation of Data

Now the real fun can begin, for this is when you begin to discover what all these results mean. What specific performance deficiencies exist? What is causing them?

The process of data interpretation moves data through a "funnel," as depicted in Figure 13. You begin with dozens, perhaps hundreds, of data results, which are the actual facts tabulated from the raw data. These results are indisputable; they involve no interpretation at all. You will have just completed the formatting of these results, which you will be taking with you to a client meeting.

As the funnel depicted in Figure 13 indicates, from these many results you draw a few conclusions. The funnel narrows because conclusions are usually reasoned deductions from several pieces of data. We are now beginning to reduce the amount of information with which we must deal. For example, consider again Figure 11. The following conclusions could be drawn from the various results depicted there: The two levels of management appear to have similar needs; and the largest deficien-

Figure 13. The Data Funnel.

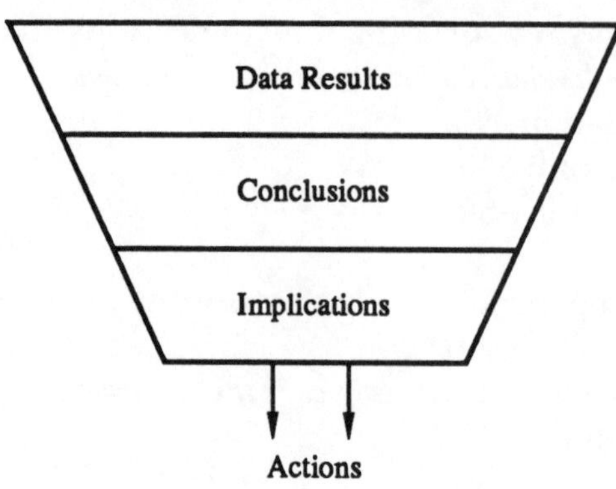

cies appear in the areas of behavioral coaching, delegation of projects, and career-planning discussions. In this example, we have reduced the many data depicted by each of the points in Figure 11 to two conclusions.

The final point of the data funnel is implications. Implications are the "so what" of the various conclusions. They often reflect the business need that initiated the project and show how the situation (as depicted by the data) will affect the business need. For example, "so what" that midlevel managers are not demonstrating the skills of behavioral coaching with their employees at the necessary frequency or level of effectiveness? "So what" that career planning with employees is not being demonstrated? If those situations did not change, what would the impact be on the organization and its business goals?

In this situation, the client felt that the impact would be severe. The organization's growth had leveled out, and opportunities for advancement had slowed considerably. High-achieving employees were becoming increasingly frustrated by the lack of opportunity for upward movement and were not being counseled by their managers about available opportunities for lateral movement or job enrichment. If this situation went unchecked, senior management felt, certain high-potential employees would begin to leave the organization. Development of managers in the how-to's of career planning and coaching seemed critical. Again, the teaming of data implications with business needs became the primary motivator of management's taking action.

Preparation for the Client Meeting

Once you are familiar with the collected data and feel confident in the various patterns and pictures that the information is painting, you need to prepare for the client meeting. More than at any other time in the process of linking training to business needs, you will be in a "where the rubber meets the road" situation. This will be a prime opportunity to influence the client's thinking and move the client toward taking the actions necessary to make certain that an appropriate training program is delivered and that skills and knowledge taught will be transferred to the job. If this opportunity for influence is lost, it may not reappear through the life of the project. In a feedback meeting, such as the one to be described here, the HRD professional is in the role of change agent, elevating any prospective training from an activity effort to an impact- and business-driven effort. Obviously, preparation is crucial.

In planning for the feedback meeting, the first need is to identify its specific purposes. The primary purpose should be agreement on actions that must be taken if the training program is to result in an impact on the business and if the business need driving the program is to be met. Some actions will be for the HRD professional to take; others will be for management to take. You will be reviewing information about skill and knowledge deficiencies, as well as about their causes. Since some of the causes may be related to the work environment of the future learners, management action may be required. (Your client should have accepted this possibility when you had the initial meeting, described in Chapter Five.)

There are secondary purposes of this meeting, however, which may also be important to consider. These secondary purposes may include developing management's concepts about what training can and cannot do, gaining support from management for the program about to occur, determining how the program will be evaluated, and dealing with any resistance.

In preparing for this meeting, there is one overriding issue to be considered: How collaborative will the meeting be? (We discussed possible consultant styles in Chapter Four. Block's [1981] work in this area is also relevant.) In the expert style, all results and conclusions are reported to the client by the HRD professional, who makes recommendations for action. In the collaborator style, results are presented by the HRD professional, but all conclusions and actions are determined by the client and the HRD professional working together. In the expert style, the client's role is to react to what is stated by the HRD professional, accepting or rejecting it as desired. In the collaborator style, the HRD professional does not bring any formal recommendations to the meeting. Recommendations are formulated through exchange of ideas.

Obviously, there can be gradations of these two styles along a continuum. We encourage advancement toward the collaborative end of the continuum as much as possible in making reports to clients.

In a feedback meeting, it is essential to invite the client to participate actively in determing what the results mean. Clients will bring their own perspectives from working in the organizational areas from which the data were collected. As clients help to draw conclusions from the information, it becomes more probable that they will support the implications for action. This process is yet another way to demonstrate the collaborative approach to internal HRD consulting.

Before the meeting, it is important to establish a mutual understanding with your client about how the information will be delivered. Will you be using the collaborator style (and therefore expecting the client to help decide what the results mean and what to do about them), or will you be using more of an expert style (and therefore bringing conclusions and recommendations for the client to consider)?

We had an unfortunate experience a few years ago that illustrates what can go wrong when the client and the HRD professional are not on the same wavelength. We had concluded an extensive front-end assessment whose outcomes would be used to identify learning objectives for a training program yet to be developed. There was a substantial amount of information to be reviewed with our clients. We had told our primary contact that we would bring the results from the assessment but would expect to work jointly in determining both what those results meant and their implications. Our mistake was to tell the clients how the data would be reviewed. We did not give the clients any option.

As the meeting progressed, it became obvious that the clients were growing dissatisfied. They would take some data and immediately jump into decisions for action, bypassing the step of drawing conclusions. As they became more and more impatient, we became more and more frustrated. The meeting would have been more successful if we had presented conclusions for the clients' reactions and then all built on them together. The clients' expectations for some of the services we would be providing and our own expectations regarding those services were dissimilar.

Over the years, we have found that the amount of information one needs to review with a client tends to dictate where on the "expert" to "collaborator" continuum of feedback one should place oneself. When you have a great deal of information, it becomes important to expedite the feedback process by bringing with you some conclusions and, perhaps, some recommendations. What the client must understand is that these conclusions and recommendations are merely proposed and are open for lots of discussion. We must be willing to back away from some of our conclusions and recommendations if the client does not support them. The give and take of collaboration must still occur, even in a meeting to which we bring conclusions and recommendations.

Here are a few suggestions to guide your preparation for feedback meetings.

1. Determine how the client prefers to have the data presented. Does your client like bar graphs, tables, or frequency distributions? Does the information need to be formally pre-

sented (by the use of slides, for example), or will a handout be sufficient?

2. How much time will be allotted to the meeting, and who will attend? We have found that such meetings typically take from two to four hours.
3. Review the outcomes and the agenda you expect for the meeting, and be confident that the client supports them.
4. Will you report any results that may cause emotional reactions in members of the client team? If so, consider how you will handle those situations. Can you do anything before the meeting to limit the possibility of problems?

In preparing the information to report, you need to consider the overall picture as depicted by the data. If an overriding conclusion from the data is that bosses of potential learners are not prepared to coach and reinforce new skills, then you should consider which data to present so that your client will arrive at a similar conclusion. In this manner, you begin to set priorities for the results you will review, reducing the data so that only the most critical information is discussed in the meeting. In this meeting, you will have an opportunity to influence the thinking of your client. You will want to be prepared to address the most critical information first.

One additional consideration is whether to give your client a preview of the results before the meeting. There are two schools of thought on this subject. On the one hand, providing a preview is both courteous and helpful, especially if there are real surprises in the results. Your client can help you think about how to handle that information if there will be other people at the meeting. You also are able to obtain a sense of the key client's acceptance of the results, so that you go into the meeting more confident of the client's support. On the other hand, the client may formulate opinions about what the information means and discuss it with others before the meeting. If so, you may find yourself on the defensive as the meeting begins. You will have to spend time explaining why the results are what they are, rather than working with your client to determine what the results mean. It becomes more difficult to exert influence when you are in a defensive posture.

Our general rule is not to offer a preview of data before the meeting. We never send the data report ahead to a client so that he or she has a copy of the information as it will be presented. When we do give a preview of information, we do it in person or over the telephone, highlighting the major results and seeking reactions from our client. We tend to offer a preview either when we have some concern regarding the results and how they will be received or when the client has clearly expressed the desire to have a preview.

Reporting of Data

Over the years, we have participated in many feedback meetings. Those experiences have afforded us the opportunity to create a model for how meetings typically flow. On the basis of our model, we offer the following suggestions.

State the Purpose of the Meeting. As in any other meeting, it is important to give an overview of what you expect to accomplish. (Again, the purposes and expected outcomes should have been agreed to by your client.)

Outline the Agenda and Structure. Here, you note the various topics to be reviewed in the meeting. At this time, it is wise to indicate the role of the clients in the discussion. How active do you expect them to be in drawing conclusions and implications for action? (Again, their role and yours should have been agreed to by your client before the meeting.) You should also confirm the amount of time available for the meeting.

Present the Data, Agree on Conclusions, and Discuss Implications and Recommendations. Go through this sequence for each major category of data.

Present the data, and seek reactions. Because you probably have not sent the data ahead to be previewed, this is the first time each person will be seeing them. As you review the data, seek reactions. Do your clients indicate (through comments and nodding) that the results are no surprise? Or do comments indicate that your clients do not understand how you obtained the results? In the former case, you have some certainty that the clients are accepting the results, even though those results may be disappointing. In the latter case, you do not have that certainty. You need to probe for understanding of what is causing concern in the clients, for if they do not accept the findings, they will never agree to conclusions or implications for action. You must feel confident that your clients are accepting the results before you move on.

Agree on conclusions that you and the clients can all support. Consensus is important. Since conclusions involve some interpretation, everyone may not see the results in the same way. Therefore, as the facilitator of the meeting, you need to work through any disagreements and to articulate conclusions that everyone can support.

Determine the implications for both the training department and line management. Remember that implications are the "so what" of the conclusions. These will involve even more interpretation and therefore may present a greater opportunity for differences of opinion. Implications must reflect the business needs that prompted the investigation of a training project. Because the actions to be taken will come directly from these implications, it is essential to facilitate agreement and consensus.

Discuss and agree on recommendations for action. Some actions will be for management to take (such as altering the reward system so as to include accountability for demonstrating what will be taught). Other actions will be for the training department to take (such as including in the training program a specific module or segment not previously considered).

Finalize All Decisions. Two or three categories of data may have been discussed, and now is the time to agree on the actions in total.

Check for Client's Concerns. While it is crucial to be aware of concerns throughout the meeting, end the meeting in the certainty that all concerns have been addressed. Sometimes you can do this by asking everyone individually whether there are additional concerns or issues to be discussed.

Finalize Actions and Responsibilities. A "to do" list should be created during the meeting. At this point, you should be satisfied that everyone has the same understanding of what actions will be performed next and by whom.

The kinds of actions that result from the meeting will depend somewhat on the types of information you are reviewing and the original purposes of your project. If you are focusing on performance effectiveness assessment, for example, then the agreements and actions resulting from your meeting might include the following:

- Agreement on competencies required for success in a specific job or function (these competencies become criteria for job performance, which incumbents and managers alike will need to understand and support)
- Agreement on competencies (skills and knowledge) to be taught in a training program (these would typically be translated into learning objectives)
- Agreement on where the greatest performance deficiencies exist and identification of priority for training
- Agreement on whether a training program or other developmental means will be used to teach desired skills and knowledge

As you can see, many of the actions emanating from performance effectiveness assessment will be for the training department to take.

If what you have completed is a cause analysis, you and your clients may reach agreements on the following items:

- Causes of current performance deficiencies
- Specific actions that management must take to reduce or eliminate organizational barriers to learners' application of the desired skills and knowledge
- Specific aspects of the situation that can or cannot be addressed by training efforts

Most actions for management will be identified through cause analysis.

Regardless of which data were reviewed or what actions have resulted, it is important to send a brief letter or memo to everyone who participated in the assessment. Summarize the findings, and thank the people who gave their time and energy. This also encourages employees to cooperate in the future, for it is evident that something is being done as a result of the information that was collected.

Things That Can Go Wrong

A feedback meeting is an opportunity to link training to business needs and to gain management's assurance that the desired changes will result from this effort. Things can go wrong in the meeting, however. Clients may express resistance, either to the information that is being presented or to the direction that the meeting is taking. They simply may not agree among themselves about what should be done. You will want to manage the process skillfully, so that such events do not derail the entire effort. The following are some pitfalls that we have observed and been involved in. We also offer our thoughts on how to manage such problems.

Resistance. This is "a predictable, natural, emotional reaction of a client against the process of being helped and/or against the process of having to face up to difficult organizational problems" (Block, 1981, p. 113). When you experience a client as being resistant, it often is not a bad thing. It means that you are on target with your data and conclusions, causing concerns in the client. Clients can begin to resist because it may be easier to discredit or withdraw from the process than to make a commitment to taking certain actions. Your skill at recognizing resistance and facilitating people through it will make the difference between no action and the correct action.

What does resistance look like? A client may become very silent, make no comments until directly asked, and then offer only a minimal response. If this pattern of behavior continues, the client is probably resisting. Perhaps the client attacks the information, indicating all the reasons why it is not accurate or credible, or a client may continually change the subject and divert the attention of the group from what is being discussed. Each of these reactions, continued over time, is very likely an indicator that the client is resisting the process. It is important to detect a pattern. We do not mean that if the client becomes quiet for two minutes, she or he is resisting what is happening. Silence may mean that your client is thoughtfully considering what is being discussed. In your role as trainer-consultant, you must be alert to patterns of behavior.

Once you believe that resistance is a possibility, you must identify and clarify the situation. State, in a neutral manner, what you have observed by reflecting on the client's behavior. You may want to follow with a statement of that behavior's impact on you. For example, you might say, "To the last six or seven questions I have asked, you have given me very short answers. That makes it difficult for me to know what you are really thinking." Remain quiet, providing the client with an opportunity to respond to your observation or question. On the basis of the client's response, continue asking questions. You will want to probe below what you have observed to understand why the client is expressing such behavior. Is the client anxious about taking certain actions? Could the client be feeling frustrated because other people are seeing the situation differently? You need to know what is going through your client's mind, so that you can alleviate the concern or find a way to move forward by minimizing it.

One technique that we have found helpful is to draw on the other resources in the meeting. It is a rare situation in which a feedback meeting consists of only you and one client. Determine whether others share any of the concerns of the resistant client by asking if they agree or disagree with what is being said. Allow the whole group to help you work through the resistance of one member.

Remember that resistance is a good thing. It should not be ignored. We certainly cannot become defensive because of it. Resistance is not a personal attack, but a reaction to the process of being helped.

Disagreement. There will be occasions when your clients may not agree on what actions would be best. The first thing to do is to identify the aspects they do agree on and what specific aspects are causing the problem. One technique is to look for ways to build on agreement. This will require each person (including yourself) to be willing to compromise in order to reach consensus. It is also important to determine whether disagreement is a sincere difference of opinion, rather than resistance to the entire process.

If there is honest disagreement, it becomes necessary to ask the group for ideas about how it can be resolved. There are times when this situation will require the decision to be moved up one organizational level. Again, involving the client team in deciding how to resolve disagreements is important.

Too-Quick Agreement. Agreeing too quickly with everything that is proposed can be another form of resistance. In a sense, the client is saying, "Yes, yes, yes," in the hope that the meeting will end quickly. If you sense that the reason for this behavior is resistance, it must be identified and discussed. You may say to the client, for example, "You seem willing to do anything that is suggested. Why?"

Clients may also agree too quickly because it is growing late and they are tired, or because there is a high-level individual in the group with whom no one is willing to disagree. When you are getting agreement that, in your opinion, may not be sincere, you need to address that issue. You can suggest that the meeting stop and continue later (be certain to agree on the date and time), or you can test for commitment to an action by indicating what the implications of that action are for those in the room. Specify the steps that each person will need to take. Are the clients willing to take such steps? As nice as agreement sounds, you do not want it to come too easily.

Client's Wish to Review Data Before the Meeting. We said earlier that whether to provide your client with a preview of the findings is not an easy decision. We make it a practice not to send a copy of the results ahead to a client. There is too much danger that the information will be photocopied, distributed, and reacted to before we have had an opportunity to influence its interpretation. Nevertheless, there are times when it makes sense to provide a verbal overview of the major themes and discuss potential issues. Whether to conduct such a preview is a decision to be made each time you face a feedback meeting. As we have said, our preference is to avoid such previews if possible. This practice helps ensure that conclusions and implications will be reached in a collaborative manner by all who have a stake in the results.

Client's Desire for Brief Overview Rather Than In-Depth Report. We have already mentioned that a typical feedback meeting takes from two to four hours. The length of time required will depend on how much information there is to review and how many people will be at the meeting.

What if your clients say they can give you only thirty minutes? In this situation, it is important to elevate the importance of the meeting in the mind of the client. How will the client benefit from a meeting that lasts two hours instead of thirty minutes? What will the client gain from that investment of time? These benefits need to be articulated.

It is also important to point out what the client will lose by not giving more time to the process. What would not be completed if the time were not provided? As much as possible, relate these concerns to the business needs that brought you into the project in the first place.

To illustrate, perhaps the problem that started this project was a rise in customer complaints. Your client has a vested interest in seeing that these complaints are reduced. By giving you only thirty minutes of time, will your client be unable to discuss topics that are pertinent to the resolution of this problem? What problems does the client risk in the project as it moves forward? These things should be pointed out.

You may have to provide information to the client during two or three short meetings. This may be one situation when some information will need to be forwarded and reviewed ahead of time, to expedite the process. Finally, it is essential to involve your client in solving the problem. What will he or she be willing to give up, if the meeting is so short?

The proactive manner for avoiding this situation, of course, is to state clearly from the start that two or more hours of meeting time at the end of the data-collection process will be one of the costs of this project. (This agreement should have been reached in the initial meeting, described in Chapter Five.)

Now you have had your feedback meeting, and agreement has been reached on what specific skill and knowledge areas will be addressed in a training program and on what specific environmental issues will be addressed by management. At this point, the HRD professional typically moves into designing the training program or determining what program will be purchased. Trainers are then prepared to deliver the program. Learners are identified, so that they can be invited at the appropriate time, and the implementation cycle begins.

As we noted in the Preface, we will not be addressing the design and delivery of training programs; many books, articles, and workshops focus on these topics. We do, however, want to discuss the design of an evaluation and tracking system for the training effort. Identifying the results expected from a training program and then measuring to determine whether those results have occurred are just as important as accurately identifying training needs. The design of these evaluation systems begins before the training program is delivered.

Summary

The following techniques move training toward impact:

Activity **Impact**

- Whenever you collect data, tabulate them and put them in an understandable format, so that conclusions and implications can be drawn.
- When reviewing data with clients, work toward a collaborative interpretation of the information. Avoid telling the client what the results mean and what should be done because of them.
- Develop skills in data analysis and interpretation, or work with people who have those skills. Do not underestimate the importance of these skills to your success as an HRD professional.

Part Four

Building Evaluation and Tracking Systems into Training Programs

Many people think of evaluation and tracking as things that are done after the training is completed. Actually, they must be built into the design of the training system before any training takes place. What happens at the end of the training is the implementation of evaluation or tracking that was designed along with the training.

Chapter Nine focuses on how to use reaction questionnaires to obtain data not only about how well the course met the expectations of the participants but also about the quality of materials, effectiveness of instruction, pacing and sequencing of activities, and on-the-job barriers that inhibit the transfer of learning. Chapter Ten provides guidelines and examples of how to test the learners' knowledge and develop competency demonstrations for learners.

Tracking the impact of training programs is discussed in Chapters Eleven through Thirteen. Chapter Eleven provides details on how to track the amount of skill transfer that actually details on how to track the amount of skill transfer that actually occurs after training. Methods for measuring the nonobservable results of training programs are described in Chapter Twelve. The tracking of the operational impact of training efforts is examined in detail in Chapter Thirteen.

Nine

Participant Reactions: Going Beyond "Smile Sheets"

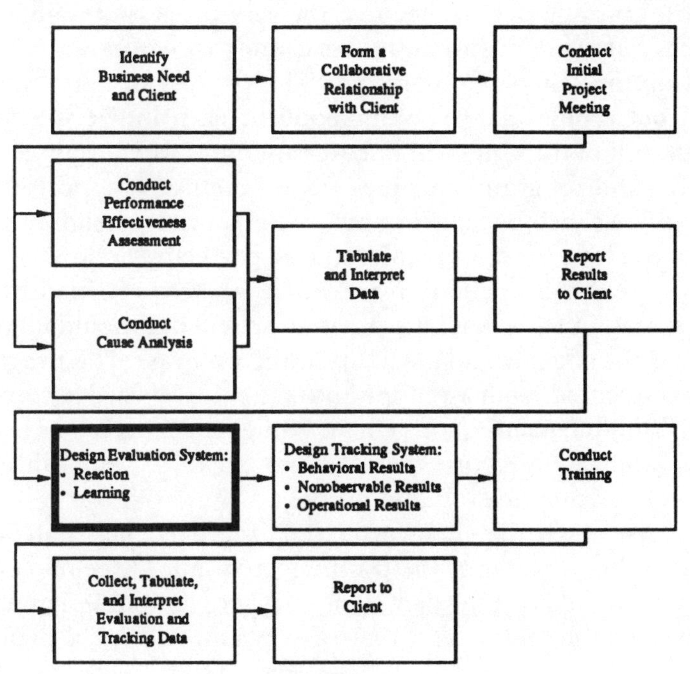

Once the feedback meeting with your clients has occurred and agreement has been reached on what specific learning outcomes need to result from a training program, you are ready to begin either designing a program or searching the market for a program you can purchase. Concurrent with the design or purchase of a program is the need to begin designing an evaluation system.

Contrary to what some people think, evaluation is really a front-end process, for two reasons. First, you often need to collect pretraining or base-line data about your population and the business need being addressed. If you want to determine how much learning has occurred, for example, it is best to determine specifically what participants know before the program and how, if at all, that has changed at its conclusion. If you want to know whether the frequency of skill or behavior use has changed because of the program, you must determine that frequency before training and compare it with what is occurring some weeks or months after the program's conclusion. Thus, an evaluation system must be readied to collect base-line data before training begins. Second, the very process of evaluation forces you to identify what you are trying to accomplish in terms of training outcomes or results. The process of determining such outcomes (what you want people to learn and be able to do as a result of training) will uncover any areas where your course design and program outcomes are not mutually supportive. By identifying such mismatches before the training design is finalized, you have an opportunity to take corrective action.

We recall a situation in which we were retained by an organization to design an evaluation system that would identify the results of a particular sales training program. The program was purchased from a vendor and was being revised according to the unique needs of this client. While that process was occurring (and before actual delivery), we began to work with the client to create the evaluation system.

We asked the client to identify the particular outcomes expected as a result of the training program. Three outcomes were described by the client: that salespeople would plan more completely for sales calls; that sales personnel would manage their time and territory more efficiently, so that more sales calls could be made in a day; and that salespeople would ask high-yield questions, revealing explicit needs of customers.

In our review of the design of the purchased program, it was evident that the first two outcomes could be expected but that the program design would allow no time to build the necessary skills to accomplish the third outcome.

We discussed this nonmatch with the clients and offered them two options to consider: first, to design into the current program learning activities that would focus on building questioning skills (this would require extending the program beyond its current length of three days) and, second, to hold off on meeting the third outcome until the next time a training program would be offered to this group of sales personnel (tentatively, the following spring). These clients opted for the second alternative, since they did not want to remove sales personnel from the field for longer than three consecutive days.

Because we were clarifying outcomes for a training program as part of the evaluation process, this nonmatch was discovered. We were able to resolve this situation by working proactively with the clients in a problem-solving mode. We avoided having an unhappy client at the conclusion of the project, upset because sales personnel were unable to ask questions more skillfully and wondering why this topic had not been included in the course.

Acknowledging that evaluation is a front-end process, we now need to define what *evaluation* means. Kirkpatrick (1983) has defined four possible levels of evaluation. We have used Kirkpatrick's levels as a foundation for our work in this area. These levels are described here, with some modification to reflect our own work.

Four Levels of Evaluation

Level I: Reaction Evaluation. The first level of training program evaluation is the reaction, or critique, evaluation; in reality, it is a customer satisfaction index. It lets you know your participants' degree of satisfaction with a program's design and delivery. This is a crucial piece of information. If people are not satisfied with the learning experience, they probably will not use what they have learned and will undoubtedly advise others not to attend.

Typically, questionnaires are distributed and completed at the conclusion of a training program. Often, such questionnaires inquire about the participants' reactions to program content, learning activities, and level of instruction. This level of evaluation is important for training efforts. Unfortunately, it is often discredited by HRD professionals. Perhaps you have heard this type of evaluation referred to as a "happiness index," a "smile sheet," or a "whoopie sheet."

If you are dissatisfied with the quality of information obtained from your Level I evaluations, we suggest that you examine the type of questions asked. If the quality of the information you are obtaining is low, perhaps the questions being asked are of the same caliber. In this chapter, we will provide tips and techniques for developing good Level I evaluations. They are a critical part of evaluation and should be used consistently in the delivery of training programs.

Level II: Learning Evaluation. If you want to know whether participants have learned what you intended them to learn, then you should use a Level II evaluation. This evaluation level essentially reveals whether participants have learned the stated objectives of the program and is a type of quality-assurance index for training. In the objectives for courses, HRD professionals typically indicate what participants will know and be able to do as a result of attending the program. What data do we have to verify that the objectives were met? What if the same program is delivered by more than one instructor? How can we be sure that the learning objectives are accomplished regardless of who the instructor is? Those are the types of questions that a Level II evaluation effort addresses.

Typical ways through which people evaluate at this level are paper-and-pencil tests and observed simulations or skill demonstrations. In Chapter Ten, we will provide some techniques and ideas to use when designing your own Level II evaluations.

Level III (Type A): Behavior or Skill Application Evaluation. If you want to know whether participants are using on the job what they have been taught, then you will need to do a Level III evaluation. Every HRD professional has experienced the frustration of knowing that people have learned skills that they never use on the job. The learning of skills is in itself no guarantee that they will be transferred. This level of evaluation helps us determine the ultimate test of training effectiveness: "Are people applying what was learned?" We have divided this third level of evaluation into two types. In Type A, we are concerned with skills or behavior that can be observed. (Chapter Eleven is devoted to this level of evaluation.)

Level III (Type B): Evaluation of Nonobservable Results. Some desired results of training programs cannot be seen or heard. For example, participants may mentally use certain problem-solving techniques in analyzing causes of production problems. Such analysis, however, cannot be observed; it is occurring in the minds of participants. What if a training program has as its desired outcome that participants be committed to the vision and future direction of the corporation? This result, called *commitment*, is hard to observe, but it can be measured. (In Chapter Twelve, we will discuss the how-to's of evaluating nonobservable training results.)

Level IV: Impact or Results Evaluation. Most HRD professionals' not-so-secret dream is to be able to prove that a training program has resulted in a monetary return on investment to the organization. We often hear people discuss "bottom-line impact" and whether training can cause a change in the "bottom line" ("Training Evaluation . . .," 1986, pp. 1, 3). We do not believe that training can be solely responsible for such results, but we do know that training can contribute to such impacts on a business. You must complete Level IV evaluation if you want to know what impact a particular training program has had on a unit, division, or department in your organization. (Chapter Thirteen will discuss how to design this type of evaluation.)

In consideration of which evaluation level(s) to use in any particular training program, Exhibit 3 may prove helpful (we have also identified the chapter in this book dedicated to each

Exhibit 3. Levels of Evaluation.

If you want to know . . .	*Then you must use . . .*	*This level is discussed in . . .*
Did participants like the program?	Level I	Chapter Nine
Did participants learn the objectives of the program?	Level II	Chapter Ten
Are participants applying the skills and behavior taught in the program?	Level III: Type A	Chapter Eleven
Are participants applying non-observable outcomes to the job?	Level III: Type B	Chapter Twelve
In the application of skills, has there been any impact on the business?	Level IV	Chapter Thirteen

level of evaluation). If you want to know the answers to all five questions listed in Exhibit 3, then all five evaluations must be designed; no one level will address all five questions.

Frequency of Use of Each Evaluation Level

In 1987, we had the opportunity to be participants in the Training Directors' Forum, which is sponsored by Lakewood Publications' *Training Directors' Forum Newsletter* and *TRAINING: The Magazine of Human Resources Development*. Approximately 150 training professionals attended this event. Most people in attendance were managers or directors of HRD; all had functional responsibility for some aspect of the training efforts of their organizations. In this forum, we were asked to make a presentation on the measurement of training results. In preparation for that presentation, we collected information from the participants via a questionnaire.

Among other things, participants were asked to indicate the frequency with which they currently implemented each of the four levels of evaluation (Level III was identified as evaluation of behavior application only). The results of this diagnostic effort are noted in Figure 14. From these results, we concluded that Level I evaluations are routine; that there is a large variation in the frequency with which respondents complete Level II evaluations; that, while one-third of the respondents indicated no evaluation at Level III, approximately 70 percent of the respondents do utilize this level of evaluation at least occasionally; and that the majority of HRD professionals in this study do not evaluate at Level IV.

To the degree that these HRD managers and directors are representative of their peers throughout North America today, we certainly see an area of vulnerability. For some strange reason, management is only now beginning to ask us to determine the results of what we do; historically, we have been held accountable only for our activity. In essence, we create our own HRD Catch-22 syndrome: We are not requested to determine results information; we are busy people, and so we do not do what we are not requested to do. As a result, management continues to be uncertain about our value. We have colluded with management to keep ourselves in an uncertain place, and our contribution to the organization is left ambiguous. It is up to HRD professionals to break this dynamic, take the initiative, and begin to determine results, even though we are not being asked to do so.

We want to make one more point before we look at Level I evaluations in depth: You may have heard the terms *formative* and *summative* evaluation and wondered what they mean. Formative evaluation occurs during the design and delivery of the training program. Information is collected to determine the appropriateness and effectiveness of the program's learning activities and content. For example, if you conduct a field test on a training program (before offering it to the organization at large) in order to determine whether the learning design is effective, you are completing a type of formative evaluation. On the basis of the data collected, the program will probably be reformed before it is offered to others.

Summative evaluation measures the results of a training program or activity. It is typically done on programs that are completely developed (or formed) and is a way of determining how effective the programs are. While decisions may be made from collected information to modify a program's design, the

Figure 14. Results from Participants at the Training Directors' Forum, 1987: Percentage of Respondents Indicating Use of Each Evaluation Level.

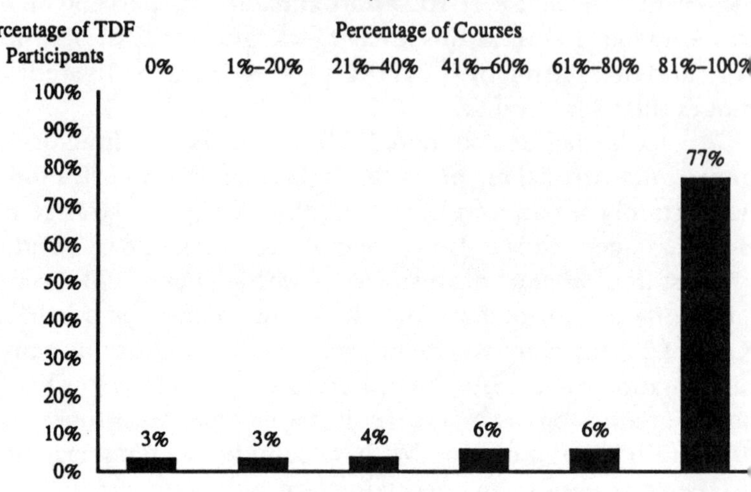

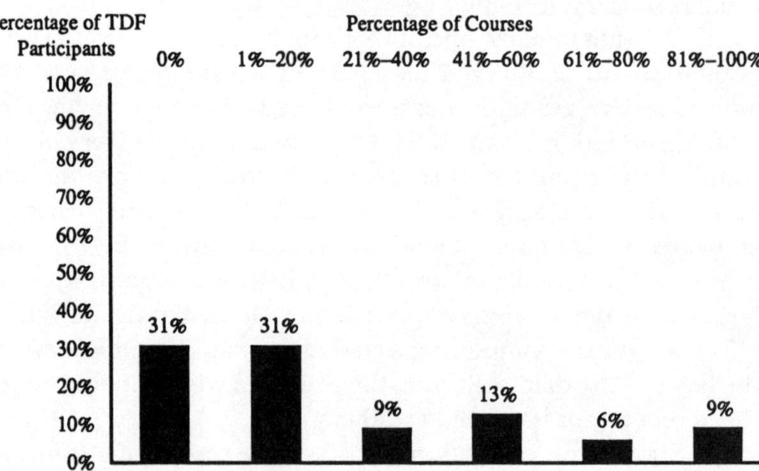

Figure 14. Results from Participants at the Training Directors' Forum, 1987: Percentage of Respondents Indicating Use of Each Evaluation Level, Cont'd.

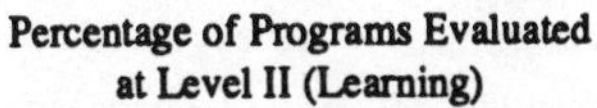

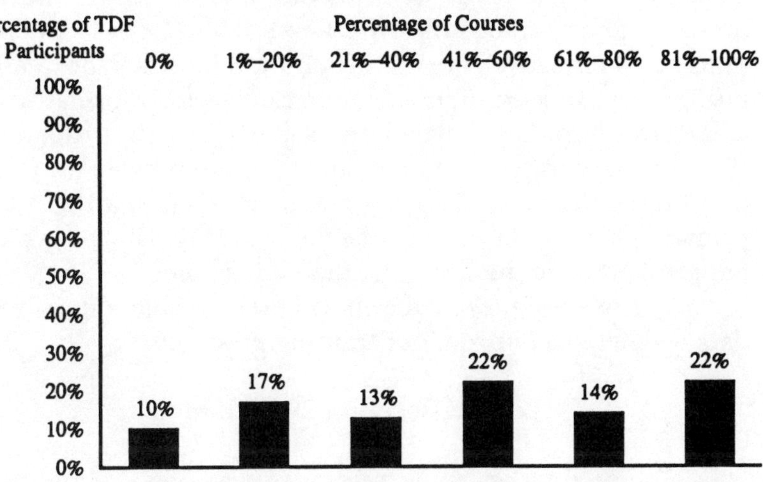

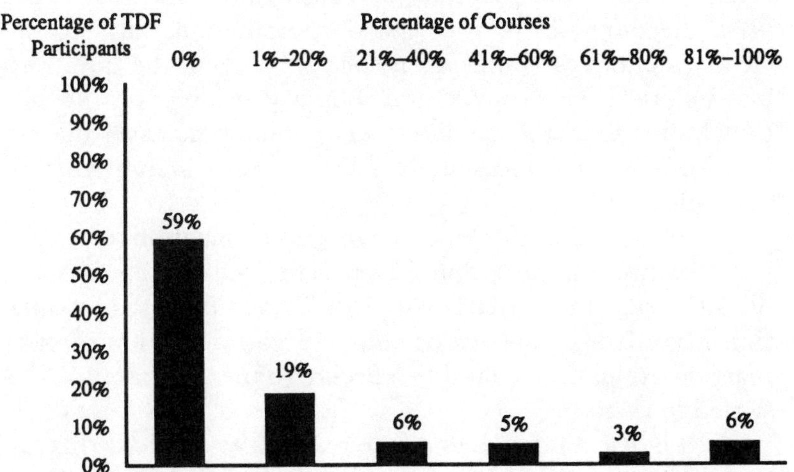

Source: Data presented at Training Directors' Forum, Boca Raton, Fla., 1987, sponsored by *Training Directors' Forum* newsletter and *TRAINING: The Magazine for Human Resources Development*. Reprinted with permission of Lakewood Publications.

primary purpose for this type of evaluation is to identify the impact of the program on individuals and on the organization.

Level I evaluations are a type of formative evaluation. Generally, their purpose is to provide information regarding how a program can be improved. Level III and Level IV evaluations are summative. They indicate the kinds and degree of results. Level II (learning) evaluation can be either formative or summative; its nature depends on the purpose of the evaluation. If the primary purpose of the evaluation is to provide information on the design of the program, then it is formative; if the primary purpose is to determine the degree to which learning has resulted from the program, then it is summative.

Let us look now in depth at Level I evaluations, whose data will help us improve our training programs.

Level I: Reaction Evaluation

As noted earlier, many training professionals belittle reaction evaluation, saying that it produces no useful information. If you feel this way about your own reaction evaluations, one or both of these problems may be causing your dissatisfaction. First, the purposes of your reaction evaluations may not be clearly identified or may be incorrect. Second, the questions may be poorly constructed and so may provide poor information. Moreover, there are other, very common mistakes that we have seen HRD professionals make in constructing reaction evaluations.

It is a mistake to create one reaction evaluation to be used for every training program. This practice reflects the "one size fits all" idea. Unfortunately, this idea is no more true of evaluations than it is of dresses or suits. At least a portion of each reaction evaluation should be specific to the program it is designed to evaluate.

It is also a mistake to create reaction evaluations that are composed almost entirely (or only) of open-ended questions. The problem with this questionnaire format is that few HRD professionals actually take the time to do content analysis on the information that is collected. The information is thumbed through, and what is missed are the subtle patterns in the data. It is impossible to make good decisions on the basis of untabulated data. Unless you are prepared to content-analyze open-ended data, we recommend that your reaction evaluations primarily contain closed questions.

Another mistake is to use unbalanced questions, which predominantly ask for positive or negative comments on the program. For example, to ask what parts of a program were most interesting is a positively biased question; it assumes that something was most interesting and encourages positive comments. We have seen reaction evaluations that ask up to five questions in a positive format and pose only one that seeks critical feedback; we have also seen the reverse. One client with whom we worked was distressed when her reaction evaluations for a program provided no positive comments. In reviewing the form, we found that all the questions were in the negative mode. Reaction evaluations should be balanced to include as many questions that seek positive reactions as questions that seek criticism.

Still another common mistake is HRD professionals' failure to maximize this opportunity to collect useful information. Hundreds of people, maybe thousands, probably attend your training programs in a year. What an opportunity to gather information on your organization! Nevertheless, we commonly ask questions only about the program itself. Do you inquire about what, if anything, will make it difficult for your participants to use their new skills on the job? Do you ask questions to determine whether the managers of your participants can be expected to model, coach, and reinforce the new skills? Do you ascertain how motivated or confident your participants are to apply what they have been taught? Not to do so is to miss a great opportunity for data collection.

A final common mistake is to allow insufficient time for participants to complete reaction evaluations. How often are the evaluation forms distributed late in the day, after the training program has already reached or extended its time limit? How much thought will participants give to completing such evaluations when they are in a hurry to catch planes or beat the traffic or are just plain tired? Time should be allocated for the completion of reaction evaluations, just as time is set aside for coffee breaks. Plan for the formal program to end at least twenty minutes before the stated time. Then use that time to have people complete reaction evaluations.

Acknowledging that these are all common mistakes, let us look now at how to develop and use reaction evaluations effectively.

Determine the Purposes of Reaction Evaluations

Purposes represent what you want to know and the decisions you want to make as a result of the information you collect. What can you know as a result of reaction evalution? Perhaps this list of questions will provide you with some ideas.

1. Did the program meet the expectations of the people who attended it?
2. What aspects of the program were most helpful? most interesting? most informative?
3. What aspects of the program were least helpful? least interesting? least informative?
4. What were participants' reactions to the program's design? pacing? materials? precourse work?
5. What were participants' reactions to the expertise and facilitative style demonstrated by the instructor(s)?
6. Do people feel confident to use what they have learned?
7. Do people value what they have learned?
8. Do people intend to use what they have learned? How?
9. What barriers, if any, do people believe will inhibit their ability to use what they have learned?
10. Were the room and environmental conditions satisfactory?

Decisions you may make on the basis of the tabulated data may be guided by the following questions.

1. How, if at all, should the program's content, pacing, or materials be changed?

2. How, if at all, should the program's learning activities be modified or redesigned?
3. How, if at all, should the instructor be coached to modify or change his or her facilitation of the program?
4. What influence is necessary with line management to ensure that the skills being taught will be transferred to the job?
5. What precourse work might be helpful in preparing participants for the program?
6. Are there precourse requirements or experiences that should be used as criteria for selecting participants in the future?

Determine How Data Will Be Tabulated

Will you be computer-tabulating the information from your reaction evaluations? We strongly advise this. Will someone be asked to tick off or content-analyze responses to form a compilation of results? The method you select to tabulate the evaluations will affect how they are constructed and the kinds of questions you can ask.

If you will be using a computer to tabulate the data, then you will want to construct a form both compatible with your computer software and convenient for personnel to input. Always check out any parameters that may apply before you create your questions.

Create High-Yield Questions

Entire books are written on the subject of how to ask the right questions right. For example, consider this question: "What did you think of the course?" This is an ineffective attempt to obtain important information. Questions asked in this manner will yield little useful information. We hope to provide you with some tips on this subject and encourage you to investigate the area of question design more completely, if that is a need of yours.

Ask specific, closed questions. For example, if you want to

Exhibit 4. Sample Scale.

	Not Applicable	*Deficient*	*Adequate*	*Good*	*Very Good*	*Excellent*
Please rate the instructor on the following points.						
Knowledge of subject matter	0	1	2	3	4	5
Ability to communicate clear instructions for case studies and exercises	0	1	2	3	4	5
Effectiveness in making group presentations	0	1	2	3	4	5
Effectiveness in encouraging questions and discussions from the group	0	1	2	3	4	5
Effectiveness in responding to questions from the group	0	1	2	3	4	5

know how the participants felt about the instructor in the program, do not ask participants to comment on the level of instruction. Rather, provide a scale, and ask about specific competencies that the instructor should have demonstrated (see Exhibit 4).

Another question, which can be closed off in designing reaction evaluations, focuses on finding what aspects of the program the participants found most helpful or interesting. Rather than ask that question in an open-ended manner, list the actual learning modules, and ask participants to indicate which, if any, were most interesting. The question could read as follows: "Listed below are the primary learning units from this workshop. Please indicate with a check mark those units that were the most interesting (or helpful, or relevant, and so on). Check all those that are true for you."

If you use a Likert scale, respondents check the points on the scale that best represent what is true for them. When using such a scale, consider whether it will be odd or even. An odd scale always has a midpoint, typically labeled "neutral," "no opinion," "moderate," and so on. An even scale, by contrast, has no such midpoint. If you have a 1 to 6 scale, you are forcing respondents off the midpoint and requiring them to indicate a preference for one side of the scale or the other. Consider which form would be most appropriate. We have found that even scales are often preferable for determining frequency of use or level of agreement with something. Odd scales are best for questions that might legitimately yield a "50 percent" response—for example, "Considering all you have learned in this program, how much of it will you be able to apply on the job?"

As much as possible, construct questions so that they are asked in a neutral manner. Do not ask, "What part of the program was most interesting?" Phrase the question to say, "Which part of the program, if any, was most interesting to you?" Such phrasing gives the participant permission to skip the question or to indicate that no part was the most interesting.

Ask questions that will yield personal responses. Do not ask participants to comment on what they think the others in the group experienced; ask them about what they have experienced. Do not ask, "To what degree did the participants in the program feel encouraged to ask questions?" Ask, "To what degree did you feel encouraged to ask questions?"

While some questions asked in a reaction evaluation are always relevant, regardless of the training program, we do not believe that "one size fits all" when it comes to designing these evaluations. Some part or section of the evaluation should focus directly on the learning and outcomes desired from the specific program. For example, you might list the program's objectives and ask individuals to indicate the degree to which those objectives were met. The question might appear as follows:

To what extent was each of the following program objectives met for you? Please note the point on the scale that best represents your opinion. The objectives of this program were:

1. A better understanding of the laws and policies that a supervisor needs to consider when hiring employees.

0	1	2	3	4	5	6
Not Met			Somewhat Met			Fully Met

2. Increased skill in the ability to ask candidates questions that comply with EEO and Affirmative Action laws.

0	1	2	3	4	5	6
Not Met			Somewhat Met			Fully Met

It is also important to determine the degree of confidence a participant feels to use the skills taught, as well as the participant's level of value for the skills that were taught. As noted in Chapter Seven, if a participant lacks either confidence or value for what was taught, the probability of skill transfer is reduced. In assessing levels of confidence or value, it is important to address the specific learning from the program (see Exhibit 5).

Finally, another opportunity to ask course-specific questions focuses on identifying potential work environment barriers that could inhibit or even prevent participants from using the skills that were taught. (Again, refer to Chapter Seven for a more complete description of these barriers.) Here, we want to note that obtaining this information from a reaction evaluation is an opportunity not to miss. The data will certainly alert you to any potential problem that may be awaiting participants as they return to their jobs and attempt to use the newly learned skills.

Exhibit 6 shows a question used to determine work environment obstacles. It is taken from a reaction evaluation developed for a workshop on negotiation skills. This format can work in any reaction evaluation. You will need to include the specific barriers that could limit use of skills by your participants.

Exhibit 7 illustrates some other questions we have used in

Exhibit 5. Evaluation of Confidence and Value.

Listed below are the major negotiation strategies and tactics taught in this program. Indicate on the scales provided (a) your level of confidence to demonstrate the strategy or tactic and (b) the degree to which you believe this strategy or tactic is important in accomplishing effective negotiated agreements with clients.

My level of confidence to demonstrate this strategy or tactic effectively						*The degree of importance I place on this strategy or tactic*				
Low		*Moderate*		*High*		*Low*		*Moderate*		*High*
1	2	3	4	5	1. Determine what specific interests and objectives I have in the negotiation.	1	2	3	4	5
1	2	3	4	5	2. Determine what specific interests and objectives the client has in the negotiation.	1	2	3	4	5
1	2	3	4	5	3. Determine my best "walk-away" alternative agreement before entering the negotiation itself.	1	2	3	4	5

Exhibit 6. Sample Question.

There are times when individuals want to apply what they have learned, but organizational "barriers" make it difficult to do so.

Which of the following barriers, if any, will make it difficult for you to use what you have learned in this workshop? Please check all items that are true for you.

a. ___ The downside risk of negotiating aggressively is too great in this organization.
b. ___ I am uncertain about whether people on my team would want me to negotiate in this manner.
c. ___ I lack people to talk to who could help me plan negotiation meetings using these strategies.
d. ___ There is no clear expectation from senior management that I will use these approaches when negotiating fees with clients.
e. ___ I have not seen or heard others around me using these approaches.
f. ___ Other: Please explain. ______________________

Exhibit 7. Questions for Reaction Evaluations.

To determine whether the pacing of the workshop and the degree of difficulty in the workshop were appropriate to the audience:

The pace of this workshop was:
a. ___ too slow
b. ___ just right
c. ___ too fast

In my opinion, the content of this course was:
a. ___ too basic
b. ___ about right
c. ___ too difficult

To determine what the reaction of the participants was to actual learning activities or program materials:

Please rate the effectiveness of the following program activities in helping you achieve the course objectives. Use the following scale except where otherwise indicated. Circle only one response to each question.

Excellent = outstanding; superior; exemplary
Very good = well above average; very competent; few if any weaknesses
Good = above average; may need minor improvements
Adequate = about average; could use improvement
Deficient = definite weaknesses; inadequate in many respects
Not Applicable = does not apply to this course or instructor

	Not Applicable	*Deficient*	*Adequate*	*Good*	*Very Good*	*Excellent*
General class discussions	0	1	2	3	4	5
Group presentations	0	1	2	3	4	5
Discussion of case studies and exercises	0	1	2	3	4	5
Role plays	0	1	2	3	4	5
Work in small groups on case studies and exercises	0	1	2	3	4	5
Audiovisual aids	0	1	2	3	4	5
Course materials	0	1	2	3	4	5

To determine overall reaction to the training program:

On the basis of information you received before the program and comments you may have heard from others who have attended this workshop, you probably had some expectations for it. To what degree were those expectations met?

a. ___ This workshop substantially exceeded my expectations.
b. ___ This workshop exceeded my expectations.

Exhibit 7. Questions for Reaction Evaluations, Cont'd.

c. ___ This workshop met my expectations.
d. ___ This workshop partially met my expectations.
e. ___ This workshop did not meet my expectations.

What is your overall rating for this program?

1	2	3	4	5	6	7	8	9
Poor		*Fair*		*Good*		*Very Good*		*Excellent*

To identify what percentage of the new skills participants expect to be able to use on the job:

How much of what you learned in this course do you expect to use on the job?

a. ___ all
b. ___ almost all
c. ___ about 50 percent
d. ___ very little
e. ___ none

reaction evaluations. These have proved helpful for obtaining information about reactions to program content and learning design. You can adapt them to your own reaction evaluations, as appropriate.

Common Questions About Reaction Evaluations

Should Respondents Be Asked to Sign Evaluations? This is truly an issue of personal preference, for there are pros and cons either way. Our personal preference is to request the name of the individual who is responding. This way, if respondents are displeased with the program, we have an opportunity to contact them and discuss it more completely. Some people feel that the request to sign a questionnaire may inhibit responses. We know of no research that supports this theory, but it may be an issue in some programs and some organizations. Therefore, one suggestion would be to make the signature optional and leave that decision to the participant.

How Long Should It Take to Complete a Reaction Evaluation? If you use closed questions in your questionnaire, your evaluation will have more pages, but closed questions often require less time to complete. We target ten to fifteen minutes as the ideal length of time. Again, it is important to allocate sufficient time at the end of the program so that people are doing this on your time, and not on theirs.

Are There Other Ways to Collect This Type of Information Besides End-of-Course Evaluations? Yes, but most of these alternatives will require more of your time to administer and tabulate. One option would be to have a series of prepared questions, which are posed to the entire class at the conclusion of the program. This would be similar to a large-group discussion or a focus-group format.

We know HRD professionals who take time to conduct follow-up interviews with participants over the phone about one or two weeks after the course has concluded and while it is still fresh in their minds. Again, if you select this option, it is important to have prepared questions, so that you are consistently asking the same questions of each person you interview. While you may improvise some questions on the basis of the responses you obtain, it is important to ensure that you are collecting data directed at your evaluation purposes.

Some organizations use a daily evaluation at the conclusion of each day of the program. This should be a very short evaluation, which is used to provide a quick check on how things are going. This information should be tabulated the same night and reviewed with participants the next morning. It provides the instructor with an opportunity to make a midcourse correction (if there is any discontent among the participants regarding material, pacing, and so forth).

Sometimes HRD professionals give reaction evaluations to participants and ask that these evaluations be returned through interoffice mail at some point in the future. We personally do not recommend this option. Our experience is that less than half of these questionnaires will be returned. If it is important to collect this type of information (and we think it is), then it is equally important to allocate time during the workshop to obtain it.

Other Issues Regarding Level I Evaluations

How Data from Reaction Evaluations Can Be Used. There is only one reason to take the time to collect any type of information: for you and others to make decisions. Therefore, once you have tabulated the reaction data, it is important to draw conclusions and implications. This interpretive process is no different from the one described in Chapter Eight. We have known HRD professionals who compared reaction evaluation results for particular courses instructed by various people to determine whether results were similar or different. You can also compare results of a program when it is delivered to different parts of your organization. Do you get the same reaction results when people from marketing attend as when people from operations attend? You will certainly want to determine any patterns for anticipated work environment barriers to the application of new skills.

Asking Instructors for Their Reactions. One of our clients has a policy of collecting reaction evaluation information not only from participants but also from instructors. Instructors can give you their reactions to a program's content and design, their observations on how participants responded to a program's design (as well as on how prepared the participants were), and their thoughts about how well prepared they themselves were to deliver a program and about what might be helpful to them in the future. Questions can be asked to determine the degree to which instructors believe that a program's exercises, case studies, and skill practices enhance learning. Instructors can also indicate whether content moves in a logical manner, with each learning module built on the content of a previous one.

Finally, you can obtain information about the instructors' own preparation for a program. Was it adequate? Did instructors have enough documentation and preparation time? Was there enough administrative support? Over time, certain patterns and trends will appear, and it will be possible to take any necessary action.

A final point about reaction evaluations: Once you have

created one, be certain to test it with one or two groups before you finalize it. After the initial use of the questionnaire, review the information you received—not only to determine participants' reactions but also to ascertain how effective the evaluation questionnaire itself is. Are there questions that a large group of people skipped? This probably means that they either did not understand the question or that it was not pertinent to them. You may want to consider rephrasing such questions. If you are using a Likert scale on your form, check whether people are using the entire scale or are just going down one end of it and checking "always" or "agree" every time. When someone checks the same response to every question, it usually means that he or she is not reading the questions or that the questions are not discriminating enough. Before you photocopy your evaluation form hundreds of times, make certain that the information you receive is helpful and allows you to make good decisions. You may need to edit the form a few times before you get it right.

Summary

The following techniques move training toward impact:

Activity **Impact**

- Design an evaluation system for the training program as the program is being created or purchased. Evaluation is a front-end process.
- Design reaction evaluations to contain primarily closed questions. Tabulate and draw conclusions from all data each time you collect reaction information.
- Ask questions on your reaction evaluations to obtain information on learners' confidence and values, as well as on learners' perceptions of the work environment and its readiness to support new skills.

Ten

Participant Learning: Assessing Development of Knowledge and Skills

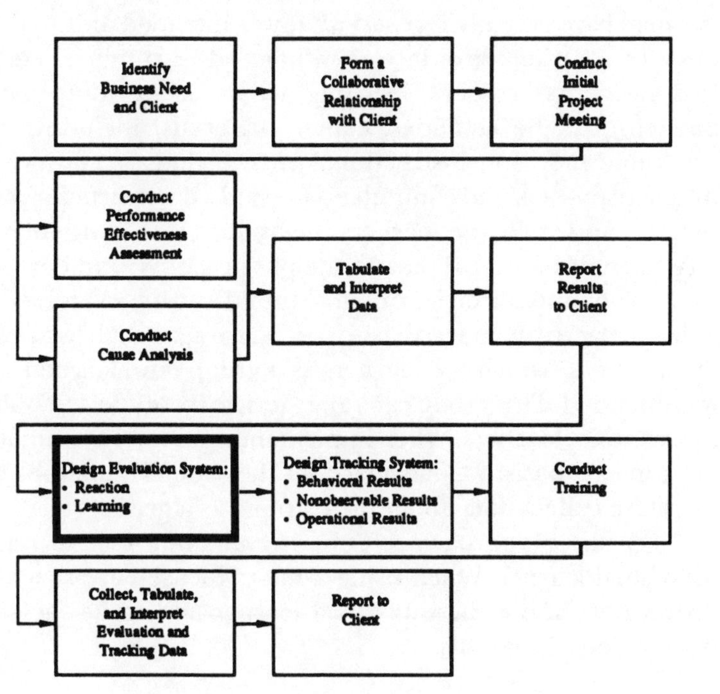

In Chapter Nine, we discussed how to use Level I reaction evaluations to determine learners' degree of satisfaction with training. In this chapter, we will examine Level II learning measures, which are used to determine the amount of learning that took place during the training.

Most of us have experienced Level II learning measures in the form of tests, when we were students. Usually, those measures were paper-and-pencil tests. For example, our knowledge of American history might be measured through a test that involved such items as "On what day was the Battle of Bunker Hill fought?" In other courses, we may have been tested on our skill, rather than on our knowledge. For example, in a typing course, we might have taken a typing test, in which the number of words accurately typed per minute would be a measurement of our skill.

This chapter will focus on how to design and implement learning measures, or tests, in two primary areas—knowledge acquisition and skill development. There are two primary purposes of Level II measures: to determine the degree to which learners have actually learned what was intended and to determine how a number of factors influenced learning. These factors are course content; learning activities, including the sequencing of the activities; course materials, including how accessible they are; instructional aids, including audiovisual, interactive video, and computer-based aids; the instructor's competence and style; the learners themselves, including their capabilities and motivation; and the physical environment.

The amount of learning acquired can be examined on either a macro or a micro basis. The macro approach focuses on the degree to which the learners as a group have learned what was intended. This group can range in size from a few people to thousands of learners. When implementing a Level II evaluation on a macro basis, we can make all these determinations and therefore collect data about the learners as a group.

A micro approach to Level II evaluation focuses on the individual learner. When using a micro-focused approach, we collect data about the individual learner and make the same type of determinations.

Now, one might ask, "Why should we be concerned about learning measures when implementing a Training-for-Impact approach? After all, that approach focuses on the learning that is actually applied on the job, not the learning that takes place in the classroom."

That is a good question. Let us reexamine the results formula:

Learning Experience × Work Environment = Business Results

Business results are the use of newly learned skills on the job. A 0 on either side of the multiplication sign will yield no results. In reality, either the learning experience or the work environment can sabotage the results.

As HRD professionals, we have the responsibility of ensuring that learning has actually occurred. Learning measures are a way of determining how effective a learning experience has been.

How to Design a Level II Evaluation

Let us examine what needs to be done in designing and developing learning measures. The process that we are about to describe pertains to either macro or micro evaluation.

Determine Who Will Use the Data to Make What Decisions. When you do this, you are really defining the purpose of the study. We have found that asking who will make what decisions enables us to focus on the primary purposes of the study. In most instances, the data will be used by the training program manager and other HRD staff members to make decisions regarding the amount of learning that is taking place. If the data are to be used to determine when a person has developed the skills and knowledge required for a position, then line managers will probably want access to the data. For instance, if a manager-trainee program is developing new managers who are to be appointed to retail stores only after acquiring certain skills and knowledge, then retail managers will need access to the data to make that decision. In this situation, the purposes of the study might be the following:

- To determine when a trainee has developed sufficient skills and knowledge to become qualified and thus to be appointed as a retail store manager (micro purpose)
- To determine any areas where a trainee is having problems, so that additional tutoring can be provided (micro purpose)
- To determine areas where all trainees are having problems, so that the course content and activities can be modified (macro purpose)

Determine Which Learning Outcomes Must Be Measured to Provide Sufficient Data for Decisions. In this step, you identify the learning outcomes that, when measured, will enable you to make a decision about learners' competence. In the case of retail store managers, two job-related competencies may be the ability to merchandise and to control inventory; thus, the learning outcomes in these two areas of the program would need to be measured.

Link Learning Outcomes to Specific Learning Activities. In this step, you identify the learning activities, the content, and the instructional materials that will enable learners to develop the skills or knowledge to be measured. By doing this, you identify factors that will require examination in greater detail (if a problem occurs with learners' development of skills or knowledge), and you do a final check to ensure that what is being measured is actually being taught. While this second benefit may seem trivial, we have come across situations where what was to be measured was not being taught. Granted, this should have been taken care of when line managers and/or the HRD professional determined what decisions they wanted to make. Because the content of programs evolves over time, however, linking outcomes to activities is a double check to make sure that you are measuring what is being taught.

Develop Tests of Knowledge and Skills. This step deals with the development of the actual learning tests, most of which fall into one of two categories: knowledge tests or competency demonstrations. Knowledge tests are used to measure the amount of knowledge acquired by learners. Competency demonstrations are used to measure the amount of skill acquired. (We will discuss knowledge tests and competency demonstrations in more detail later in this chapter.)

Determine How Data Will Be Tabulated and Reported. Tabulation of data can often be more challenging than administration of knowledge tests and competency demonstrations. Therefore, it is imperative at this stage that the tabulation process and the reporting be finalized. Flowcharts should be developed; the time and resources required should be thoroughly planned. (Many of the issues that we discussed in Chapter Eight also pertain to Level II evaluation.)

The caution here is to make sure that you determine how the data will be tabulated and reported before you complete the development of the knowledge tests and competency demonstrations.

Pilot the Learning Tests. The purpose of this step is to ensure that instructions for the tests and simulations are clear; that the tests and simulations are structured so that a competent person can satisfactorily complete them; that they are not too difficult, even for those who have mastered the learning outcomes; and that they are not so easy that even those who have not acquired the learning can complete them.

Piloting the learning measures should be done with the learners themselves, or with people of very similar skills and knowledge in the areas being tested. The tests should be administered just as they would be in the actual Level II evaluation. In other words, pilot these learning tests in the same manner that you would administer them during or after the training program.

It is difficult to provide specific guidelines about the number of people who should participate in piloting the learning tests. Generally, we look for discernible patterns that will provide us with sufficient data to make these decisions. For example, if three or four competent people could not complete a knowledge test or a competency demonstration, then we would review that test or demonstration to detect its flaws. In another situation, we may need twenty-four people to participate in a competency demonstration to provide sufficient data to calibrate it. In short, we use enough individuals to enable us to determine a pattern.

Revise the Tests as Necessary. In this step, we modify and change the tests on the basis of data patterns and conclusions from the pilot. The amount of modification may range from no revision at all to complete rewriting of a simulation.

Validate the Tests and Establish Norms or Standards. Now that the learning tests are usable, we must validate them and establish norms or standards. When validating a test, we determine that it truly measures what it was designed to measure—that is, that the more knowledgeable people test higher on the knowledge test than the less knowledgeable people do. In the case of a competency demonstration, we determine that individuals with the required skills are able to complete the simulation satisfactorily, while those who lack the necessary competencies are not.

When validating tests, we can use the test results to develop norms. These become a reference against which later test scores can be compared. We will use this norm-referenced approach if our purpose is to enable the learners to compare their scores with those of others who have already taken the knowledge test. Norms can also be developed for well-designed competency demonstrations.

When we use a criterion-referenced approach, we are rating the learner against specific criteria. There are specific items on a knowledge test that the learner must answer correctly to have a passing score. In the case of the competency demonstration, there are certain key skills that the learner must demonstrate to meet the criteria (to pass).

Whether the performance standards will be norm-referenced or criterion-referenced depends on the purpose of the Level II evaluation. If the evaluation is to identify people who are qualified to perform a certain function, then criterion-referenced standards should be used. For example, with respect to the retail store managers mentioned earlier, if management wants them qualified to manage stores, then the Level II tests would be criterion-referenced. If, however, management wants to know which trainees have greater knowledge and skills as compared to other trainees, then the norm-referenced approach would be used.

An Example of Level II Evaluation

Let us now follow this process through an actual situation in an organization that installed and serviced vending equipment in thousands of retail establishments throughout the United States. In this organization, there were hundreds of service technicians who installed and serviced equipment.

A front-end analysis had determined that good diagnostic and problem-solving skills were needed for service technicians to be able to repair equipment efficiently. As a consequence, the technical training function developed an interactive video self-study course that provided service technicians with the problem-solving techniques related to specific types of equipment. Also included were simulations on solving major malfunctions that might occur.

Step 1. The key decision makers were the district service managers, and they wanted to determine which service technicians could accurately diagnose and solve malfunctions on the equipment. In addition, the technical training department wanted to determine which learning activities of the self-study course enabled service technicians to devleop the necessary skills and knowledge and which ones were not able to develop a sufficient level of competency in service technicians.

The primary purpose of the study was to determine which service technicians could accurately diagnose and solve the equipment problems within the prescribed time parameters. The secondary purpose of the study was to determine which learning activities were helping and which were hindering the service technicians in the development of the needed competencies.

Step 2. The decision was made to measure both the knowledge and the skill components of the service technicians' problem-solving ability. The knowledge tests would focus on the functions of each component of the equipment and on the symptoms that might occur when a component was not operating correctly. In the competency demonstration, the service technicians would be given a set of malfunction symptoms and be asked to determine the causes.

Step 3. The knowledge tests were linked to three major learning modules in the program. The first module provided information on each major component of the equipment. The second module covered malfunctions that could be easily repaired on site. The third module provided information about malfunctions that would require replacement components.

The competency demonstration consisted of two simulations, given as a posttest after completion of all three modules. The second and third modules had similar but not identical practice simulations.

Step 4. The knowledge tests used a multiple-choice format and referred to specific content within the three modules. Interactive video simulations were developed for the competency demonstration. For each set of malfunction symptoms, four diagnostic paths were programmed into the simulation. A correct path was available, along with three incorrect paths that contained some of the most common errors made by service technicians in diagnosing these malfunctions. Each service technician was asked to complete two of the four simulations satisfactorily.

Step 5. The test results were tabulated by computer. They could be retrieved from the computer by the technical trainer and could then be passed on to the district service manager.

Step 6. The learning measures were tested with newly trained but competent service technicians. Each item on the knowledge test was examined to determine whether both the questions and the answers were understandable. For the compentency demonstrations, each decision by each service technician was recorded by the computer, so that the percentage of correct and incorrect decisions could be tracked. In addition, each service technician was interviewed after taking the tests, and some questions focused on the reasons for incorrect diagnosis of the malfunctions. In some cases, that interview provided information on how to clarify the malfunction symptoms or the available diagnostic options in future simulations. Thus, the possibility of a misinterpreted question or answer was reduced.

Step 7. On the basis of the information from the pilot groups, the knowledge tests and competency demonstrations were revised.

Step 8. As the program was rolled out into the field, data on both the knowledge tests and the competency demonstrations were collected and sent to the technical training department. These data were used to establish norms for the knowledge tests and the competency demonstrations. The norms were published after the first one hundred newly trained service technicians had completed the self-study course and the Level II tests. These norms were used by the technical trainers and the service managers to make decisions about service technicians who could accurately and efficiently diagnose equipment malfunctions and about technicians who needed additional training.

Knowledge Tests

Four types of knowledge tests, most frequently used for Level II evaluation, will be discussed in this section, along with their advantages and disadvantages.

Essay/Open-Answer Tests. This format uses open-ended questions and asks the individual to write each answer in narrative form. For example, a typical question at the end of a workshop on influencing might be "Describe the four major types of influencing strategies, including when to use each, the factors that would make each effective, and the limitations of each."

The advantages of this type of test are that the test is easy to construct, allows for considerable freedom in answering questions, and adapts well to "why" and "how" questions. Some disadvantages of this format are that each answer must be read and graded by a knowledgeable person; that the test must be manually scored, rather than computer-scored; and that an individual's writing ability may affect his or her score.

Write-In or Short-Answer Tests. This approach involves test items that are sentences with key words missing: "The influencing approach that involves painting an image of the future and the benefits of achieving that goal is called ____ ____."

The advantages of this approach are that there is a limited number of correct answers, so that the test can be scored either manually or by computer by a person who has the correct answers; that there is very little subjectivity involved in scoring; that the test adapts well to problems that have only a small number of correct answers; and that the test instructions are easy to understand. The disadvantages are that the format does not adapt well to "how" or "why" questions, the test items can cue the individual to the correct answers, and the tests cannot be machine-scored.

Binary (Including True/False) Tests. This type of test involves questions in which the individual is given two choices and is asked to select the correct one: "A manager who believes that employees cannot be trusted and will work only when being closely controlled is called (a) a Theory X manager; (b) a Theory Y manager."

Also included in this category are true/false questions: "When reviewing a person's performance, you should compare the person's actual results to the performance standards agreed upon for that employee (answer *true* or *false*)."

The advantages of binary test items are that the tests are easy to score; that the tests can be machine-scored, computer-scored, or manually tabulated; and that the test instructions are easy to understand. The major disadvantages are that the questions are limited in scope by virtue of the individual's being given two answers, one of which must be correct; that the test writer must have a high degree of content knowledge, along with the ability to construct unambiguous statements; that there is a tendency for the individual being tested to view these as "trick" questions, to read something into a statement that is not intended, and to have trouble answering the questions; and that an individual who truly does not know the answer is often tempted to guess. Rae (1986) notes two important rules to follow in developing a binary test. First, "The question must consist of only one question, and that question must be clear to the reader so that it does not have to be puzzled over for its meaning. Otherwise, the person being tested may be confused. The intention is to test the knowledge of the person, not to test their ability to interpret ambiguity." Second, "One of the answers given (as an option) must be correct, and there must be no doubt or ambiguity about the correct or true answer" (p. 76).

Multiple-Choice Tests. Multiple-choice questions vary from binary questions in that more than two choices (usually up to five) are offered. Here is a sample multiple-choice question: "Greater pressure aids carbonation because (a) it makes water boil; (b) CO_2 breaks down chemically; (c) it forces CO_2 molecules in between water molecules; (d) CO_2 clings to the inside of the glass; (e) none of the above." Typically, there is one correct answer, with the remaining answers being wrong or obviously not applying to the situation. To make multiple-choice questions more difficult, the choices may include "all of the above" and "none of the above."

The advantages of multiple-choice tests are that they are easy to score, either by machine or by computer; that the questions can be more complex than binary questions; and that, when given a well-constructed test with a penalty for wrong answers, participants are less tempted to guess at answers, because sheer guesses will most likely result in a greater number of incorrect answers. Some of the disadvantages of multiple-choice questions are that they do not adapt well to complex answers, such as those dealing with rationales; that they take more time to develop than binary questions, primarily because the test writer needs to be able to develop logical wrong answers; and that, as with binary questions, individuals may feel that there are some trick questions and thus read into those questions more than the tester intended.

Competency Demonstrations: Testing for Skill

When we wish to measure the amount of skill that has been developed in a learning situation, we should use a competency demonstration. In other words, the learners are provided an opportunity to demonstrate their competencies while being observed by a trained evaluator. This would be very similar to the auditioning of actors for the cast of a stage production. In auditions, actors are usually given several pages of script to read and deliver in a believable manner, thus demonstrating their acting skill.

So it is with skill testing in Level II evaluations. We develop simulations or activities that enable the learners to demonstrate their use of the newly learned skills. They are then observed by people who can objectively assess the learners' performance. These competency demonstrations can be part of the learning activities, where the learners are assessed as they participate. Frequently, the competency demonstration is a separate event, placed near or at the end of the learning experience.

In this section, we will discuss the measurement of learning, rather than how to design simulations, because that topic alone could be the subject of another book. Needless to say, the simulation needs to be well designed and should duplicate a real-life situation. Assuming that we do have well-designed simulations for the competency demonstrations, let us discuss several types of learning measures.

Behavioral Checklist. The behavioral checklist provides the observer with a list of behaviors that the learners should demonstrate as they successfully handle the simulation. An example of one type of behavioral checklist is shown in Figure 15. When the observer sees the learner effectively demonstrating a specific skill during the simulation, the observer puts a checkmark in the "Effective" column. If the learner is less than effective or misses an opportunity to demonstrate the skill, the observer will check "Not Effective" or "Missed Opportunity." The training of observers in how to observe and assess skill use against specific criteria is essential if you are to get assessments that have high interrater reliability.

The advantages of this approach are that the checklist is easy to develop, if the learner outcomes are well articulated; that the training of the observers is relatively easy; that the rating system is easily understood; and that it can also be used as a

Figure 15. Behavioral Checklist.

Simulation # ____________ Manager ____________

Date ____________ Time ____________

Listen and Respond with Empathy

	Effective	*Not Effective*	*Missed Opportunity*
Maintain eye contact			
Nod head affirmatively			
Verbally acknowledge with "yes," "right," and so on			
Let other person finish speaking			
Repeat your understanding in your own words			
State the other person's emotions or feelings			

Observer ____________

feedback tool during the training of the learners. The disadvantages of this approach are that it does not allow for a qualitative rating of skill levels when learning is performed at various levels of competence; that it does not adapt well to variations of the prescribed behaviors, even when those variations may also be effective; and that, if poorly designed, the checklist can allow for subjectivity on the part of the observer.

Behaviorally Anchored Rating Scale (BARS). This approach uses a scale with behavioral anchors, wherein each anchor describes a level of competence. It is shown in Figure 16. Each increment on the scale is behaviorally described, so that the observers are able to note the behavior that they have observed, with little or no interpretation.

The advantages of the BARS approach are that it provides

a mechanism for assessing the differences in skill level of the learners; that, by providing behavioral anchors, it removes the subjectivity that results from observer interpretation; that it is relatively easy to train observers to use the scale; and that it can also be used as a feedback tool during the training of the learners. The disadvantages of the BARS approach are that it is time-consuming and difficult to develop a scale; that the scale is difficult or impossible to use if the learner deviates from the prescribed method of handling a situation; and that the observation worksheet is inherently more complex than the behavioral checklist.

Behavioral Frequency Worksheet. Another approach is to count the frequency of specific effective and ineffective behaviors. Here, the observer, using a frequency worksheet, counts each time the learner uses an effective or ineffective behavior. This approach differs from the behavioral checklist in that the observer notes each time that the learner demonstrates a behavior; when using the behavioral checklist, the observer makes one

Figure 16. Behaviorally Anchored Rating Scale.

For "Listening and Responding," the learner demonstrated the level of skill indicated.

5	Learner accurately identified the feelings of the other person, indicated what those feelings were, provided a summary of what the other person had just said, and asked if his or her understanding of the message was accurate.
4	Learner accurately identified the feelings of the other person, indicated to the other person what those feelings were, and provided a summary of what the other person had just said.
3	Learner provided the other person with a summary of what the person had just said.
2	Learner gave an answer to the other person without summarizing what the other person had just said.
1	Learner interrupted the other person and gave his or her own point of view.

Figure 17. Behavioral Frequency Worksheet.

Simulation # ______________ Manager ______________________

Date ____________________ Time ______________________

General Principles	*Effective*	*Ineffective*
Maintain self-esteem	/	~~////~~ ///
Listen and respond with understanding	~~////~~ ~~////~~ ~~////~~ /	~~////~~ /
Ask for ideas	~~////~~ ~~////~~ //	///
Build on ideas	~~////~~ ///	////
Check for understanding	///	~~////~~ /

Observer ______________________

overall assessment of the learner's effectiveness for each skill. An example of a behavioral frequency worksheet is shown in Figure 17. The assessment of a person's competency is based on the frequency with which that person uses effective and ineffective behaviors. Many times, a desirable profile of frequencies can be used as a standard for judging learners' competence.

The advantages of this approach are that it produces highly reliable data, because the basic measurement is frequency, rather than quality; that it focuses on the use of key effective and ineffective behaviors; that it works well even when the learner deviates from the prescribed approach; and that it can also be used as a feedback tool during the training of the learners. The disadvantages of this approach are that it does not provide for incremental rating of a person's skill level, as the BARS approach does, and that it requires considerable training of observers before they are able to accurately record the frequency data.

Figure 18. Behavioral Observation Scale.

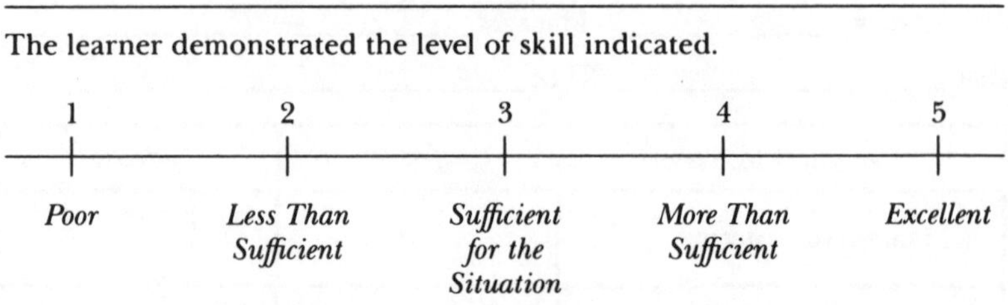

Behavioral Observation Scale (BOS). This scale (also often called a Likert scale) has the observer make a judgment of the appropriate use of the learner's behavior and enter that judgment on the scale. A sample BOS is shown in Figure 18.

The advantages of this approach are that the BOS is easy to construct and easy to tabulate. The disadvantages are that the rating depends on observers' ability to observe and make judgments about learners' behavior; that it is difficult to train the observers to observe and judge behaviors to a level of expertise that will provide interrater reliability; and that the BOS does not provide either frequency or behavioral data (if needed, these data would have to be collected through a supplemental method).

Effectiveness Rating Worksheet. Another approach is to assess the effectiveness with which the learner has handled a competency demonstration. In this approach, the effectiveness criteria are established for each segment and for the entire simulation. The criteria focus more on the result of the learner's actions than on the learner's behavior. The evaluators observe and then rate the learner's effectiveness in handling each segment. Effectiveness criteria used for a simulation in which a supervisor is discussing poor work habits with an employee are shown in Figure 19.

The advantages of this approach are that effectiveness criteria have high credibility with many people, including line managers and learners, because they focus on the results of the learners' actions; that the training of the observers is relatively easy; and that the approach can be used for feedback during the

Figure 19. Effectiveness Rating Worksheet.

	Yes	*No*
Concern about the impact of the employee's work habit is clearly stated by the supervisor.		
Reasons for the poor work habit are stated by the employee.		
Ideas for solving the problem are generated by both.		
Specific action is agreed to by both.		
Follow-up date is set.		
Total Discussion		

training of the learners. The disadvantages of this approach are that there is less emphasis on the need for the learner to follow the procedures and that it does not adapt so well to the measuring of skill levels as the BARS or behavior analysis approaches do.

The Best-Solution Approach. For some simulations, several solutions are acceptable. Many times, however, one or two are clearly the best solutions, because they represent more effective or efficient ways of handling the situation. This is often the case in fact-finding and problem-solving simulations, in which obtaining all relevant facts and seeing the relationships between them are essential to developing a best solution. While there may be several acceptable answers, one or two clearly demonstrate the best interpretation of facts and the most creative problem-solving process. This approach gives a higher score to those who develop the best solutions. Those who develop an acceptable solution receive lower but positive scores. Those arriving at no solutions or at unacceptable solutions may receive negative scores.

The advantages of this approach are that it acknowledges that some solutions are better than others and that there is a specific rank-ordering of answers for each simulation. The disadvantages are that it does not directly assess the skill levels of the learners; that it may not directly assess how solutions were reached; and that, if a person is "given" a best solution before taking the competency demonstration, that person would probably receive a high rating.

Increased Objectivity

Developing and maintaining a high degree of objectivity in the observers of competency demonstrations are an ongoing concern. On the one hand, observers often have pet words or phrases. When a pet phrase is used by a learner in a simulation, the observer will rate that behavior unduly highly. On the other hand, some observers have certain "turn-off" phrases or actions that cause them to rate the learner unduly low. We are reminded of one observer who particularly liked action verbs and disliked verbs indicating intent. When observing managers in simulations, she would rate too highly those who used such phrases as "I will discuss that with John tomorrow," and she would underrate such phrases as "I intend to discuss that with John tomorrow." Let us examine some ways to increase the objectivity of assessments.

Using Multiple Observers. The use of multiple observers provides a mechanism for identifying ratings that are unduly high or low. In using this approach, it is best to have each observer enter his or her assessments individually on worksheets. When assessments differ by a predetermined margin, the observers can discuss the observed behavior and agree on an assessment.

Training Observers. Training observers in behavioral observation and assessment skills is an excellent way to increase objectivity and reliability. The training usually consists of a thorough description of effective and ineffective behavior. Observers assess videotaped learners in simulations. They compare their own ratings to predetermined ratings. They continue this process until every observer has evaluated a given situation in the same manner. This training not only increases interrater reliability and objectivity but also reduces the amount of time devoted to discussing differing ratings during actual competency demonstrations. In addition, if all observers are perceived as rating consistently, there will be fewer complaints from learners who are participating in the competency demonstrations.

Videotaping and Audiotaping. Videotaping or audiotaping the competency demonstration provides not only documentation of the demonstration but also an opportunity to get second, third, or even fourth opinions, as needed. Whenever there is some disagreement over a rating, other independent observers can view or hear the simulation and provide additional assessments. Another benefit is using the videotapes or audiotapes as feedback tools with learners. Thus, the learner can see and discuss things that were done or not done that affected the rating.

The advantages of videotaping over audiotaping include the ability to observe the learner's nonverbal behavior and the ability to clearly identify who is talking. The advantages of the audiotaping include simpler and less obtrusive equipment.

Measuring Attitudes and Values

Training objectives often involve the changing of learners' attitudes or values; for example, we may wish to change employees' attitudes toward product quality. In this situation, we would most likely wish to track the learner's on-the-job behavior (Level III) and job performance (Level IV). We may also elect to test the participant's knowledge of quality and skills in using specific quality improvement techniques (Level II). Also, we would want to measure the change in the learners' attitudes and values.

In another situation where managers have received training that includes information about the organization's values and ethics, it may be important to your client—and to you—to know whether the training has changed managers' values or beliefs about ethics. When it is important that key decision makers have information about such changes in attitudes or values, you must decide how to measure such changes. (We do not discuss in this chapter how to measure changes in values or beliefs; see Chapter Twelve.)

Issues

Certification Versus Development. The issue that creates the greatest amount of emotion regarding Level II evaluation is how the data will be used. When the data are to be used for certification or qualification, the measures become gateways through which people must pass to be able to work in jobs for which they have been trained. Failure to pass through denies the person the privilege of working in his or her field.

If the learning measures are used for developmental purposes, the data are used to highlight areas where a person is strong or where more training and development are needed. Here, people usually continue to work in their chosen fields, even though they may need more development.

In implementing a Level II measurement system to be used for certification, it is imperative that you have the full support of your client and that together you conduct a potential-problem analysis and agree on how to handle each issue that will arise. In addition, you and your client must develop a plan for communicating the certification system to all who are affected by it.

You must also be knowledgeable about the legal and technical aspects of knowledge tests and competency demonstrations when these are vehicles for determining qualifications for selection or promotion.

It is easier to implement a certification process for a new position or a new operation than for current jobs. When you are changing current procedures, however, resistance to the certification process will be much greater. No matter how strong your reasons are for implementing the certification process, there will be tremendous resistance from people who are already working and performing in the area where certification will be required in the future. Usually, some people who have been working in the area cannot be certified without additional training. This is difficult for them and their supervisors to accept. Your client must point this out in advance and reassure them that the certification process will be implemented uniformly and fairly.

Organizations implementing certification into currently operating areas often use grandfather clauses, which allow people who are in the area to continue to operate as they did before. Our feeling is that a grandfather clause should not be open-ended. It should state a reasonable period of time (possibly a year) during which those already working will be required to demonstrate their competency to become certified.

It is important to allow those who cannot pass the competency demonstration the first time an opportunity to receive additional training and to try a competency demonstration again. In this way, the process will be perceived more as a developmental than a screening process.

For Level II certification to work well, the performance standards need to be clearly articulated and accepted by line managers, particularly your client. Once standards have been agreed on, your measurement system must assess individuals as accurately and objectively as possible against these criteria. There should be no bending of the rules, because the first time the requirements are waived for one person, the floodgates are open, and other people will want the same waiver.

What Can Go Wrong

Obviously, any system can have problems. Here, we would like to discuss three of the most common problems of Level II evaluation.

Lack of Rigor. We have seen instances in which knowledge tests and competency demonstrations were initially established and used effectively. They were able to achieve their objectives, whether those involved certification or development. Over time, however, and particularly with turnover among key staff people, the administration of the tests and simulations became less rigorous. In some cases, the tests became obsolete; in others, the simulations became common knowledge among those who were participating in the training. Both of these situations reduced the credibility of the measures in the eyes of the evaluators, instructors, and learners. Thus, there was a tendency to bend the rules or give the benefit of a doubt, and the Level II measurements gradually became compromised.

In other situations, we have seen the documentation become haphazard. Often, learners who were having problems would be well documented, while the documentation of successful learners was almost nonexistent. This system would work only until a supposedly successful certified learner was not able to perform on the job, and the lack of documentation became an embarrassment to everyone.

Failure to Inform Learners in Advance. When Level II measurement is sprung on learners during training, there generally are some who will strongly resist it. Dealing with their objections—and, many times, with the objections of their bosses—takes an undue amount of time and effort. If learners and their bosses are aware in advance of the Level II measures and of their benefits and rationales, then support and cooperation are more likely.

Data Collection Without a Plan. From time to time, we have seen HRD professionals who collect Level II data but have no plan for using them. In other words, key decision makers have not been identified, the purpose of data collection has not been established, and there is no plan for using the data. The explanation is often "We wanted to have these data just in case we needed them." This approach not only takes a lot of time and effort but also can become a barrier to use of the Level II data in the future. For example, your client may ask, "How come you never did anything with all the data you collected in the XYZ program?" We recognize that Level II data are often collected and used during the piloting of new training efforts. Once the piloting is completed, however, and if there is no clear purpose for the Level II data, we suggest that no more be collected until a specific purpose becomes apparent.

Level II evaluation is crucial, particularly when we train people according to specific criteria or performance standards. It provides invaluable information about the degree to which learners have learned what was intended. It also can provide valuable information about participants' ability to meet standards before they are given new job responsibilities. Level II measurements can provide accurate readings about the effectiveness of a learning experience. Nevertheless, we also need information about the extent to which newly trained employees use their new skills on the job. This topic will be discussed in Chapter Eleven.

Summary

The following techniques move training toward impact:

Activity **Impact**

- Design a Level II evaluation system that will demonstrate that learning does take place during the training.
- Involve your client in designing the Level II evaluation, so that the client understands and accepts the evaluation data.
- Pilot and validate all knowledge tests and competency demonstrations.
- Monitor, on an ongoing basis, the use of the knowledge tests and competency demonstrations, so that rigor can be maintained and standards will not be compromised.

Eleven

Behavioral Results: Evaluating Transfer of Learning to the Job

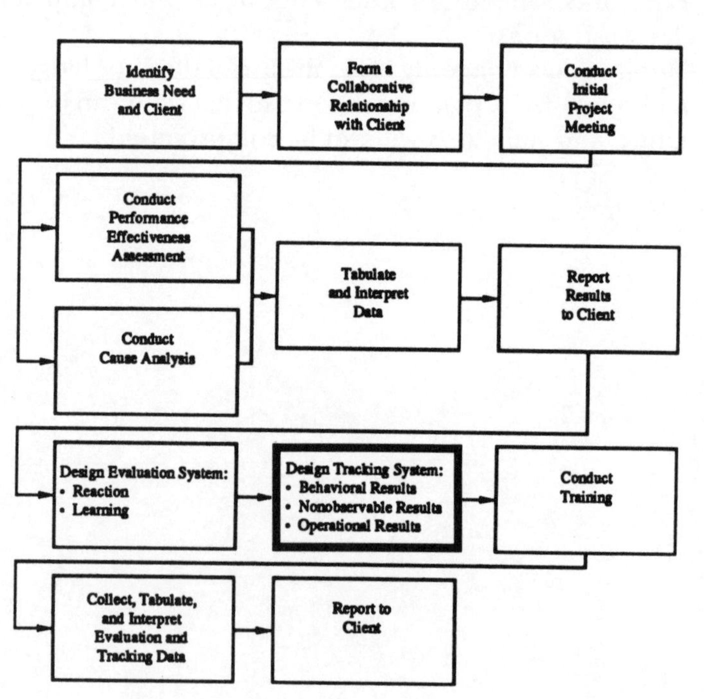

Thus far, we have concentrated on how to evaluate at the reaction and learning levels. Now we will be shifting our focus to concentrate on the evaluation of the application of learning. There are four categories of learning outcomes that can be evaluated for application: affective learning outcomes, cognitive learning outcomes, behavioral or skill learning outcomes, and operational outcomes.

Affective learning outcomes focus on attitudes, values, and beliefs of participants. Much of the affirmative action training that occurred in the 1970s and the 1980s had affective objectives associated with it. The hope was that participants would believe that women and minorities had not been provided equal opportunity and that now it was important to correct that situation.

Cognitive learning outcomes represent the concepts, principles, and knowledge sets that participants are to learn and then use on the job. Almost all training programs include some cognitive outcomes; for example, participants are provided with information on policies and practices of the organization or are given knowledge about products and services.

Behavioral or skill learning outcomes address what participants are to be physically able to do. These outcomes can be observed by others. When we build the technical skill of replacing a part in a boiler unit, or when we develop the managerial skill of coaching, we are addressing this kind of learning outcome.

Operational outcomes occur on the job as a result of all of the other outcomes. When sales increase, customer complaints are reduced, or waste declines, these are operational outcomes. They are not taught in a class; they result from what has been presented to and used by participants.

In Kirkpatrick's (1983) model, Level III evaluation focuses on behavior or skill application. As we indicated in Chapter Nine, we prefer to view Level III evaluations as being of two types: Type A (focusing on behavior application) and Type B (focusing on nonobservable results). Level IV evaluation is also an important part of results evaluation. We have created a phrase, "tracking for change," to refer to all these evaluations. In essence, the HRD professional who designs and implements any Level III or Level IV evaluation is tracking the degree to which change has occurred after a training program. In this chapter, we will discuss how to design a Level III evaluation that focuses on behavioral application. (We use the terms *behavior* and *skill* interchangeably, to mean anything that we teach people to do that can be observed.)

The decision to track behavioral or skill change after a training program actually represents a decision to answer two questions: Are people using the skills and behaviors they have been taught? Is the work environment supporting the use of these skills and behaviors? The second question must be addressed in evaluating behavioral change, because skill transfer is a function of learning and of a work environment that supports and encourages the use of that learning. Once again we see the operation of this formula:

Learning Experience × Work Environment = Business Results

In tracking behavioral change, you are truly evaluating that equation and the degree to which items on both sides of the multiplication sign were operative during your particular program or project.

Purposes for Tracking Behavioral and Skill Change

Recall that purposes are either major questions you wish to address or major decisions you wish to make as a result of collected information. With that in mind, the questions to ask during a tracking evaluation can be any or all of the following.

1. Are people applying on the job what they have been taught?
2. Which behaviors or skills are being used with the greatest frequency? Which are being used with the least frequency?
3. Which behaviors or skills taught in the program are not being used at all? What are the primary reasons for lack of skill transfer?
4. Is the degree of skill transfer similar or different in com-

parisons of people by area of the company, position in the company, and so forth?

5. Has the business need that initiated the request for training been met?
6. Are there new business needs that are not being met?

Decisions that can be made as a result of tracking involve these questions.

1. How, if at all, should the program be redesigned to increase its impact on the organization?
2. How, if at all, should the work environment of the learners be modified to increase support of the skills taught?
3. Should the job experience and/or the learning requirements for entrance into the program be modified?

Note that none of these objectives focuses on proving what percentage of change is due to training. In considering why a plane takes flight, would we think in terms of what percentage of that result is due to the plane's engine and what percentage is due to the wings? Obviously, without both parts, the plane could not become airborne. The same is true in tracking for behavioral change: The learning experience must have been effective, and the work environment must be supportive; otherwise, there will be no results. When we measure behavioral change, we are focusing on whether the partnership of training and management worked; we are not interested in identifying which partner had the greater impact.

In determining purposes for a behavioral tracking study, one of your first decisions must be whether to evaluate results for individuals or for the group of people who attended your program. *Microevaluation* means the evaluation of individuals: To what degree is John Doe using the learning from a specific program when on the job? The purpose of this evaluation is to assist John Doe in his skill development. A typical situation would be that of employees' being conditionally hired into an organization. Banks, for example, often hire tellers conditionally. To be retained, new hires must successfully complete a training program. If they are unable to complete the competency test, they are let go. It becomes very important to have specific information on each teller-trainee in such a situation. The identities of these people are known; the information collected during the training process is used to develop and evaluate these individuals.

In contrast, *macroevaluation* focuses on groups of people. Here, the purpose is to determine what percentage of people who attended a program are using skills on the job. The overriding purpose is not to develop individuals, but rather to identify the benefits being returned to the organization for investing in this program. Perhaps you delivered a sales training program to one hundred sales professionals and wanted to determine the degree to which this group is using the skills taught in handling objections from customers. All the purposes of tracking for change would be applicable if you wanted to do macroevaluation. Such a focus usually requires that you protect the identity of the people being evaluated. (As we discuss this process more completely, the need for confidentiality will become clear.) Therefore, a basic decision must be made at the start of your evaluation effort: Do you wish to know results for specific individuals (for developmental purposes), or do you need to determine what benefits have accrued to the organization because a program was offered (for purposes of determining the costs and benefits of the program)? The majority of this chapter will focus on macroevaluation. The how-to's of microevaluation are also described near the conclusion of the chapter.

Common Mistakes in Evaluating Application of Learning

Several years ago, we had a conversation with a trainer who had just completed a follow-up evaluation on a particular program. The results seemed impressive. He had written them into a report and proudly sent them off to several members of management to read. Days passed. He heard no comments or reactions to this report. He then phoned a few of the managers, only to be told, "I haven't got to it yet," or that the managers had glanced through it but had little recall of what was in it. What did this training manager learn from that experience? He concluded that managers were not interested in this type of information and that he would never do such an evaluation again.

This training professional made some key strategic errors. These are errors we have observed more than once. Generally, such errors fall into two categories: errors in positioning the tracking effort and errors related to data collection.

Positioning errors include the following.

1. The purposes of the evaluation effort are never identified, or the only purpose is to justify training.
2. There is no involvement of clients, nor is any effort made to determine what type of information those individuals would find meaningful and credible.
3. Results are reported in a written memo, rather than in a face-to-face meeting with all clients and others who have a stake. (Interpretation of results should be interactive, as described in Chapter Eight.)
4. Training is conducted apart from any business need, and management's interest in evaluation is low.

Errors related to data collection include the following.

1. Evaluation occurs only after the program has been conducted. No base-line information is collected against which posttraining results can be compared.
2. Only the learners are asked to provide information on change or results. No other sources of information are used.
3. The questions asked of people are of poor construction. They are too broad—"Are you communicating better?"—and result in data that lack meaning and even credibility to the people who review the information.

Acknowledging that these errors need to be avoided, let us now turn our attention to effectively tracking for change.

Five Critical Questions

To track for behavioral change, you will need to answer five questions.

1. Who is the client for this training project and, therefore, for the information to be collected?
2. What is the business need behind the training request?
3. What outcomes, in behavioral terms, are expected from the program?
4. How will you and the client know whether these behavioral outcomes have occurred?
5. After the training program, how long should you wait to determine whether these outcomes have occurred?

Questions 1 and 2. The first two questions are primarily strategic. They focus on the program's strategy for implementation and evaluation. By making certain that you have a client and a business need, you increase the probability that when you complete your evaluation you will find results to report. As we have indicated before, results from training occur because the learning experience has been effective and because the work environment is supportive. Training implemented without a tie to a business need or to a client has a reduced probability of yielding results to the organization, and management is less likely to want to work with you to ensure that the work environment will encourage skill transfer. The first step of reporting results from training efforts is to implement the program so that results are virtually assured. Having a client and a business need helps to increase the odds for success.

Another benefit of having a client is that you will have someone to report the results to when your evaluation effort is done. Without a client, who will believe or even care about your reported success? With whom will you celebrate? What if you find that there are skill-transfer problems? With whom will you work to change those results? Without a client, you are left with limited decisions about the information you collect.

The benefit of having a business need is that when you

measure results from a training program, you will want to measure whether that business need has been met. This is the type of information that holds interest for your client.

Consider a true example. A manufacturing firm wanted to modify the organizational culture at one of its larger plants. Approximately one thousand people worked there. The wage-earning employees belonged to a union. There was a history of low trust between the union and management, as well as an almost adversarial quality between the two groups when they faced common business dilemmas. Plant management acknowledged these business problems and wanted to take appropriate action. Part of the cause was the inability of supervisors to be participative with their employees: They were not seeking out employees' ideas or acknowledging the contributions made by employees. As a result, the employees felt isolated from management and unappreciated. Supervisors lacked the skills and confidence to demonstrate such behavior; many supervisors even believed that the union agreement prohibited them from being participative with employees. A decision was made to provide supervisors with a training program that would build skills in how to handle employees' complaints, coach for improved performance, and acknowledge positive performance. The program would also inform supervisors about the union agreement. The primary purpose of the tracking done on this program was to determine whether actions taken by management and skills taught in the training program were helping to change the work climate. The driving force of the tracking effort was to determine the degree to which this business problem was being eliminated; evaluating the training program was just a part of the overall effort.

Thus, you are evaluating more than just a course. We want to concentrate in this chapter on critical questions that focus on the data-collection methodology used for tracking behavioral change. Again, it is important to collect information that will be meaningful and credible to your client and to other individuals who will be reviewing it. It is also important not to put a great deal of time and resources into evaluation of a program if your client is going to "shoot holes" through the information and not believe the results. This situation can be avoided if the data-collection methods are sound and agreed to by your client.

Question 3. Would you attempt to evaluate any of these behavioral outcomes? "Salespeople will sell more effectively." "Managers will actively listen." "Clerks will demonstrate customer-oriented behavior."

Such outcomes, while behavioral in nature, are much too broad and ambiguous to be measured. The criteria to be used in measuring each outcome are left up to individuals to decide. To truly measure behavioral outcomes, we must identify discrete behaviors—defined as individual units of behavior (not unseen, low-key behaviors, as one of our clients thought). While we cannot measure "sales effectiveness" as an outcome, we can measure salespeople's ability to describe a product to a customer by noting its benefits and not its features or to gain agreement with the client on a follow-up date for the next contact. While measuring "active listening" is impossible, as stated, we can measure whether managers check for understanding by restating what has just been said before they respond to the comments or whether managers acknowledge any feelings that have been expressed.

These are examples of discrete behaviors, because they can be seen or heard by others. Therefore, it is possible to measure whether they are occurring. Clearly, discrete behaviors are related to but different from behavioral objectives for a training program. For example, an objective from a vendor's program with which we are familiar indicates that, as a result of attending the training program, "customer service representatives (CSRs) will be able to effectively handle customer complaint calls." While this may suffice as a program objective, it is not sufficient for our needs if we want to measure whether CSRs are demonstrating the desired skill. We must define *effective* behaviorally by determining what specific techniques or steps the CSRs will be taught to use when taking complaint calls. In this case, the discrete behaviors are the following:

- Confirm the customer's name.
- Ask questions to identify the nature of the complaint.

- Complete the company form, filling in all information requested.
- Summarize the CSR's understanding of the complaint.
- Indicate what actions the CSR can and cannot take relevant to this complaint.
- Confirm when the customer will hear next from the company regarding this complaint.
- Acknowledge, throughout the conversation, any feelings that the customer may have expressed.
- Thank the customer for bringing the complaint to the attention of the company.

Each of these behaviors is discrete, for it can be seen or heard by others. We need to determine the frequency with which each of these behaviors was demonstrated before training and compare that with how often the behaviors are used after training.

Another factor to consider is whether the training program's design actually does build skills. If participants are expected to do something, they should be given an opportunity to practice. To expect people to learn something and then make the operational leap by themselves is asking for trouble. For example, if you wanted to teach someone how to pilot a plane, you might design a training program in which the participant would hear about the theory of aerodynamics and perhaps view a film illustrating the inside of a cockpit, with its various controls and dials. Participants could be tested to determine their ability to read and interpret information from such dials. All of this would be training at the cognitive level. If, on the basis of this design, the participant were then expected to pilot an airplane successfully, there could be disastrous results. To spring from the cognitive to the behavioral level of performance, the learner must be provided with an opportunity to practice flying a plane in a simulator, where no harm would come while the necessary skills were being built.

Thus, for a training program to be a candidate for tracking at this level, its outcomes must be behavioral (able to be seen or heard), and the skills required to demonstrate the outcome need to be developed in the training program itself.

The flowchart illustrated in Figure 20 shows the decision points that should be reviewed in identifying behavioral outcomes. (Clearly, there are many training programs in which only part of the program can be measured at this level, because only part of the program provides behavioral outcomes.)

A final point regarding the identification of discrete behavioral outcomes: It is the rare training program that will have these discrete, behavioral outcomes listed for you. We have found that the two primary sources for locating these types of discrete behaviors are subject-matter experts (the individuals who designed the program or instruct it effectively) and the instructor's guide for the program. You need to isolate the specific techniques, behaviors, steps, or skills being taught to participants regarding a behavioral objective. Once that list is composed, you and your clients must agree on which behavioral outcomes are most important to evaluate. You may wish to collect information on all of them, or you may require information only on some. The more behavioral outcomes you measure, the longer and more complex your tracking system will become.

Question 4. Once the specific behavioral outcomes you wish to measure have been identified, the next issue is to decide how to collect information to determine whether those outcomes are happening. When it comes to measurement of human behavior, you have three methodology choices: behavioral observation, interviews, and questionnaires.

When using behavioral observation, you and other skilled observers go where your participants are and observe them as they perform their jobs, and you record the frequency with which individuals are demonstrating the desired behaviors.

We have conducted this type of evaluation effort for clients. In one instance, we were asked to determine whether district managers were using coaching and counseling skills when meeting with their representatives. Three representative districts were selected for our study. A consultant was paired with a district manager; together, they visited a number of representatives. While the manager conducted a one-to-one meeting

Figure 20. Identifying Behavioral Outcomes to Be Tracked.

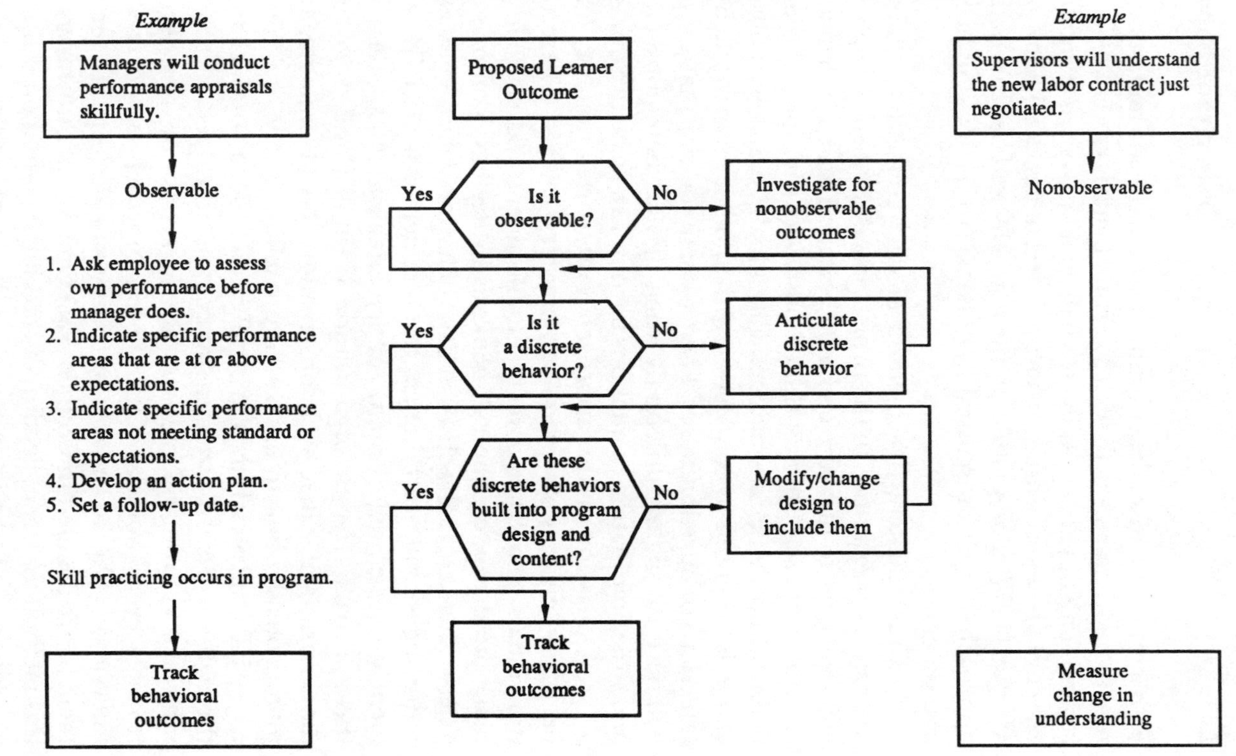

with a representative, the consultant sat to one side and actually noted the frequency with which certain behaviors were demonstrated. This approach, known as behavior analysis, is extremely effective in determining behavioral frequency. Rackham and Morgan (1977) have written on the how, why, and benefits of this approach; it is also discussed in Rossett's (1987) book on needs assessment.

Unfortunately, this method of data collection is labor-intensive. For example, in the project just described, it required eighteen days to measure eighteen people. This approach also requires the use of highly skilled observers who have all been trained to code behaviors identically. Finally, behavioral observation is best used in connection with another method, such as interviews or questionnaires. There is some concern that people will perform slightly differently when they are being observed, and so a combination of methods becomes an attractive option.

A variation on this approach is often used. You may have heard of "mystery shoppers" or "mystery callers." These are individuals who enter a retail establishment and pretend to make purchases, or who call banks as if they have complaints. These callers are really observing the behavior of employees and reporting whether certain behaviors are demonstrated. Department stores, as well as many service establishments, often use this approach. If your organization is similar, and if you are developing skills that such observations could evaluate, you might consider how to use this approach.

HRD professionals typically track behavioral change through surveys. In essence, surveys are developed to collect information from people who are in a position to observe learners every workday. One survey approach is the use of interviews. (The advantages and disadvantages of this survey method are detailed in Chapter Six.) One distinct advantage of this method for the collection of tracking information is that it affords you the opportunity to collect actual incidents, or stories, of how participants have used the techniques taught in a program, and with what results. This is basically an adaptation of the "critical incident" interview technique, in which past participants in a program are asked to think of specific situations where they have applied whatever skills were taught. Participants are asked several questions that illuminate the contexts in which skills were applied, the specific techniques or skills that were used, and the results to individuals, their work units, and their organizations. Such qualitative data give depth to the more quantified information that may also have been collected.

We used this approach as part of an overall tracking system in an organization that had implemented a program on influencing. In this program, individuals were taught how to influence people in the organization over whom they had no authority. Approximately three months after the conclusion of the program, we telephoned a sample of the participants. We learned of several instances in which the skills had been applied and yielded positive results. For example, we learned of agreements that had been made and had expedited the completion of a project, afforded access to previously unavailable resources, and won support for a particular approach to a project.

Focus-group interviews are also an option to be considered. In this approach, you bring together a group of people who have attended the program and ask them, "What do you recall from the program? How have you been able to apply that learning to your job?" It is also important to inquire about anything that has made it difficult or impossible to use what was taught.

We used this approach with a Canadian corporation. Each year, this corporation delivers a program to young professionals (people who have been with the organization for two or three years). The overall purpose of this program is to provide information about the company's business plan and direction. It is felt that such information will assist employees in making decisions and exercising judgments back on the job. It is also hoped that the program will increase the motivation of these professionals to remain with the firm and recognize the career possibilities and challenges that it offers. Many of the learning outcomes for this program are cognitive. Clearly, however, participants are expected to benefit from the information they are given as they make career decisions or seek information relevant to projects. Our clients wanted to know whether these outcomes were occurring and what, if anything, could be done to enhance the program. Considering the cost of the program (approximately $300,000 a year), it was important to identify its benefits.

We used focus-group interviews as the primary method of data collection. We heard many examples of ways in which past participants had used information from the program back on the job. We also learned clearly about aspects of the program that were yielding little or no impact over time. In some cases, people could not even recall that a subject had been part of the program's agenda. The clients were given a great deal of information with which to make decisions about what to continue and what to modify in the program design. The clients also received information on how the work environment was affecting the ability of participants to gain the full benefit of what was learned.

Thus, one-to-one interviews and focus-group interviews are both good methodology choices for evaluating skill transfer. The primary disadvantage of this methodology is that it is labor-intensive. One individual may be able to interview eight to ten people in a day. Focus groups require a great deal of effort to organize. The information that is collected must then be analyzed (and we have already discussed how much time that can take). We find that interviews are a great supplement to a data-collection system, but rarely do we use them as our only source of information. Almost always, questionnaires are our primary method.

The general advantages and disadvantages of questionnaires are described in Chapter Six, so we will not review them here. What is pertinent regarding this method for tracking is its cost efficiency. You can collect questionnaire data from a few hundred people for less money than it would take to collect and analyze interview data from fifty people. In some instances, interviewing is not an option, because of the numbers of people and their geographical locations.

The primary consideration in the use of questionnaires is the anticipated response rate. Without a good response rate, you are left with little from which to draw conclusions. In one organization in which we worked, a decision was made to track skill application after a supervisory training program. Unfortunately, there was little trust between management and employees; therefore, employees were suspicious of the tracking effort. More questionnaires ended up on the shop floor than being returned. We actually received back only 10 percent of the questionnaires, and most of those were blank. Obviously, better planning at the start (such as meeting with union leaders to obtain their support) would have alerted us to this possibility and to the fact that questionnaires should not be used in such situations.

When we use questionnaires to measure behavioral change, we typically use an even scale, of either six or eight points. A typical scale for one of our questionnaires would look like this:

1 = This is a behavior I never use.
2 = This is a behavior I rarely use (less than 15 percent of the time).
3 = This is a behavior I use very infrequently (less than 33 percent of the time).
4 = This is a behavior I use infrequently (less than 50 percent of the time).
5 = This is a behavior I use frequently (more than 50 percent of the time).
6 = This is a behavior I use very frequently (more than 67 percent of the time).
7 = This is a behavior I almost always use (about 90 percent of the time).
8 = This is a behavior I always use.

In each instance, the respondents indicate the frequency with which they use a particular behavior in a situation that we have described in the questionnaire. We prefer even scales, because they show the tendency of someone to do or not do something. It is doubtful that a behavior is demonstrated exactly 50 percent of the time; we want to determine whether people are closer to the high or the low end of the scale.

For an example of how we might collect behavioral data,

consider the following situation, which involves selling skills. In this program, participants were trained to prepare for sales calls in a specific manner. We asked each participant to indicate, on an eight-point scale such as the one just described, the frequency with which they did the following things:

- Identified and wrote down the call objectives before the call
- Developed questions that would focus on facts regarding the prospect's situation
- Identified possible objections of the prospect, and how those objections could be overcome
- Identified the specific piece of information to use in opening the conversation.

Before the training program and again three months after, participants were asked to indicate how often they did such preparation. The means were then compared, to determine what change, if any, had occurred.

In summary, when you select methods for tracking behavior, you need to consider the following questions.

1. What human resources are available to you for data collection? Interviews and observation will require a lot of labor.
2. What skills do you and the others who will implement the tracking system have? Observation requires a great deal of skill. Do you have people on staff who can do this?
3. How many people do you need to collect information from? If hundreds of people need to be included and sampling is not acceptable, then questionnaires may be your only option.

As noted previously, we typically use questionnaires as our primary method of data collection (providing us with quantified data on behavior usage) and support them with interview data that provide a more qualitative set of information or "stories" on how the skills have been applied.

Once you have determined the data-collection method(s) you will use, the next decision is to identify your sources of information. By *sources*, we mean the categories of people from whom you will be seeking information. Again, there are choices to be made. While learners are always a source of information, providing self-reports on the frequency of their use of behaviors, you need to consider at least one additional source. For example, you could collect information from managers of learners (the direct superiors of people who have been taught), employees of learners (the direct subordinates of people who have been taught), or third-party sources (anyone outside the learner-employee-manager chain who has information related to the behavioral outcomes being assessed—for example, co-workers of learners or customers of learners).

In determining whom to collect information from, you should select people who are in a position to directly observe the learners as they use the skills taught in the program. For example, if you wanted to measure the selling behavior of people who open bank accounts and sell bank services, your sources (besides learners) could be co-workers and bank customers. If you wanted to measure how supervisors were handling employees' complaints, then you probably would need to collect information from supervisors and their employees. In evaluating management training programs, we have found that the two most common sources of information are learners and their employees, because employees are often the only sources present when the managers are using the skills we are tracking.

While you must select a minimum of two sources of information, three sources are preferable. Once the results are in, you will be determining the degree to which the learners' self-report information is similar to or different from information collected from others who observe those learners. You will be looking for consistency. For instance, perhaps you have trained supervisors in the skills of conducting performance appraisals. One of the behavioral outcomes you would expect is that supervisors would ask employees to evaluate their own performance before appraisal. If your tracking results indicate that supervisors report doing this with high frequency, and if their employees report a similarly high frequency, there is a good probability that this behavior is occurring. With each additional source of information, you increase your confidence (and that of your client) that the reported results are an accurate reflection of what is happening.

There is one additional consideration in developing a tracking methodology and deciding on sources of information. It is vital to determine what types of information your client will find meaningful and credible. We have worked with some clients who were biased against questionnaires and some who were biased against interviews. Oddly, such biases usually reflect the same concern: "Nobody will be honest in answering your questions." It then becomes important to develop a data-collection system that uses other methods in addition to, or instead of, the method that the client is concerned about. It is also important to learn from your client what sources of information would be of interest to him or her. For example, we tracked a training program that had been conducted for a bank. Employees were being taught selling skills. The client clearly said that customers' feedback would be very important, and so we made sure that it was collected. Sometimes a client will specifically indicate a source of information not to use. At times, clients are hesitant about collecting information from employees. If you are delivering a supervisory or managerial training program in which employees are your only other source of information, this can be a problem. Our position is to understand the source of the client's concerns and work hard to design a process that addresses those concerns. What is important is that the final data-collection method use approaches and sources of information that both you and your client will find meaningful and acceptable. You want the information to be accepted, regardless of what it shows.

Question 5. There is no one answer to the question of how long to wait before tracking for behavioral results. You must judge that on the basis of the following criteria.

1. What set of skills are you tracking, and how frequently can learners use those skills on the job? You can measure behavioral results sooner if the skills in question are used daily;

you will wait longer if the skills are used only weekly or monthly.

2. Who, besides the learners, will be your sources of information, and how frequently can they observe the skills in question? For instance, if you will be using managers of learners as a source of information, how often can they observe the skills you want them to report on? Can they observe the skills daily? weekly? monthly? The rule is that the less frequently your sources can observe skills, the longer you will need to wait to measure results, because it is preferable to have people report on patterns of what they see.
3. How long will it take for a new norm to be established? You will want to wait long enough for the work environment to have its impact on use of the behavior or skills (whether that impact is good or bad).

Figure 21 illustrates two graphs. Graph A illustrates what so often happens with skill transfer. People who attend a program have a given level of skills, which provide some level of results. During the training program, the skill set is enhanced, and people leave the program planning to use some or all of what was taught. Back on the job, they attempt to use the new skills and find that their results dip below what they were before the program. Consider a fast and accurate typist who attends a training program on word processing and then returns to the workplace to work with the new technology. While he may be performing many of the functions properly, he is probably doing that at a slower rate, and with more errors. Perhaps a salesperson attends a training program and learns the steps to be included in planning for a sales call. Back on the job, those steps are completed, and the salesperson finds, at least initially, that fewer calls can be made in a day, because more time is taken for planning.

Immediately after learners leave a training program, the new skills are most vulnerable to extinction. If the work environment does not support and encourage participants to use the

Figure 21. Transfer of Skill Training.

A. Skill Training:
What So Often Happens

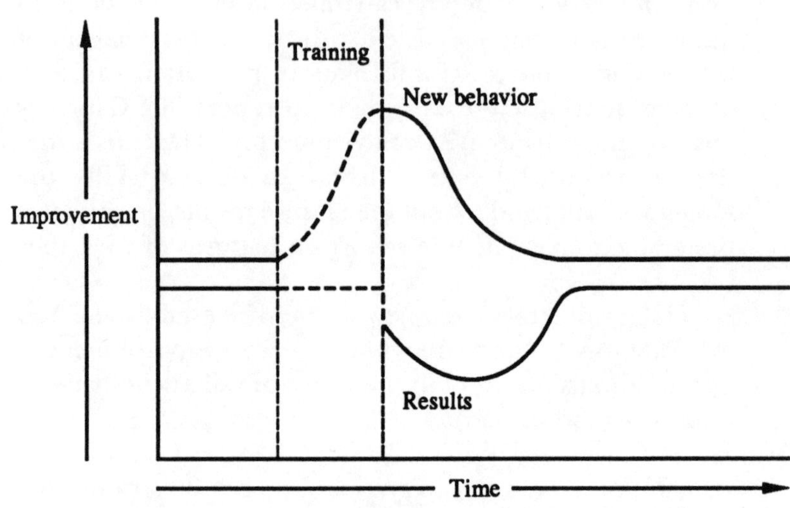

B. Skill Training:
What Should Happen

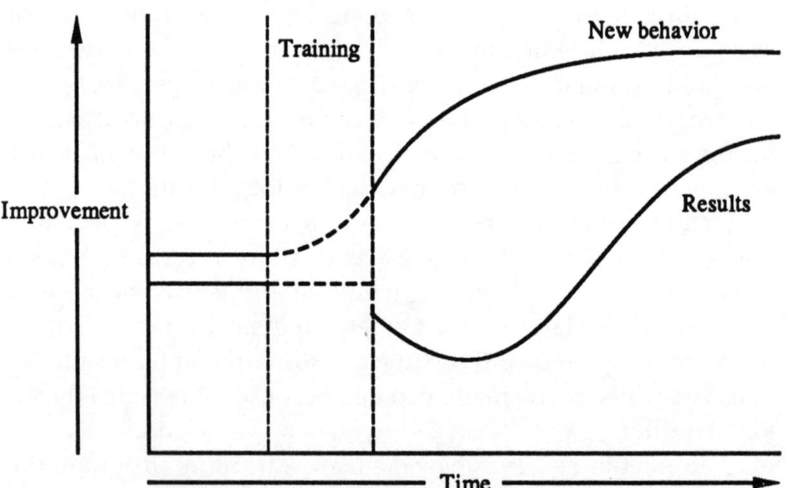

Source: Rackham, 1979, p. 14. Copyright 1979, *Training and Development Journal*, American Society for Training and Development. Reprinted with Permission.

skills (even though the initial results may be disappointing), if managers are not prepared to coach and reinforce the skills, and if learners are punished for reduced results rather than rewarded for use of these new approaches or techniques, then up to 87 percent of the skills can disappear (Rackham, 1979). If you measure results too soon, you may be measuring the decline that appears immediately after training, when people are trying to apply the learning; you will not be measuring what will be the actual norm over time. As illustrated in part A of Figure 21, this new norm becomes the same as the old one.

Part B of Figure 21 presents a different scenario. Here, learners are using skills after a program and do experience the decline in results. In this case, the work environment is reinforcing the use of these skills, so that learners continue to use them. Eventually (assuming that what learners were taught is workable behavior), results will begin to surpass what was true before, but the behavior will level out. This is when you should take a posttraining "snapshot" of what is occurring. The data collected at this point are what you will compare to what was collected at the start of the training program (your base-line information). Essentially, you are indicating that, barring any significant action by you or your client, this will be the result. Is it satisfactory?

For most training in behavior and skills, the time for posttraining measurement tends to fall between three and six months after the conclusion of the program. If participants can use skills daily, and if other sources can observe the use of these skills weekly, then three months is more appropriate. If the skills can be used only monthly, and if others will observe with even less frequency, then you may need to wait up to six months. On occasion, we have measured at two months, but never sooner than that.

For determining how long you should wait to measure, we advise you to select one period of time and use that for all sources of information in your study. For example, if you are measuring the use of influencing skills by engineers, you may use the learners themselves, their bosses, and their peers as sources of information. Perhaps the engineers can use these skills on a few occasions each week, but the remaining two sources can observe them only a few times each month. Select a period when all sources will have been able to observe repeated use of these skills (perhaps four months after the program), and distribute questionnaires or conduct interviews at that time. It can become an administrative nightmare to have questionnaires going to learners at three months and to bosses at four months, or interviews to co-workers at five months. Make it easy on yourself (and your administrative support) by selecting one optimal time for all sources.

Including Questions About the Work Environment. It is clear by now that we believe strongly that training delivered in a vacuum, without links to business needs or assurance of management support, is of little value and will yield limited organizational impact. Therefore, once you wish to measure whether skills have been transferred to the work environment, it becomes important to measure both what has been transferred and what has not been and why. Remember that the primary purpose of this tracking effort is to provide you and your clients with data around which sound business decisions can be made. If results are disapppointing, you need to know the probable causes before you can take appropriate action. Questions about the work environment are what yield this type of information.

In Chapter Seven, we discussed work environment conditions in depth. Recall that there are three categories of these conditions: conditions of the learner, conditions of the manager, and conditions of the organization. In a tracking system, we typically include questions that help us to address the following issues in each of these categories. Regarding conditions of the learners, does the participant value the particular set of skills and behaviors taught in the program? Does the participant feel confident using the skills and behaviors taught in the program? Regarding conditions of the managers, do the managers of the learners coach and reinforce the use of these specific skills and behaviors? Do the managers of learners model the use of these specific skills and behaviors? If managers are not expected to model the use of skills (as is sometimes true in technical and operational areas), then we inquire about co-workers, foremen, and so forth who are to be setting an example by using the skills.

Regarding conditions of the organization, does the organization reward or punish people for the use of these specific skills and behaviors? What is the balance of consequences regarding these skills? Are there any interferences with the use of these specific skills or behaviors (such as conflicting policies or lack of equipment)? Does the organization provide feedback to employees indicating the impact of these particular skills and behaviors on the organization itself?

Creating Your Tracking Design

The final decision in designing a tracking system for a training program concerns the number of times you need to collect information. Three designs can yield reliable, meaningful information.

Pre- and Posttracking Design. This design is represented as follows:

Pre	*Training*	*Post*
X (baseline)	yes	X

In this design, individuals who will be attending a program are questioned about their use of specific skills and behaviors before the start of the program. Other sources of information are also asked to report on this skill use. All this information collectively provides you with a baseline against which to compare any change.

Participants then attend the program. Some weeks or months after the program concludes, they are questioned again. This time, they report on the frequency of skill use since the program's conclusion. Other sources are questioned in a similar manner. These data are compared to what was collected before training.

The obvious advantage of this design is that you are comparing apples with apples by comparing the actual participants to themselves. The primary disadvantage is that you have almost no way of isolating training as a primary cause of any change: There is no control group of untrained personnel.

Trained/Untrained Design. This design can be represented as follows:

	Pre	*Training*	*Post*
Participants	X	yes	X
Nonparticipants	X	no	X
	(baseline)		

In this design, individuals who are similar to participants are selected as a control group. Nonparticipants must be matched to the group of participants as closely as possible. When we have used this design, we have attempted to control such variables as boss, area of the organization, job function, and experience level. In this option, nonparticipants are asked to complete questionnaires or to be interviewed before the start of the training program. Other sources who will be reporting on the nonparticipants are also questioned at this time. Therefore, you are establishing a baseline for this group, as well as for the group of participants. These two baselines should be very similar; if they are not, then you do not have matched groups, and it will be difficult to draw many conclusions from your results.

Participants attend the program; nonparticipants do not. Some weeks or months after the program, both groups and their respective sources are questioned again. Obviously, results for participants should indicate a higher frequency of skill use than among nonparticipants. To the degree that this is true, you have increased the certainty that training was a primary contributor to change, because both groups have been managed similarly, both have similar job functions, and both have been similarly affected by external forces.

While this design is strong, there are difficulties associated with it. Administratively, it is more work to evaluate two separate groups of people. The larger issue, however, deals with the ethics of withholding training from a group of people for the purpose of evaluating the program. In many organizations and many training situations, this would not be possible. It could result in a certain group of people being set up to fail.

We like to consider this design option when there are natural opportunities to use it. For example, if you are about to introduce a program in which nine hundred people will eventually participate, and if it will take one year to complete the training, then some people do need to come last. Therefore, to partner some individuals with the initial participants is not to withhold training from anyone.

We also encourage the use of this design when you are piloting a training program. It would be helpful to verify that the program will be effective and will result in training impact. Conduct the program with a few groups of people, and partner these individuals with others, who are not trained during the pilot. Withhold broad implementation of the program until results of the pilot are obtained. Once the program is implemented widely, bring in the nonparticipants of the pilot effort as the next group to be trained. This is a nice way of thanking them for their cooperation in your evaluation effort, and they will truly benefit, for the program will undoubtedly have been modified or the work environment altered as a result of the initial results.

"Pre," "Then," and "Post" Design. This design can be represented as follows:

Pre	*Training*	*Post*
X	yes	X
(baseline)	X	

This third design is the one we now most frequently use with clients. We thank Mezoff (1981) for bringing it to our attention. In this design, information collected on participants before the start of the program serves as the baseline. Participants attend the training program. At its conclusion, they are immediately asked to complete an adapted questionnaire. The focus of this questionnaire is to ask participants to think back, prior to the training program, to the frequency with which they demonstrated the skills taught in the program. The frequency that is noted is referred to as a "then" score, since they are thinking back to "then" when they respond.

Research has indicated that participants will lower their self-report scores, because now they understand more fully what is meant. Let us assume you are training supervisors to coach employees who have performance problems. Perhaps one of the discrete behaviors supervisors will be encouraged to use is to describe the performance problem in specific terms. Before training, attending supervisors may believe that they are doing this quite often. During the program, they come to understand just how specific descriptions of problems need to be. Rather than saying, "Your output has dropped off in the last week," supervisors are taught to say, "Your output for the past week was 40.3 finished units, but the standard is 45.0 finished units." As participants come to be aware of how specific they should be in describing problems, they frequently lower their self-report scores.

If you compare participants' "pre" self-reports to their "then" self-reports, it becomes clear whether awareness has been raised about competence in particular areas. Since awareness of an inability to perform is the first step toward behavioral change, this is a positive result. Comparison of "then" scores to "post" scores will also illustrate a greater change than comparison of "pre" scores to "post" scores.

When you are considering the use of a "then" questionnaire, it is important to recall that it should be distributed immediately after the training program ends, before the learners have had an opportunity to apply the new skills to the job. This questionnaire is usually distributed along with the questionnaire for reaction evaluation.

Tracking After Training Has Already Occurred. This kind of situation calls for a "post only" design, which is flawed in many ways. The primary problem is that there is no base-line information against which to compare the "post" results. How do you know whether these results are better than, worse than, or the same as what would have been true if no training had occurred? If you are faced with this type of situation, we encourage one of two actions.

First, you can select a group of people similar to those who have attended the program. These people should not have attended the course but should be as similar as possible to those who have. Evaluate the use of certain kinds of behavior by both groups. Those who have been trained should show a higher frequency than those who have not been trained. We used such a design with a corporation that had implemented an influencing program. We selected individuals who were trained and individuals who had not yet attended the program. Information was collected on both groups from three sources: the participants and nonparticipants, their co-workers, and their bosses. We also interviewed some of the participants. The results indicated a difference between the two groups, and that difference was more obvious for certain kinds of behavior than for others.

Second, you could decline to evaluate results for people who have completed the program. Instead, you could start by evaluating, on a "pre-post" basis, those who are about to come to the program. Inferences could be made regarding previous results by reviewing what is obtained for this group.

If neither of these options is possible, we encourage you not to track programs when no "pre" data exist. Instead, look for another opportunity to evaluate.

Results Obtained Through Behavioral Tracking

Increase in Use of Desired Behaviors. In a large communications company, there was a need to develop supervisors' skills in handling system crises (occasions when both the primary and the clone computer failed simultaneously). Management knew that the decision-making processes being used by supervisors were inconsistent and not always appropriate. Front-end work clearly identified where the information flow during a system crisis could be improved and where decision making could be enhanced. A training program was developed and delivered to build the skills of supervisors in handling crises. The program was tracked to determine whether supervisors were using their new skills back on the job.

Information was collected from three sources: supervisors, their direct managers, and the vice-presidents and directors of the various units. Behavior was evaluated on a five-point scale, with 1 being low frequency and 5 high frequency. Results for a representative sample of behaviors are noted in Table 7. There were a dozen behaviors evaluated, but these results are

Table 7. Results of Tracking Behavior Frequency.

	"Pre" Frequency			*"Post" Frequency*		
	Supervisor (Learners)	*Manager*	*VP/ Director*	*Supervisor (Learners)*	*Manager*	*VP/ Director*
Behavior 1	3.6	3.5	3.5	4.5	4.7	5.0
Behavior 2	3.6	3.7	2.5	4.2	4.7	4.0

representative of the total study. Clearly there was change in frequency as noted by all sources.

Reduction in Variance Within a Group. Another type of result that occurs through training is that the trained people become more similar to one another in their display of desired behaviors than they were before training. Variance is measured by the standard deviation that occurs for each discrete behavior. Before training, there are often many behaviors that display a standard deviation of 1.5 or greater when data are collected on an eight-point scale. This indicates a wide degree of variation in how people within a source group are reporting the use of behaviors. After the program, "post" results often indicate that standard deviations have dropped to less than 0.5 on the same scale. This indicates that participants are now viewed as more similar in the frequency with which they use the behavior and that the mean (whatever it is) is an accurate picture of more people in the group.

In a large hospital, we developed a tracking system to determine the use of caring behavior with patients and their guests by the hospital staff. Ten behaviors were evaluated on a six-point scale. Before training, there were five standard deviations that met or exceeded 1.0; after training, there were two. Clearly, these people were more similar in how they demonstrated behaviors after training than before.

Impact of the Work Environment. What effect, if any, does the work environment have on the use of skills? In a large bank, we tracked results from a business development skills training program. Branch managers attended to learn how to sell the bank's products and services.

Information collected indicated that some work environment conditions made it difficult for branch managers to use the skills they had been taught in the program. The time required to manage the branch was in conflict with the time required to make sales calls. Branch managers also knew very clearly what their management objectives and accountabilities were; they were less certain about their accountabilities regarding sales calls. The majority of managers were uncertain about whether they were evaluated on how effectively they interpersonally managed sales calls, for example. This confusion and lack of clarity worked against their motivation to use their new skills. These issues were brought to the attention of higher managers so that they could address them in a timely manner. This is an example of how tracking data can be used to make business decisions.

Poor Course Delivery. If the ultimate test of training effectiveness is whether participants have learned the skills well enough to apply them on the job, then behavioral tracking can identify whether this has happened. In one situation in which we were involved, the client measured interpersonal skills taught to individual professional contributors. He found that certain segments of the program were consistently not being transferred to the job, while other segments were. The primary problem was identified as the participants' lack of confidence to use the skills. In the segments where transfer was low, confidence was low; where transfer occurred, confidence was high. On the basis of previous observations that the training manager had made of the program and its design, he determined that those parts of the program where skill transfer was low were delivered in a manner that was more cognitive than behavioral; therefore, people could not make the leap to skills application. As a result, the program design was changed, some material was eliminated, and the opportunity to practice skills was added. This program now yields greater results than it did before.

Problems with Course Design. Another major finding is to identify specific behaviors that people already are able to use and that do not require training. Ideally, such an analysis should be completed at the front-end stage, but we know that this is not always what happens. There are also situations in which a program has been delivered over a period of years. While people may have required training in certain behaviors at one time, it is possible that this is no longer true. Tracking the results of a program implemented over a long time provides an opportunity to determine whether the needs of learners have changed.

We had such an opportunity. A training program focused on the interpersonal skills to be used with co-workers and patients in a hospital. The program, as initially designed, required fourteen hours to complete. The first group of people who attended were tracked. They and all the sources reporting on them agreed that, before training, the frequency with which certain behaviors were used was very high. After training, frequency remained high. We then tracked a second group of people and obtained similar results. Because of these findings, the director of training decided to reduce the program's length by eliminating the material that was not required (people already were demonstrating those behaviors). The program was reduced from fourteen hours to eight hours. The savings to the organization more than paid for the tracking effort.

Microevaluation Revisited

Earlier in this chapter, we said that the measurement of behavior change can be done on a macro or a micro basis. Until now, we have been focusing on macroevaluation efforts. Now we would like to direct attention to microevaluation.

The purpose of microevaluation is to identify the change in behavior of a particular individual. Typically, this process is used when a person needs to be certified as competent to perform in a job. This method requires that the identity of the individual be known to you; it will likely require that all information be reported to the individual's manager or supervisor.

Microevaluation starts with the same five critical questions that must be addressed in macroevaluation. The answers to these questions are often different, however.

Question 1: Who Is the Client? In a microevaluation, the client is typically the boss of the learner. Recall that a client is the "go/no go" individual who needs to be involved in decisions made relevant to the training project, usually the individual's boss in a "micro" situation.

Question 2: What Is the Business Need for the Training? Here the answer may be similar to what is true in a macroevaluation study. For new hires, the business need would be to certify that the individuals are able to successfully perform on the job. This provides a return to the organization for its hiring investment.

Question 3: What Are the Outcomes to Be Measured in Behavioral Terms? The answer here is typically the same as in macroevaluation. These outcomes are listed and provided to both the individual and his or her manager so that everyone knows and agrees on what the learner must be able to do.

Question 4: How Will You Know the Outcomes Have Occurred? In this case, you will probably use direct observation (either yours, the manager's, or both). It is unlikely that you will develop interviews or questionnaires to collect this information.

Question 5: How Long to Wait to Measure? Again, the same criteria need to be considered here as for a macroevaluation study. The time line may be shortened, however, depending on requirements for the job into which the individual is to be placed.

The role of the HRD professional during this process is threefold.

1. Clearly identify what is expected and ensure that both the manager and employee know and understand those expectations.
2. Provide the employees with quality learning experiences so that they are able to achieve the learning outcomes.
3. Provide appropriate coaching to the managers so that they understand what role they must play and what actions they must take if the new skills are to be transferred to the job.

Throughout this process, it is important for the employee to realize that information is being collected and reported to others. The employee should also understand why.

Common Questions About Behavioral Tracking

How Do You Ensure That Individuals from Whom Information Must Be Collected Will Respond and Cooperate? Without cooperation and a willingness to provide honest information, and without a high response rate to questionnaires, any tracking effort is doomed. Here are some tips on how to elicit the cooperation you need.

1. Inform people, through a memo signed by the client, of the project and its purposes.
2. Let people know how the information will be used.
3. Assure those involved that they will receive a summary of the final results. When this summary is sent, be certain to acknowledge any actions taken as a result of the evaluation.
4. Focus on the actions that will be taken as a result of the information (how the training program will be improved, what can be done to make certain that people are supported in the skills).
5. Advise people of how they will benefit from this effort (future participants will experience an improved program, and any work environment barriers will be addressed).

If you are using a questionnaire to collect the information, be certain that your questionnaire is easy to understand, the directions are clear, it will require less than twenty minutes to complete, and so on. You will know whether this is true if you pilot your questionnaire.

How Do You Influence Line Managers to Recognize the Benefits? Managers often express little or no interest in evaluation. Our best response to this dilemma is to put the training into a business context. Determine what it will cost the client and the organization to conduct the program. Recently, we made a keynote presentation to a group of managers in a large organization. The organization was moving from an instructor-based to a technology-based approach to training. We wanted line managers to be committed to doing what they could to make this conversion successful. We began our presentation by saying that the cost of this conversion would be just under $1 million. (This figure did not include the cost of off-the-job time once the training was available.) Do line managers want to know what returns will be realized from such an investment? They certainly do.

How Do You Know That Your Results Are Not Influenced by the Hawthorne Effect? Because observers are paying attention, their mere presence can change the results of a study. This phenomenon is known as the Hawthorne effect. What does this have to do with tracking studies?

In our opinion, it is unlikely that observers have much effect on the results of a tracking study whose tools of measurement are questionnaires and interviews. This is because information is collected from those who are in a position to observe the learners anyway; there is no special observation. We find it difficult to believe that the Hawthorne effect would exist during the entire three to six months after a training program. This is merely an opinion, but it is one that we strongly hold.

Rackham (1988) conducted extensive research on the use of selling behaviors at Motorola Corporation. His primary method of data collection was behavior observation (in which the Hawthorne effect is more likely to occur). By dividing a group of trained individuals in half and following their respective sales over time, he determined that "there was a Hawthorne effect at work but that, as with most Hawthorne effects, its impact was short-lived" (p. 184).

How Can You Be Certain That You Have Received Honest Information? This question deals with the issue of ensuring that people tell you exactly what they are doing or observing, even though they think it may not be what you want to hear. Several things can be done to guarantee candor.

1. If a macroevaluation is planned, do not use names or code the questionnaires in any manner.
2. Inform people about how the information will and will not be used. Let them know how it will be reported (for example, by groups of people, and not by individuals).
3. Make certain that the behaviors you inquire about are dis-

cretely identified. (You will get more honest information if you ask me to indicate the frequency with which I stand and greet a customer who approaches my desk than if you ask me the frequency with which I am courteous to the customer.)

Should You Use Hard Statistics to Report Results? This question focuses on the fact that we report results descriptively, using means, frequencies, standard deviations, and so on. We do not choose such statistics as correlation coefficients. In Chapter Eight, we described our rationale for doing this. Those comments are applicable here, too.

How Long Does It Take to Create and Administer This Type of Evaluation? We have found that if you use questionnaires as the method of collecting information, and if these questionnaires are computer-tabulated, then it will require between eight and ten staff days to develop the evaluation process (before training) and interpret and report the results (after training). If interviews or observation are used as methods of data collection, this time will increase.

Are There Short-Form Approaches to Collecting This Type of Information? As in any other data-collection effort, things can be done to make it simpler.

1. Follow up by phone with a sample of people after a training program. Do this approximately three months after the program concludes. Develop an interview guide to standardize the questions asked of all participants. Develop questions that focus on how the individual has used the skills on the job or on what (if anything) has made it difficult to do so.
2. Rather than asking about discrete behaviors, ask about more global aspects of the program. For example, one client with whom we worked wanted to evaluate a training program where participants had identified specific projects to be implemented back on the job. The follow-up questionnaire asked if participants had in fact implemented the projects. If so, we wanted to know the results. If not, we

wanted to know why. In approximately three questions, a major part of the program was investigated.

While it is possible to simplify the data-collection system, there are still certain things you should always be doing. Have a client who wants this information; someone other than you should be interested in the results. Ask about the use of skills, and determine the impact of the work environment. Finally, always have more than learners' self-report information to review. If you cannot do these things, then do not track at all.

Summary

The following techniques move training toward impact:

Activity **Impact**

- Select a few programs each year that build discrete behaviors or skills, and evaluate them at the results level. Do a good job of evaluating a few programs, rather than a less effective job of evaluating many.
- Have a client to whom you can report information and who will celebrate your success or work with you to resolve any problems.
- Collect base-line and follow-up information from at least two sources. This adds to the credibility and reliability of your information.
- Use the information to make business decisions regarding the course. Have your client involved in the decision-making process.

Twelve

Nonobservable Results: Identifying Changes in Values, Beliefs, and Cognitive Skills

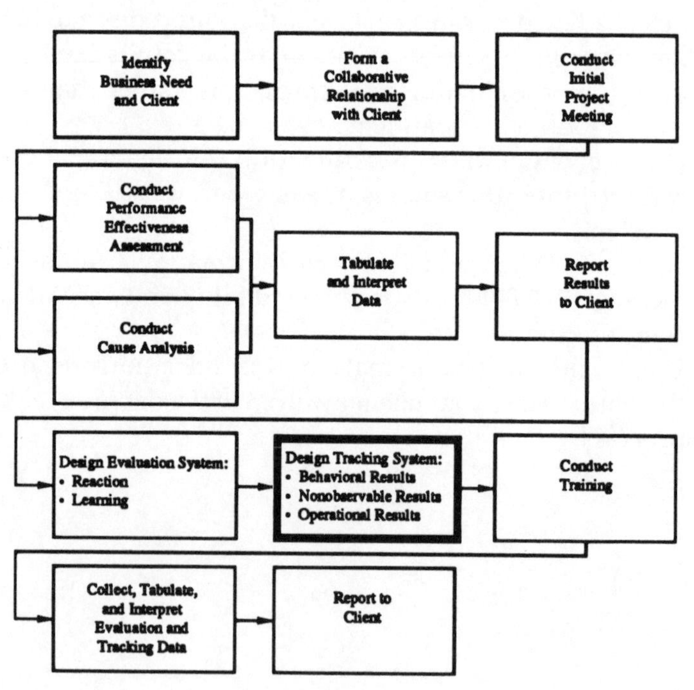

Tracking results that are behavioral (and therefore can be seen or heard) is relatively easy, compared to tracking the results that we will discuss in this chapter. How can you measure results that cannot be observed?

Consider the following outcomes, which various clients of ours have wanted to measure: "Participants will leave the program committed to the vision statement of the president." "Operators will be able to analyze why an alarm went off in the control cab." "When faced with an angry customer, the company representatives will talk to themselves (a method called 'self-talk') in order to control their behavior." Such outcomes are related to individual beliefs or mental abilities. While the result of a decision can be observed, the actual analytical process someone uses to come to that decision is nonobservable. How can you determine what people believe or value as a result of a training program? The measurement of such outcomes is the focus of this chapter.

What Are Nonobservable Outcomes?

It would be helpful to describe what we mean by *nonobservable outcomes*. In Chapter Eleven, four categories of training results were identified: affective results, cognitive results, behavioral results, and operational results. It is really the first two categories that this chapter addresses. Affective learning has been described by Krathwohl, Bloom, and Masia (1964). Generally, this domain focuses on learning that influences the values and beliefs of an individual. At the lowest end of the affective scale, participants develop an awareness of values or beliefs that are new or different for them (for example, the realization that the organization believes that well-planned performance appraisals will result in improved employee performance). Higher on the affective scale is the participants' acceptance of this belief. It is this outcome—changed personal values or beliefs—that we will address here.

Examples of such values and beliefs that we have measured include the following:

- Growth in the value of working collaboratively rather than competitively with other employees in the organization
- A sense of ownership in plant operation and the belief that it is important to get involved in solving problems, even if they are not one's direct job responsibility
- Tellers' belief that it is important to sell banking services to customers

Cognitive results are discussed in depth by Bloom (1956). At the lowest end of the cognitive scale, people develop the ability to identify and describe things. Perhaps we have trained people to identify which tool to use in repairing a particular piece of equipment or have taught them which policy to review in taking disciplinary action with an employee. Cognitive knowledge is evaluated by testing, a process discussed in detail in Chapter Ten. What we will concern ourselves with here is the higher end of the cognitive scale: the ability to analyze situations, make decisions, and solve problems. We refer to this category of results as *mental skills*, because they exist in the mind and contrast with behavioral skills, which can be observed. Some examples of the use of mental skills are the following:

- Operators determining why the quality of water is not within the purity standards required for plant operation
- Sales personnel selecting product benefits that are most relevant to the needs of particular customers
- Supervisors creating legal and appropriate questions to ask job candidates

Thus, nonobservable results are changes in the values and beliefs of participants and increased sophistication of their mental skills. In both instances, the result of training is within the participant; it is not observable by others.

Five Questions for Tracking Nonobservable Results

In Chapter Eleven, we discussed the critical questions for addressing the measurement of behavioral outcomes from training. The same questions need to be considered in tracking nonobservable results. For this chapter, we have adapted them as follows.

1. Who is the client?
2. What is the business need?
3. What are the specific outcomes, in terms of mental skills, values, and benefits?
4. What method will you use to measure outcomes?
5. How long should you wait to measure nonobservable results?

Question 1. We hope that the need for a partnership with the program's client is obvious by now. Whatever results are desired, they should be those in which the client has a vested interest and those that help the client meet a business need. Before designing the tracking system, it is important to find out what types of information will be meaningful to the client. This ensures that the results (good or disappointing) will be accepted by the client, since the information will be collected in a manner that the client values. It is also important to have a partner so that there is someone to go to with the results you obtain. If there is a successful outcome, then the client is someone with whom you can enjoy the success. If there is a problem, then the client can assist you in determining what steps should be taken.

The need to have a client does not change, even though the results desired from training may be nonobservable. (If additional information on this subject would prove helpful, we suggest that you review Chapters Three and Four of this book.)

Question 2. If the values or beliefs of participants are to be modified, or if their mental skills are to be enhanced, there should be a business purpose with which those beliefs or skills can be linked. With such a link, there is a clear reason for participants to use what was learned; without such a connection, the motivation to apply what was learned is greatly reduced.

A few years ago, we had the opportunity to work with an organization and measure nonobservable results from a training program that was linked to a business need. The president of this firm had established a vision for how the organization was to operate by the year 2000. This vision focused on three areas: the revenue goal for the organization by the year 2000, the manner in which customers were to be served, and the role of managers in developing employees to their fullest potential. It was important to the president that all managers in the organization both understand and be committed to this vision. The president was seeking help from the training department to communicate this vision, so that the managers would be energized by it and would see the possibilities of leading others in the manner espoused by the vision. Thus, this president sought nonobservable results. He wanted to modify the beliefs of his managers.

The training program developed for this need focused very little on skill building; rather, the learning design focused on activities that would help managers develop a deep understanding of the president's vision, its implications, and its potential benefits. To determine whether the managers had understood the vision, various learning measures were made throughout the training program. To determine whether the managers were committed to the vision, information was collected before the program, immediately afterward, and again some months later. To the degree that the data indicated growth in commitment (and the data did), the president's business need had been met, even though the program did not build observable skills or directly affect the operations of the organization.

Question 3. The HRD professional must articulate the outcomes to be measured in terms as specific as possible. For example, with respect to mental skills, it is impossible to measure that "operators can solve technical problems" or that "managers can make ethical decisions." These outcomes are far too broad to be measured and are open to a great deal of interpretation by whoever provides the data. What are technical problems, and what is an ethical decision? What makes the solution of a technical problem good or poor? What determines that an ethical decision is appropriate? It is impossible to look only at the end result to evaluate a nonobservable outcome. What we seek are data to indicate the processes by which decisions are made and problems are solved.

To turn mental skills into specific outcomes, we need to describe the specific analytical processes we hope people will use, as well as the specific problems we want them to address. To track mental skills, we would ask people, for example, to "determine the source of fuel leaks by checking the most probable causes first and, using the information obtained, working down to the least probable causes," or we would ask them to "make ethical decisions about the selling of products outside the United States by considering the needs of the customer, the values of the organization, and the laws and regulatory codes that are applicable."

When we are considering values and beliefs, we must also work to state specific outcomes. It is not possible to measure the degree to which managers believe in affirmative action or whether an organization supports customer-service activities. Again, these statements are much too broad and are open to much interpretation by any respondent. What affirmative action practices or policies do you want to know about? What is customer service? These outcomes could be measured if they were stated as follows: "To what degree do managers believe that women are underutilized in the organization?" "To what degree do managers believe that equal pay for comparable work is a good policy?" "To what degree do sales personnel believe that handling a customer's complaint effectively is more important than bringing in a new account?"

When you define the mental skills, values, or beliefs that are to be measured, it is important that your client agree to them. This not only demonstrates a collaborative partnership but also ensures that any training will be directed at the desired outcomes.

Question 4. Multiple sources of data are required for measuring behavioral outcomes. With nonobservable outcomes, you generally have only one possible source of information: the participant in the training program. Nonobservable outcomes exist within the individual; by definition, they are not directly observable by others.

Regarding mental skills, we have found the best measurement method to be one-to-one interviews with participants.

Interviews are sometimes conducted after the training program. The participant is asked if he or she has had an opportunity to solve a particular type of problem since the training program ended. If so, questions are asked to help the participant reconstruct the thought process that he or she used. That information is then compared to what the participant was taught to do. Such a comparison indicates the degree to which the participant used learning from the training program in an on-the-job situation.

We used such a method to measure nonobservable results of a training program on negotiation of customer fees. Some of the skills taught were observable (for instance, generating various possibilities and options for agreement before deciding on a specific course of action). Other skills used in preparation for the negotiation sessions were nonobservable (for example, considering the interests of each party; determining objectives, selecting a strategy, and deciding on the best alternative to a negotiated agreement). It is unlikely that anyone other than participants would know whether these analytical skills were being used, and so interviews were conducted with the participants. They were asked to describe specifically what they had done to prepare for negotiation. Their responses were compared to prescribed analytical steps. Participants were also asked to describe how the completion of these steps had affected actual negotations.

With regard to the measurement of values or beliefs, we have found that questionnaires with closed questions are the best method. Open-ended questions invite many problems, particularly in coding data. According to Sudman and Bradburn (1982, p. 148), closed questions "are more difficult to construct" but "easier to analyze and less subject to interviewer and coder variances."

There are times when the values and beliefs you wish to assess can be measured on standardized tests. Such tests have been developed by suppliers and are sold for use in organizations. These tests have several advantages. They usually have been validated as specific measures of values or attitudes. You can feel confident that they are measuring what you want them to measure. They usually provide norms so that any degree of change can be compared to change in a larger group outside your organization. They may also be less expensive than developing your own tests.

They have disadvantages, however. They may use terminology different from that used in your organization or your course. They may also measure only some aspects of the values or beliefs that you wish to measure. In this instance, you may need to create an addendum.

Some years ago, we used a standardized test in association with a supervisory training program. There were nonobservable outcomes desired from this program; specifically, it was hoped that supervisors would leave the program believing that employees were a source of valuable ideas and that participative management practices would yield increased commitment and involvement of employees. The Leadership Style Survey (Learning Dynamics, Inc., 1979) was used to determine the degree to which supervisors held such beliefs before training. Sixty days after training, the same instrument was administered again. The results showed significant change and indicated that supervisors' values had been affected by training.

Often it will be necessary to create your own questionnaire, usually because no standardized instrument is available to meet your needs. There will be other times when you may want to create only a few questions, as part of a larger tracking effort. When designing questions becomes necessary, we have found that the use of an agree/disagree Likert scale is most helpful. The learner is provided with a statement and is given an opportunity to express a level of agreement or disagreement. For example:

I believe the most effective way for people to work in our organization is to be cooperative, not competitive.

1	2	3	4	5	6
Strongly Disagree	Disagree	Somewhat Disagree	Somewhat Agree	Agree	Strongly Agree

A second way to determine values or beliefs is to develop questions that ask the individual to rank preferences. When doing this, it is important to limit the number of items to be ranked, so that people can remember them. If there are more than three or four items to be ranked, it is important that the individual be able to see all the options. For example:

Please review the items below and indicate with a "1" which one item is most important to you to achieve a good quality of life. Indicate with a "2" that which is next most important; use a "3" to indicate the third most important.

Rank	*Item*
____	A job which pays me well.
____	A loving family and home life.
____	A feeling of achievement in what I do.

A few years ago, we collected information on values for a banking client. The training department was conducting a program that taught branch managers how to make sales calls at small commercial establishments. In this manner, the branch managers were actually becoming calling officers for the bank. Much of the training program was designed to build the skills necessary to ask prospective customers questions to identify their needs. Managers were then to describe banking services that would meet those needs.

Some value outcomes were also desired. One value involved the importance that a calling officer placed on planning for a sales call. We asked participants to indicate their level of agreement with this statement: "Identifying the specific objectives for a sales call before making the call is a key to the success of any call."

Two different groups of people attended this program, and both began the training with similar levels of agreement with the statement. After training, however, one group had increased its valuing of this selling step, while the other had reduced its valuing of this step. How would you interpret this information? Clearly, it needs to be interpreted in light of all other results, but this one result alone alerted us and our client that there was a potential problem with the latter group.

Question 5. When we are measuring beliefs and values, we have found it very important to collect base-line information before the training program, to ask the same questions again immediately after the program, and to collect data again a few months later. This is because we want to see trends in beliefs and values. If the training program is having the desired effect, then the values and beliefs should be moving in the desired direction by the end of the course. If the work environment is reinforcing the beliefs and values, that movement will continue after the program's conclusion. We have seen apparent movement when a program ended, but, when we measured a few months later, this positive movement was no longer evident. Thus, trends and patterns become very important in the measurement of beliefs and values.

With higher-end mental skills (such as decision making and problem solving), we have not found the collection of "pre" information to be so crucial. We view it as nice to get, if that is possible. Of course, information cannot be collected immediately when a program ends, because participants are unlikely to have experienced real on-the-job situations that could be reported. Generally, mental skills will require two to three months before any interviews can occur. This delay helps ensure that at least several of the participants will have experienced situations in which the new analytical and mental skills were applied.

The measurement of nonobservable outcomes is certainly not easy, but it is possible. When these are the kinds of results your client seeks, they should be tracked. We hope this chapter has provided you with some ideas on how to do just that.

Summary

The following techniques move training toward impact.

Activity **Impact**

- Determine what specific mental skills, values, or beliefs your client wants as outcomes of training. Do not overlook this category of results; it is important to many line managers.
- Interview a few participants some months after training to identify how they were able to apply the mental skills. Report your findings to your client.
- Develop a few questions to measure change in beliefs or values, and ask these questions before training, in the reaction evaluation, and again some months later. Report your results to your client.

Thirteen

Operational Results: Measuring Impact on the Business

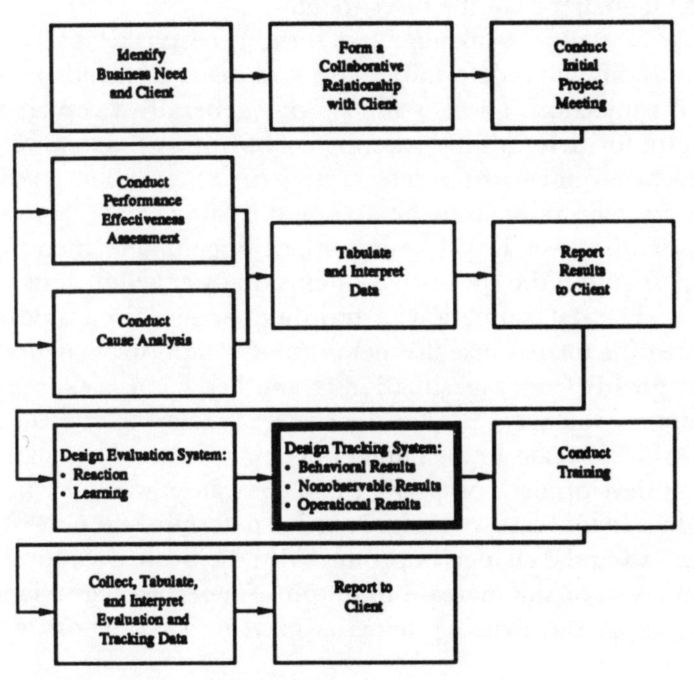

"How much will this supervisory training contribute to the bottom line?" "In computing the cost of this training, did you include the cost of lost sales opportunities?" "How do you know that the 23 percent improvement in productivity was due to training?" These are the questions that we, as HRD professionals, are likely to hear, particularly when we are presenting a training program to management for approval, or when we are discussing the results of a successful program. Not to have substantive answers may send chills up and down our spine.

This chapter will focus on how to track the impact of a training effort in operational, or hard data, terms. Generally, this is done by calculating both the costs and the benefits of training. The benefits are then compared to the costs. Certainly, you hope to show that the benefits of training were greater than the costs. This type of tracking is often referred to as cost-benefit analysis.

Return on investment is a term also used to describe this process. The costs of training are the investment, and the benefits of training are the return. Again, the hope is that the return will be greater than the investment.

Actually, the calculation of training costs is relatively easy; what is difficult is determining the cost items to include in your final projection. There is still no one generally accepted procedure for determining training costs. In this chapter, we will present a framework for determining costs that we feel is easy to use and will most likely be accepted by your client. For every project, however, it will be important to gain agreement from your client on the specific cost items that you will include.

The determination of training benefits is considerably more difficult, because the methods for computing benefits will vary greatly from one situation to another. For a sales training program, you may calculate the change in sales volume, the size of an average sale, or the number of new accounts; for a management development program, those indicators would be meaningless. In that case, you might need to determine the benefits by calculating the change in productivity, the decrease in production costs, or the increase in output. For a customer relations workshop, the primary benefits may be a reduction in the number of customer complaints or the amount of repeat business obtained. Obviously, each type of training (and even each specific course) will dictate what operational benefits you may be monitoring. Thus, part of the front-end work of determining operational benefits from training is to identify the specific operational indicators that are both related to this training effort and possible to monitor.

When benefits can be computed in terms of dollars, you must go through the process of adding up the derived benefits by totaling the sales increases, the decrease in production costs, and so on. You then divide that dollar amount by the total dollar cost of the program. The result is the cost-benefit ratio for the course. For example, if the total benefits of a program were $50,000 and the total cost was $20,000, then the cost-benefit ratio would be 2:5. Some people might prefer to say that the total return of the program was $50,000, while the investment was $20,000, and so the return on investment was 2:5. However the formula is expressed, the company would have received $2.50 for every $1.00 spent on the training program.

Sometimes the benefits of a training program cannot be easily expressed in dollar values. Consider, for example, the start-up of a new operation, wherein the key desired benefit would be to start up on time, with employees capable of fulfilling their new responsibilities. This is an example of a business opportunity that your clients want to maximize. Turning the start-up into dollars returned (as compared to what the dollars would have been if the training had not occurred) will not be easy. Another example of calculating benefits that are not easily expressed in dollar values would be determining the impact of training on turnover. Turnover is usually reported as a percentage of the employee population. While it is possible to obtain dollar values on this statistic, such a value would require detective work to determine the cost of hiring and training new employees to replace those who have left. Such figures are not always available.

Clearly, training can contribute to operational results in an organization. It is important, however, to consider results both with and without dollar values. As HRD professionals, we should not overlook the nondollar benefits that are valuable to our clients when we perform operational tracking efforts on training programs.

Purposes of Tracking Operational Results

We have already said that the major purpose of tracking operational results is to determine whether the value of the resulting benefits outweighs the cost of training, but not all operational tracking studies are conducted to illustrate what the return on investment has been. Other purposes include the following.

1. You may want to determine whether training is having an impact on a specific business factor. For example, you may want to know whether sales have increased or whether customer complaints have decreased. These findings need not involve the question of whether benefits outweigh costs.
2. You may want to determine whether similar operational results are being obtained in various parts of an organization.
3. You may want to determine which skills taught in the classroom are having the greatest positive impacts on operational results. For instance, are newly learned questioning/responding skills and empathy/caring skills having equal impact on customers' image of the business? Is one set of skills more positively affecting that image?

The key is to articulate a clear purpose for the tracking effort. The HRD professional and the client must identify objectives in specific terms. Compare the difference in level of specificity for each of the following purposes of a tracking effort: (1) "This study will determine whether there is an increase in productivity because of training." (2) "This study will identify to what degree waste is reduced for both the day and twilight shifts in Assembly 1 after delivery of the operator training program." The second purpose narrows in on a specific, measurable unit (waste) in a specific area of the company (Assembly 1) and identifies specific groups of people to be evaluated (day and twilight shifts). This is the desired level of specificity for operational tracking.

Seven Critical Questions

When establishing a system for tracking operational change, you need to address each of the following questions.

1. Who is the client, and what is the business need for the training effort?
2. If the training is addressing a business problem, what is the cause of the problem? If the training is addressing a business opportunity, what are the major components that have to be in place to maximize this opportunity?
3. What operational results do you and your client want to track?
4. What knowledge and skills being taught in the training are causally linked to the operational results that you are about to track?
5. What is the total cost of developing and implementing the training program?
6. What information will you use to determine whether the desired operational results are occurring? What are the sources of that information?
7. How long must you wait to determine whether the operational results are occurring?

Question 1

In Chapter Three, we dealt with identification of the client and of a specific business need that is driving the request for training. Therefore, in this chapter, we will only reiterate that a business need and a client should be present. If you obtain results from your training effort, it would be best to have some people (other than yourself) to care about the results and celebrate success with you. If results do not occur, it is helpful if there are others who care enough about that situation to want to change it. This means that you must have a client or a client team for the project.

Question 2

This question focuses more specifically on the business need. This need may be a problem, if some aspect of operational performance is a source of pain to your clients. To design training that will bring about change in the business problem, you must identify the cause of that problem. You must also determine that at least a part of the cause is lack of skills or knowledge on the part of people being considered for training. When this is the case, training can be expected to contribute to the solving of the business problem.

For instance, an organization may be experiencing high turnover. Turnover previously was 5 percent for a particular job, but for the past year it has been rising and is now 17 percent. Would you expect to see a reduction in turnover if supervisors were taught to be more participative in their approach to employees, more empathetic toward these employees, and more conscientious in maintaining and even building these employees' self-esteem? To know if the training will affect turnover, you must know the cause of turnover. Exit interviews become a primary source of information in such cases. Let us say that the data from exit interviews indicate that employees are leaving because their supervisors are not involving them in decisions, are not training them to perform (yet expect them to do so without error), and so on. If the supervisors are trained in the identified skills and then use those skills on the job, a reduction in turnover should result over time. Returning to the data from exit interviews, you may find that the primary reason why people are leaving the organization is that a competitor has opened a major office in town and is paying fifty cents an hour more for the same job. Developing supervisors will not affect turnover much, if at all, in this instance. Thus, to track at the operational level, you must know the business need and, if that need is a business problem, you must know that employees' lack of skills or knowledge is at least part of the cause. In such cases, training attacks the cause of the problem and should contribute to operational change. When you track operational results from training, you are actually determining whether the business need was met, not just whether the course was successful.

In dealing with a business opportunity, you should make certain that all the necessary components are in place to enable employees to perform successfully and that the skills taught will be transferred. This means that the needed skills and knowledge are identified and delivered to employees and that the work environment will support the use of the new skills and knowledge. If you develop supervisors to be empathetic, to be participative, and to maintain the self-esteem of employees, then supervisors will apply those skills only if they are encouraged to do so by their own managers and by the organization. (Chapters Six and Seven discuss the need to identify performance deficiencies and their causes.) It is clear that tracking operational results requires a thorough front-end assessment and data to support the expectation that training can work operationally on a business need. This means that training addresses the causes of a problem and that the work environment supports the skills being learned.

Question 3

This question refers to the identification of the operational results that will be tracked. Most organizations have operational data on literally hundreds of indicators. How do you narrow that list down to those very few that your training effort can affect?

When addressing this question, you should first review the original symptoms that your client mentioned when the project began. Were loan officers avoiding certain types of loans because of their inability to analyze customers' situations and assess risks? Were supervisors unable to diagnose certain equipment malfunctions, causing the production line to be down for longer periods than it should have been?

The measurements your client first used to identify the problem will often be the measurements to use in tracking operational results. Your front-end assessment and conversations with your client may also identify more operational results that training could affect.

Certainly, some training endeavors lend themselves to operational tracking more readily than others. For example, sales training is often measured operationally by such indicators as increased sales, increased size of orders, and add-on sales. Table 8 lists typical kinds of operational results that can be tracked by three kinds of training.

For some types of training, it is very difficult and even impossible to look for operational results. The training of middle- and upper-level managers is an example. We have had little success in causally linking middle-management training to operational results at the organizational level. Such training often deals with issues that may affect a multitude of operational results at various times over several years. In such situations, we have successfully interviewed managers to identify specific situations in which they have used the training and to determine what specific results were realized. This provides anecdotal records of individual results, which are quite important; it does not, however, determine organizationwide results.

While you do not want to overlook an opportunity to measure training results at the operational level, you also do not want to commit yourself to influencing operational indicators when training may have little effect. What you need is a clear indication that a causal relationship exists between the skills and knowlege you are about to develop and the operational indicator you wish to measure. Let us look more completely at causal relationships.

Question 4

Here, you make certain that the skills and knowledge being taught in the classroom are causally linked to the operational indicators being measured. (We discussed causal relationships in depth in Chapter Seven.)

In some instances, causal links are quite evident; but how do you determine the causal relationship for training programs

Table 8. Operational Indicators for Tracking.

If you do . . .	*You may be able to track . . .*
Sales training	Ratio of new accounts to old accounts
	Call-to-close ratio
	Average sale size[a]
	Sales volume[a]
	Percentage of objections overcome
	Items per order
	Add-on sales[a]
Training for supervisory/ management development	Decreased rejection rate[a]
	Increased output[a]
	Reduced absenteeism[a]
	Reduced tardiness[a]
	Reduced number of grievances
	Reduced turnover
	Decreased waste[a]
	Increased number of employees' suggestions adopted
	Decrease in production costs[a]
	Reduced cost of new hires[a]
	Reduced overtime[a]
	Climate-survey data
Customer-relations training	Accuracy of orders and information[a]
	Size of orders and transactions[a]
	Number of escalated complaints
	Adherence to credit procedures[a]
	Customer satisfaction
	Number of referrals
	Number of lost customers[a]
	Amount of repeat business[a]
	Number of transactions per day[a]

[a] This indicator is easily expressed in dollars; other indicators would require some effort to interpret in terms of dollars.

that are providing people with interpersonal skills, planning skills, networking skills, and a host of other skills that the front-end assessment indicates are important? We have found the following methods to be useful in establishing causal links.

Research the Literature. Imagine that you wish to provide purchasing agents with new negotiating skills. They currently use a bargaining approach to negotiation. In other words, they approach suppliers and indicate the need to reduce costs. Discussing the cost of an item is the only strategy these purchasing agents use.

You research the literature and find that a negotiating style based on win-win encounters has been found to be most effective. In this strategy, the purchasing agent works to understand what the supplier wants to accomplish and at the same time indicates what the organization wants to accomplish. The agent and the supplier then discuss ways to achieve their respective goals, so that both can feel that they have won in the eventual agreement. The research indicates that when this approach is used in negotiations, there is a better agreement for both parties than when a bargaining approach is used.

Now you build or purchase a course that teaches your purchasing agents how to use these researched skills. You have established a causal link between the behaviors you teach and negotiation results, because you have reviewed the current research about negotiation. You know that the use of certain skills is causally linked to negotiating success, because others have validated the link. If you develop these negotiation skills in the purchasing agents who then use them on the job, the resulting negotiated agreements should reflect the desired results.

Observe Competent, Successful Performers. With this method, you perform your own research. Typically, you observe what successful people do, as well as the conditions under which they perform. For example, you may want to determine what behavior a successful telemarketer uses to close a sale over the telephone. You would observe or listen to phone conversations made by people whose records indicate that they are successful in closing sales. You would note the specific behavior used. You would also observe telemarketers whose sales records indicate that they are less successful in closing sales. You would determine what behavior they were or were not using and compare it to the behavior of successful telemarketers. Such analysis allows you to isolate what successful people do differently from less successful people. Your initial research shows that use of the successful behavior results in increased sales. Thus, a causal link has been established.

Pilot the Workshop and Track for Results. This technique enables you to validate a causal link. You pilot the training workshop with actual performers and then track their on-the-job behavior along with the operational results. In most instances, tracking the results for a few weeks after training will give you enough data to determine whether the workshop skills are causally linked to operational outcomes. This method has the additional benefit of providing an opportunity to "debug" the training program. Further, it affords you a chance to determine what effect the work environment is having on the new skills. All this information can be collected before the program is implemented organizationwide.

You may have already concluded that each of these three techniques identifies the "should" of desired performance. (This, of course, is part of the front-end assessment, described in Chapter Six.) Once again, we see how crucial a well-planned front-end assessment is to the impact of a training program. Even the evaluation of results begins with front-end work.

Another important point regarding causal links is that HRD professionals who are interested in determining operational results must also evaluate skill application. To measure only operational results will put you in a vulnerable position.

For example, let us return to the training of telemarketers in the skills needed to close sales. We decide to track their sales for eight weeks. Upon review of the data, we find that sales did not increase; in fact, they went down. How can we explain such results, when our only data are the sales figures? Do these results mean that the telemarketers were trained in the wrong skills or that the telemarketers did not learn the skills? Could there be factors in the work environment that are making it difficult or impossible for the telemarketers to apply the skills? There is no way to determine the reason for the poor sales figures unless we have information about the telemarketers' use of the new skills on the job.

Conversely, if sales showed an increase, can we link the telemarketing training to the sales increases without demonstrating that the telemarketers used the new skills to obtain those sales? To do so would again put us in a vulnerable position. There may have been other variables introduced at the same time as the training. Suppose a new or improved product was introduced. Could the increase in sales have been the result of that product? No one can really determine that without information about the telemarketers' on-the-job use of the new skills.

Thus, to validate the causal link, we must gather both Level III behavioral data and Level IV operational data. In the case of the telemarketers we would hope to demonstrate that the newly learned skills, applied on the job, have increased sales. When you track operational data, you must also track on-the-job behavior and the impact of the work environment.

Question 5

Here, you must determine the cost of the training project. Obviously, this information will be needed if you are going to compute a cost-benefit ratio or return on investment. While many HRD professionals indicate that they do determine the cost of training, we have found great variation in what items they include in computing costs. When we calculate costs for training, we do so by looking at five categories: direct costs, indirect costs, development costs, overhead costs, and compensation for participants.

Direct Costs. These are costs directly associated with the delivery of the learning activities. They include course materials (reproduced or purchased), instructional aids, equipment rental, travel, food and other refreshments, and the instructor's salary and benefits. These costs are so directly tied to the delivery of a particular program that if you canceled the program the day before you planned to conduct it, you would not incur them. (While program materials may have been reproduced or purchased, they would not be consumed, and so they would be available for a future program.)

Indirect Costs. These costs are incurred in support of learning activities but cannot be identified with any particular program. These are also costs that, even if the program were canceled at the last minute, could not be recovered. Examples would be costs for clerical and administrative support, course materials already sent to participants, and time spent by the training staff in planning the program's implementation. Expenses for marketing the program (for example, direct-mail costs) would also be considered indirect costs. Marketing may have cost $2,000. If there is insufficient registration and if the program is canceled, the $2,000 cannot be recovered.

Development Costs. All costs incurred during the development of the program go in this category. Typically, these include the development of videotapes, computer-based instructional programming, design of program materials, instructor preparation, piloting of the program, and any necessary redesign. This category also includes the cost of the front-end assessment, or that portion of the assessment directly attributed to the program. In addition, the costs of evaluation and tracking are included here. If a program is to be conducted for a few years, this cost is often amortized over that period. For example, one-third of the development cost may be charged off in the first year of implementation, one-third in the second year, and one-third in the last year. Otherwise, there is a real "bulge" in the budget, because of development costs during the first year.

Overhead Costs. These costs are not directly related to a training program but are essential to the smooth operation of the training department. If you have audiovisual equipment that has been purchased specifically for your department, there is a cost to maintain that equipment. Some portion of that annual cost should be charged to the various training programs. If you have classroom space available to you, there is an overhead cost for supplying heat and lighting. The cost of supporting that space for days when the classroom is used for particular courses should be charged to those programs.

Compensation for Participants. These costs comprise the salaries and benefits paid to participants for the time they are in a program. If the program is two days long, salaries and benefits for your participants for those two days are costs of the program. Typically, HRD professionals do not know what individual people are earning. Therefore, we obtain this information by asking the compensation department to provide a figure for an average salary paid to the various levels of people who will be attending.

This average salary is then multiplied by the number of people attending the program, to derive a compensation estimate.

It has been our experience that many HRD professionals include only direct costs in their cost estimates. It is important at least to consider the other cost categories and ask whether your client is expecting any of these costs to be charged to the training project. You do not want your client to accuse you of making return on investment look artificially high by keeping cost figures artificially low. This is just another example of the types of decisions on which you will want to collaborate with your client.

Question 6

Once you know the costs of training and what operational benefits to measure, you need to identify what information should be collected. You may have already agreed with your client to track the call-to-close ratio or the turnover reduction. What specific organizational information must you obtain? Is this information already reported in a manner that will be helpful, or do you need to reformat it?

Some years ago, we were asked to measure the results of a sales training program for a large corporation. We were to determine the degree to which district managers were coaching and developing their sales representatives using the techniques and behavior taught in the training program. It was hoped that, as a result of district managers' using these skills, sales representatives would be more effective in their contacts with prospective customers, and more products would be sold. This program was being measured at both the behavioral and operational levels.

To determine whether sales had increased or whether add-on sales were occurring, we needed access to the company's sales reports (obviously, not something we would typically see). We also found that sales were reported for all representatives as a group within a district, but we needed information on specific individual sales representatives only. Therefore, working with our client, we had to formulate a data-reporting system that would allow the individual reporting we required but still provide the organization with the district data it needed.

Front-end work is extremely important to the evaluation of results. During meetings before the start of training, identify with your client the operational indicators to be tracked. Ask your client which indicators will be used to determine results and will therefore be most meaningful and credible. If you use these indicators, they will most likely meet the client's needs and will not be challenged for their reliability.

Here are some additional guidelines that we have found helpful for identifying specific operational information to collect.

1. Use indicators for which the organization is already collecting data. If the organization is collecting this information, it must be viewed as helpful and important. It also means that managers understand it. We once worked with a client on a program that could have affected absenteeism. This organization, however, did not collect data on absenteeism and saw it as of no real importance (it was not seen as a business need).
2. Deal with the raw data directly. In other words, avoid having someone else review the data and report to you. You want access to the raw data in the same form in which managers will see them. This affords you the opportunity to determine what trends or patterns are appearing.
3. Request additional or new reports only if they are absolutely necessary. If you do require this type of information, ask for it over a relatively short period of time. Try to use data that are already collected, and avoid setting up new systems for which other people will have to supply data. This would involve additional costs for the organization and another source of possible resistance for you.

Question 7

The last of our questions focuses on the issue of how long to wait before stopping the clock and performing the calculations to determine what return on investment has been. In Chapter Eleven, we said you should usually wait three to six months. For operational results, however, you can usually expect to wait even longer, for two reasons.

First, if people begin to use new skills the day after training, there will still be a delay before operational indicators will reflect a change. For example, we were involved in a project that taught clerks how to handle complaint calls effectively, in the hope that such calls could be handled at the clerical level. Even if these clerks had begun to use these skills immediately, it would have taken approximately two to three months for the operational indicators to show any change, and it would take even longer for them to become stabilized at a higher level of performance.

Second, operational indicators are often seasonal in nature. Certain products sell more in the spring than in the summer, and so production varies. You want to allow for seasonal variation. At the minimum, you want to compare like quarters: the first quarter of this year to the first quarter of last year, and so on.

We typically look at operational data on a quarterly basis and hope to see trends or patterns to show that the data are moving in the appropriate direction. Nevertheless, we would not stop the process and calculate a return on investment (if such a calculation were to be done) until a year after the project had started.

If calculation of a dollar return is not required, we collect data only for as long as we need them for tracking decisions. Sometimes we stop collecting information after only four months; sometimes we continue collecting data for more than a year. If the data are already compiled by the organization (independently of our training project), then it is simply a matter of having that information turned over to our department, so that it can be reviewed and plotted.

Interpretation of Operational Tracking Results

How do you interpret all the operational data that you have collected? In Chapter Eleven, we discussed the various types of tracking designs you may consider using. The "pre-post" and "trained/untrained" designs are the most common ones for tracking operational results from training. This means that both information on the use of behaviors and skills and information on operational indicators are collected once before training and again some months later. You compare a pretraining base line with whatever is happening some weeks or months after training.

In some situations, you may need to compare posttraining results to what was expected or anticipated, rather than to a pretraining base line. This is often the case in start-up situations where there is no history to be used as a basis of comparison. In such situations, you judge the value of training by determining whether the desired result has been produced.

What is important in all cases is that you report on both the use of behavior and the operational results that are causally linked to that behavior. For instance, in a sales situation, you might indicate the following to your client.

1. You taught salespeople how to close sales and handle complaints using certain techniques and behaviors.
2. You observed and surveyed these salespeople and determined that they were using these techniques and behaviors.
3. You monitored sales records for the past six months and found a decidedly upward trend.
4. You have concluded that training has contributed to increased sales because people are using the skills that were taught.

Notice that you do not say that training has caused sales to rise. Many other factors can affect sales increases, including managers' reinforcement of the techniques that were taught. You do not want to take full credit for the results, but you do want to illustrate how training has contributed. To be able to illustrate training's contribution, you must demonstrate the causal link between the business indicators and the skills and knowledge being offered in the training, provide effective training in those skills and knowledge, determine that the learners do use on the job what they learned during training, and monitor the operational indicators and their movement. By carrying out these four activities, you can confidently illustrate how training has contributed to operational results.

Putting It All Together: Wood Panel Plant

Several years ago, we worked with an organization that we will call Wood Panel Plant. The plant produced 72,000 wood panels each day. These panels were used as building materials by contractors and do-it-yourselfers. The plant employed three hundred hourly employees on a three-shift operation. There were forty-eight supervisors, seven shift superintendents, and a plant manager.

We were brought into the situation because of three business problems. The first was the quality of the panels. Of the panels produced each day, 2 percent were rejected because of poor quality. The most frequent reason for rejection was that the stain applied to the panels was either streaked or outside the acceptable color limits. The second problem was poor housekeeping. A visual inspection, conducted each week on the basis of a twenty-item checklist, indicated that the production area had an average of ten defects in housekeeping each week. The third problem was preventable accidents. The number of preventable accidents was higher than management wanted and was higher than the industry average.

Our assessment of performance effectiveness and causes indicated that much of the poor staining of panels was caused by machine operators who were not closely watching their machines or were careless in the settings on the machines. Our data indicated that most operators knew how to operate the machines properly; they had developed some poor work habits. In addition, our data indicated that some of the preventable accidents occurred because of poor housekeeping. For example, carelessly stacked panels would fall over onto an employee, or an employee would slip on a floor that had not been properly cleaned.

On the basis of this information, we decided with the

Figure 22. Causal Relationships.

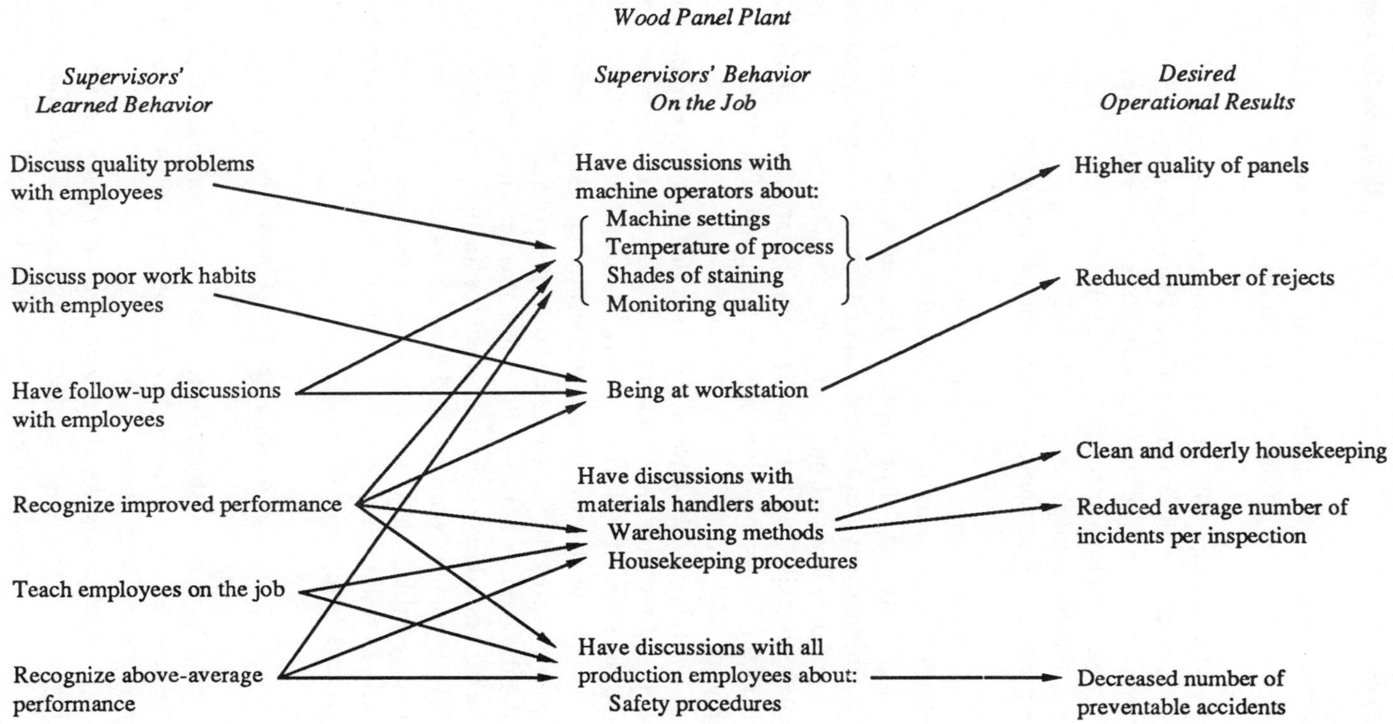

Wood Panel Plant

Supervisors' Learned Behavior

Discuss quality problems with employees

Discuss poor work habits with employees

Have follow-up discussions with employees

Recognize improved performance

Teach employees on the job

Recognize above-average performance

Supervisors' Behavior On the Job

Have discussions with machine operators about:
Machine settings
Temperature of process
Shades of staining
Monitoring quality

Being at workstation

Have discussions with materials handlers about:
Warehousing methods
Housekeeping procedures

Have discussions with all production employees about:
Safety procedures

Desired Operational Results

Higher quality of panels

Reduced number of rejects

Clean and orderly housekeeping

Reduced average number of incidents per inspection

Decreased number of preventable accidents

client to train the supervisors in the following performance-management and interpersonal skills:

- Discussing quality problems with employees
- Discussing poor work habits with employees
- Conducting follow-up discussions with employees
- Recognizing improved performance
- Teaching employees on the job
- Recognizing above-average performance.

The training program was a skill-building, behavior-modeling program. It was three days long and was conducted for all forty-eight supervisors. In addition, the seven shift superintendents and the plant manager attended a separate program, where they learned how to coach the supervisors in the use of the new skills on the job. During the front-end analysis, the causal relationships had been established. These are shown in Figure 22.

Table 9 shows how the costs of this training endeavor were determined. It is important to note that these figures are for the early 1980s. In today's economy, they would be higher.

Table 10 represents the operational results twelve months after training. Results before training, results after training, and the differences between them are also shown. Benefits that can be expressed in dollars are shown for the first year after training. It is important to note that the number of housekeeping defects decreased by eight per week. These decreases are not measurable in dollars, however, even though management saw the decreases as having real value.

Things That Can Go Wrong

As in any system, things that can go wrong will go wrong from time to time. Let us briefly comment on a few pitfalls and how to deal with them.

Operational Measurements Are Not Credible to Your Client. Every once in a while, in spite of your best efforts, the agreed-to measurements turn out to lack credibility for your client. If this is the case and you have not yet started to collect data, then ask your client what measurements would be credible. Once these have been established, you should return to the third of our seven questions for setting up a tracking system. You will need to work through all the remaining questions (after the third) to set up a workable tracking system.

Costs of Collecting Data Are High or Administrative Effort Is Excessive. Discuss the situation with your client, and attempt to do at least one of the following things: use data that are already being collected; work with those who are collecting the data to simplify the process; and collect the data for a very short period of time.

Pre- and Posttraining Data Have Become Noncomparable. Organizational changes can sometimes cause this problem. Work out an agreement with your client whereby you can adjust one set of data (usually the pretraining data) so that it will be comparable with the other set. If this is not possible, try to find a control group to provide you with data that can be compared to the posttraining data you are now collecting.

Your Client or Other Managers Want to Know How Much of the Benefit Is Due to Training Alone. You will need to indicate that no single factor, including training, could by itself have brought about the change that has taken place. The change has occurred because all factors have worked together, producing a synergistic effect, to improve performance. Attempting to say how much of the change can be strictly attributed to any one factor is an exercise in futility.

Your Client Denies Any Impact from Training. When this happens, it is better to be prepared than surprised. Make sure that you track both on-the-job behavioral change (as described in Chapter Twelve) and operational results. This way, you can show that there has been change.

Table 9. Training Cost Analysis.

Explanation	Item	Cost
Direct costs: The travel and per-diem cost is zero, because training took place adjacent to the plant. There is a cost for classroom space and audiovisual equipment, because these were rented from a local hotel. Refreshments were purchased at the same hotel. Because different supervisors attended the morning and afternoon sessions, lunch was not provided.	*Direct Costs*	
	Outside Instructor	0
	In-house instructor – 12 days × $125	$1,500.00
	Fringe benefits @ 25% of salary	$ 375.00
	Travel and per-diem expenses	0
	Materials – 56 × $60/participant	$3,360.00
	Classroom space and audiovisual equipment – 12 days @ $50	$ 600.00
	Food; refreshments – $4/day × 3 days × 56 participants	$ 672.00
	Total direct costs	$6,507.00
Indirect costs: The clerical and administrative costs reflect the amount of clerical time spent on making arrangements for the workshop facilities, sending out notices to all participants, and preparing class rosters and other miscellaneous materials.	*Indirect Costs*	
	Training management	0
	Clerical/administrative	$ 750.00
	Fringe benefits – 25% of clerical/administrative salary	$ 187.00
	Postage, shipping, telephone	0
	Pre- and postlearning materials – $4 × 56 participants	$ 224.00
	Total indirect costs (rounded to nearest dollar)	$1,161.00

Development costs: These costs represent the purchase of the training program from a vendor. Included are instructional aids, an instructor manual, videotapes, and a licensing fee. The instructor-training costs pertain to the one-week workshop that the instructor attended to become prepared to facilitate the training. Front-end assessment costs were covered by the corporate training budget.	*Development Costs*		
	Fee to purchase program		$3,600.00
	Instructor training		
	Registration fee		$1,400.00
	Travel and lodging		$ 975.00
	Salary		$ 625.00
	Benefits (25% of salary)		$ 156.00
		Total development costs	$6,756.00
Overhead costs: These represent the services that the general organization provides to the training unit. Because figures were not available, we used 10 percent of the direct, indirect, and program development costs.	*Overhead Costs*		
	General organization support		10% of direct, indirect,
	Top management's time		and development costs
		Total overhead costs	$1,443.00
Compensation for participants: This figure represents the salaries and benefits paid to all participants while they attended the workshop.	*Compensation for Participants*		
	Participants' salary and benefits (time away from the job)		
		Total compensation	$16,696.00
		Total training costs	$32,564.00
		Cost per participant	$ 581.50

Table 10. Operational Results Analysis.

Operational Results Area	*How Measured*	*Results Before Training*	*Results After Training*	*Differences (+ or −)*	*Expressed in $*
Quality of panels	% rejected	2% rejected 1,440 panels per day	1.5% rejected 1,080 panels per day	.5% 360 panels	$720 per day $172,800 per year
Housekeeping	Visual inspection using 20-item checklist	10 defects (average)	2 defects (average)	8 defects	Not measurable in $
Preventable accidents	Number of accidents	24 per year	16 per year	8 per year	
	Direct cost of each accident	$144,000 per year	$96,000 per year	$48,000	$48,000 per year
				Total savings:	$220,800.00

$$\text{ROI} = \frac{\text{Return}}{\text{Investment}} = \frac{\text{Operational Results}}{\text{Training Costs}}$$

$$= \frac{\$220{,}800}{\$32{,}564} = 6.8$$

Summary

The following techniques move training toward impact:

Activity **Impact**

- Work with your client to determine the operational results to be tracked.
- Identify the causal link between training and operational indicators.
- To have credible data, be sure to track for on-the-job behavioral change whenever you track operational results.

Part Five

Using the Training-for-Impact Approach

Now that you are familiar with the process of Training for Impact, it is important to consider how to begin using the techniques that are described. When is this approach appropriate? When should you consider a training program as an activity, not an impact, effort? How can you take "pieces" of the process and use them? And what skills are required to do all of this? These are the questions addressed in this final chapter of the book.

Fourteen

How and Where to Begin

If you have made it through this far, you may feel as if you had tried to swallow an elephant whole. There is a great deal to digest if you want to strategically implement your training efforts so that they are linked to business needs and can be measured for impact. First, let us look at what is required in the way of skill and time if you wish to implement the entire process. Then we will look at what you can do if using every step of the impact approach is not possible.

The Entire Training-for-Impact Approach

If you set out to use all the steps of the Training-for-Impact approach (including the front-end work that has been described), the project can become very large. We have been able to complete front-end work in as few as five or six days, but there are times when the period required is four and five times that amount. In the measuring of results, the same variability in length of time can be true. Considering all of that, we believe that the following ranges of time are required to fully use the impact approach: The minimum is ten to fifteen days (exclusive of time to design and deliver the training program), and the maximum is fifty to sixty days (exclusive of time to design and deliver the training). You would use the minimum if there were a limited number of meetings associated with the project; if there were a great deal of information already available that could be used in performance effectiveness assessment and cause analyses (only a limited amount of information would need to be collected); and if any measurement of results were to be accomplished through computer-tabulated questionnaires. You would use the maximum if there were several client teams that required multiple meetings; if limited information were available on performance effectiveness or on the causes of performance deficiencies (extensive front-end work would be required); and if the measurement of results were to be accomplished through the use of interviews that must be content-analyzed. Again, added to these days would be the time required to design, prepare for, and deliver the training program. We are addressing only the front- and back-end efforts associated with training programs.

We certainly know that resources are limited, and HRD professionals must consider carefully when to allocate the amount of time mentioned to any particular effort. When is it worth this type of investment? We suggest that you use the following criteria in selecting training projects to be implemented with the Training-for-Impact approach.

1. What is the cost of this training program to the organization? We have worked with clients whose costs were in excess of $100,000 each time the program was offered, and this sum reflected only the direct costs; if participants' time were included, the cost would increase. Certainly, such money should be spent strategically.
2. How much training time does the program require? If a program were to take only four hours, we would doubt the benefit of expending fifteen days on strategic front-end work and work measurement. We worked with a company

whose training program required three years. Somewhere between four hours and three years, you cross over to the side where the training time (which is a cost to the organization) warrants an investment in the strategic approaches we are suggesting here. Typically, clients with whom we work have programs averaging three to five days in length.

3. What are the potential benefits to the organization from this program? When potential benefits are in the area of increased revenues, greater productivity, and improved customer service, those benefits probably are worth an investment of time to ensure that they occur. When the benefit is that individuals will have more rapid reading skills or will be more familiar with the benefits provided by the organization, we doubt the wisdom of spending the kind of time and effort described in this book. We encourage you to use the Training-for-Impact approach when there is a specific business need being addressed by a program. In such situations, the potential benefits are often greater than the resources required for effective training.
4. Do you have a client for the project? Without a close partnership with those who have something to gain or lose from this training effort, the project is more of a Training-for-Activity approach. While it is important to offer the learning experience in a superior manner, doing the strategic work we have described here becomes very problematic, for there is no one to work with to make certain that the approach is effective.

Consider these three types of situations: Five hundred first-level managers are to be taught how to set performance goals, evaluate performance, and provide feedback to their employees. All sales personnel in an organization are being taught how to handle customer objections and close a sale. Desk clerks in a hotel chain are being provided skills in handling customers' complaints. For each of these situations, the impact approach represents a possible option and should be considered. Clearly, there is a large cost involved (five hundred managers). There are potential benefits of some magnitude (increased revenues). A link with business needs is probable (customers' improved image of the hotel).

Now consider these three situations: Three hundred line managers will attend a program to learn the major agreements reached in a new contract with organized labor. Several managers per year attend a program offered by a national consulting firm. One thousand individuals will attend a one-day program on time management. In our opinion, such training efforts do not warrant the expenditure of time required by the impact approach. While the numbers of people attending such programs may be large, their potential organizational impact is limited. In the first program, knowledge is the end result. Therefore, delivering the course so that people learn is important, but expecting measurable organizational impact is unrealistic. With regard to the second situation, the program is offered by outside resources, and a small number of managers attend each year. As a result, the HRD professional is limited with respect to the actions that can be taken if the program is not yielding the desired results. The example regarding time management may provide individual results, but to expect organizational impact is doubtful; there is probably no clear business need driving this effort.

Using Pieces of the Impact Approach

When it is not possible to implement the entire approach as described in this book, there is no need to throw the baby out with the bath water. There are aspects of the approach that can still be used and that will move you further along the continuum toward impact. The closer your program is to an impact approach, the better. Doing it all is not the only option.

For example, you may not be able to complete front-end work, but can you do any measurement of results? Such measurement may mean phoning a sample of people who attended the program to determine how the learning has helped them and what, if anything, is making it difficult to use the learning. You may not be able to measure on a follow-up basis, but can you design a reaction evaluation that is comprehensive and more in keeping with the examples in this book? Perhaps a client is not interested in completing all the front-end assessment that you feel is important, but can you get even a few days to interview some people? To the degree that the time is well planned and your purposes for collecting such information are clear, you will have better information on which to base decisions than if no front-end work is done at all.

We have provided you with some ideas at the conclusion of each chapter. The following are some additional suggestions for how you can use bits and pieces of the impact approach, if using the entire process is impossible.

1. No matter what project you have been asked to work on, ask yourself, "Who is the client? Who really cares about what happens in this effort? What can I do to influence that individual regarding the project? What can I do to identify the business need that the program may be addressing?" (Please review Chapter Three for ideas.)
2. Be alert to which of the three consulting roles you are currently working in on any project. Look to your own behavior and that of the person with whom you are working. Analyze whether your role is acceptable. Do you want to change it? (Refer to Chapter Four for some techniques in this area.)
3. When you have an opportunity to discuss a training project with management, use that time to find out more about the business context and the situation in which the training will be implemented. The more business questions raised, the more management begins to see you as a business partner, not just as someone who delivers courses. (Some of the questions used for illustration in Chapter Five may prove helpful here.)
4. Seek out information on the work environment of your participants by developing pertinent questions in your reaction evaluations. When patterns of problems begin to be identified, consider ways to bring this information to the attention of line management. You can also incorporate into the learning design of the program ways in which participants can overcome such barriers. For example, one

of our clients delivered a program to first-level managers in which they learned how to communicate corporate objectives to their staffs and set up job objectives with direct subordinates in light of the corporate objectives. Managers indicated that this had been difficult to do, because they had not been given such information by management. The program was adapted to incorporate skills in obtaining such information. (Refer to Chapters Seven and Nine for ideas on this technique.)

5. When a manager contacts you about a training program, request a project meeting. During that meeting, be certain to ask about the specific outcomes that the manager expects as a result of training. Look beyond the program to find out what the manager expects to take place back on the job. If necessary, help this manager articulate such desires, and do so in a specific manner. (Chapter Five provides some guidance here.)
6. Take time to analyze the cost of your training programs. Approach managers with information on what the program will cost per participant. Inquire about the expected benefits of this investment. If managers determine that the cost is too heavy and decide to forgo the program, all the better. You have saved yourself and the participants a lot of time, which can be spent on other, more useful efforts. (Chapter Thirteen provides guidance in this area.)
7. When a request for training results from a business problem, be certain to separate the symptoms of that problem from its causes. Ask questions of your client and others to ensure that the training will attack a cause. (Refer to Chapter Seven for the types of information you need to seek.)
8. Introduce this formula:

Learning Experience × Work Environment = Business Results

Refer back to it over time. Managers will respond to this formula and will begin to understand its implications for impact work. It then becomes easier to influence them on what actions are needed to guarantee skill transfer and business results.

Implications for Catalogue Courses

Many HRD departments have developed course catalogues or curricula over the years. Sometimes such catalogues contain only a few programs; other times, the catalogues contain several hundred. We have heard HRD professionals refer to their function as being a "little red schoolhouse" (that is, to deliver courses). What are the implications of the impact approach for such programs?

Clearly, our message has been that impact training is best done when the training program is tightly linked to a business problem or opportunity. Business needs tend to be dynamic: This year's need may not be next year's. Catalogue courses, by comparison, are often developed and appear in the catalogue over several years. In some cases, they take on a life of their own, with no one questioning the need. We worked with an organization that had such a catalogue. Included in it was a curriculum of five programs focusing on affirmative action. Managers registered to attend one of the programs as their calendars permitted. These programs had been offered relatively unchanged for fifteen years. Having just inherited responsibility for managing these programs, our client determined that it was time to find out whether they were still relevant. The data from our project clearly indicated that the programs should be dropped or substantially revised. People were attending programs that were out of touch with contemporary business needs.

Our message is not that catalogue programming is bad; often, such programs are of high quality, in both design and delivery. Our concern is that the approach by which they are implemented may be more in keeping with the activity approach than with the impact approach. You should consider several questions regarding any catalogue programs that you may have.

1. Is there any client for this program? Is there some person or group who cares whether the program results in impact?

2. Is there a current business need that this program is addressing? Do managers understand the connection between this program and such a need?
3. Is the developmental need for this program continually assessed to ensure that the need still exists?
4. Are there any work environment conditions that preclude people from applying on the job what they have learned? To what degree are such conditions being addressed?
5. Is the program being measured in any manner to determine whether it is meeting the desired outcomes?

During the 1970s and the 1980s, the HRD field focused on catalogue programs, which probably outnumbered business-driven training programs by a wide margin. HRD departments were held accountable for the number of programs that reinforced the growth of catalogues. Our prediction is that in the 1990s the number of programs in catalogues will drop. The time and energy that used to be expended on such programs will be redirected toward the types of activities described in this book. In essence, there may be fewer days of training programs, but what is delivered will yield greater impact to organizations. HRD professionals will also have time to respond to business needs with the sense of urgency that such needs demand.

Again, it is not that catalogue training programs are ineffective and should be discontinued; rather, it is our concern that the strategy for implementing such programs tends to concentrate only on the learning experience and does not address any systemic problems that may make skill transfer difficult. Such programs frequently also have weak links to current business needs. Both of these conditions mean that the potential results of training are reduced.

Skills and Structure Required in Training for Impact

Required Skills. There is much in the literature that identifies the competencies required for HRD professionals to be successful in their positions. The American Society for Training and Development (1983) has identified such competencies;

these have now been researched once again and are due to be published soon.

The types of HRD activities required in the Training-for-Impact approach also require competencies, some of which may not be considered typical in our profession. The *consulting* cluster of competencies involves negotiation skills, influencing skills, and skills in managing resistance. The *strategic* cluster of competencies involves organizational knowledge and awareness, industry knowledge, and strategic planning skills. The *diagnostic* cluster of competencies involves questioning, data-collection, and data-analysis skills. The *feedback* cluster of competencies involves skills in data presentation and meeting facilitation. The *business knowledge* cluster of competencies involves knowledge of your organization, the industry of which it is a part, and the economic, financial, and social forces that affect it.

We do not believe that each HRD professional must develop skills in each of these competency clusters, but it is important for the entire HRD department collectively to either have such competencies or be in a position to contract for lacking competencies. For example, if diagnostic work is not a specialty of anyone on the HRD staff, then contracting with an outside consultant for such services can prove wise. Perhaps an arrangement can be made to have someone on the internal staff partnered with the consultant, so that development in diagnostic work is learned as part of the contract.

Required HRD Structure and Reward Systems. HRD departments are no different from any other departments in an organization. They respond to the balance of consequences developed for the department. Therefore, it becomes important to look at the work environment of the HRD department to determine what obstacles, if any, are making it difficult to work in the impact mode. Some questions you will want to consider are the following.

1. Does the reward system for HRD professionals hold them accountable for consulting to management, performing diagnostic work, and measuring results of training? In many situations in which we have worked, the accountability sys-

tem for the HRD department was totally focused on activity indicators (numbers of programs, numbers of people); it was unacceptable for the department to deliver fewer course days and courses than in a previous year. Such a balance of consequences will propel course delivery and will not necessarily focus on the impact of that delivery. If your reward system is more driven by activity indicators, then it becomes important to influence your management in another direction. Perhaps dual accountabilities could be agreed on for a year or two, with a goal for number of courses to be delivered but also a goal for focusing on some business-driven projects that may or may not involve many course days.

2. Is the HRD function responsible for measuring results of training programs, and not just for measuring participants' reactions? Again, if the measuring of results is not a responsibility, it is unlikely that it will be given much emphasis. Activities for which stated objectives exist will always take precedence. If you are in a position where the measurement of training results is not an objective, insist that it be made one. Once it is on the objectives list, seek out a measurement opportunity and deliver on it. In doing so, you will be demonstrating the potential of the HRD department to be used in a manner different from what may have been true in the past.
3. Do members of the HRD department have time out of the classroom to devote to the front-end and follow-up activities described in this book? In some departments with which we have worked, HRD professionals were in the instructor role between 80 and 90 percent of the time. Such a class load makes it difficult to do anything besides prepare for the next course. We do not pretend to know the ideal balance of in-class and out-of-class responsibility, but we do know that activities like those described in this book will require several days a month to complete. That time must be made available to some members of the HRD staff, or else the Training-for-Impact activities cannot be accomplished.

Final Thoughts

Linking training to business needs and strategically implementing a program so that it yields measurable results to the organization are very possible accomplishments. First you must shift your thinking about the role of the HRD professional. The HRD professional must be viewed as an individual who contributes to performance effectiveness within the organization, rather than as a person who delivers training programs. With this shift in focus, the delivery of training programs becomes only part of the job; performance effectiveness can be developed in a variety of training (and nontraining) ways. This shift in focus must occur on two fronts: in management's view of HRD professionals and in HRD professionals' view of themselves.

HRD professionals who are serious about the impact approach must ensure that they have the competencies required to perform such activities. The consulting and diagnostic events associated with impact training will bear results only if the events are conducted with skill.

Finally, this type of work means taking some risks. It is safe to respond to a request for a training program just as the request was presented. It is riskier to meet with the contact and begin to influence him or her away from a course and toward the need for more information. Just as we want others in our organizations to take calculated risks, so must we be willing to do so.

The movement away from Training for Activity and toward Training for Impact will not occur overnight. It will not occur at all unless HRD professionals take a leadership role in moving the HRD function in this direction. In essence, it is up to those of us who believe in the potential of our profession to demonstrate both the leadership and the skills required to serve our organizations in this manner.

References

American Society for Training and Development. *Models for Excellence*. Alexandria, Va.: American Society for Training and Development, 1983.

American Society for Training and Development. *Serving the Corporation*. Alexandria, Va.: American Society for Training and Development, 1986.

Block, P. *Flawless Consulting: A Guide to Getting Your Expertise Used*. Austin, Tex.: Learning Concepts, 1981.

Bloom, B. (ed.). *Taxonomy of Educational Objectives: Handbook of Cognitive Domain*. New York: McKay, 1956.

Feuer, D. "Training Magazine's Industry Report 1988." *Training: The Magazine of Human Resources Development*, 1988, *25* (10), 31–34.

Kirkpatrick, D. *A Practical Guide for Supervisory Training and Development*. (2nd ed.) Reading, Mass.: Addison-Wesley, 1983.

Krathwohl, D., Bloom, B., and Masia, B. *Taxonomy of Educational Objectives—Handbook II: Affective Domain*. New York: McKay, 1964.

Learning Dynamics, Inc. *Leadership Style Survey*. Needham, Mass.: Learning Dynamics, Inc., 1979.

Mager, R., and Pipe, P. *Analyzing Performance Problems, or "You Really Oughta Wanna."* Belmont, Calif.: Fearon, 1970.

Mezoff, B. "How to Get Accurate Self-Reports of Training Outcomes." *Training and Development Journal*, 1981, *35* (9), 56–61.

Nadler, L., and Wiggs, G. D. *Managing Human Resource Development: A Practical Guide*. San Francisco: Jossey-Bass, 1986.

Rackham, N. "The Coaching Controversy." *Training and Development Journal*, 1979, *33* (11), 14.

Rackham, N. *SPIN Selling*. New York: McGraw-Hill, 1988.

Rackham, N., and Morgan, T. *Behaviour Analysis in Training*. London: McGraw-Hill, 1977.

Rae, L. *How to Measure Training Effectiveness*. New York: Nichols, 1986.

Rossett, A. *Training Needs Assessment*. Englewood Cliffs, N.J.: Educational Technology Publications, 1987.

Rummler, G. "Geary Rummler: Training Still Isn't Enough." *Training*, 1983, *20* (8), 75–76.

Spencer, L. *Calculating Human Resource Costs and Benefits*. New York: Wiley, 1986.

Sudman, S., and Bradburn, N. M. *Asking Questions: A Practical Guide to Questionnaire Design*. San Francisco: Jossey-Bass, 1982.

"Training Evaluation Is a Critical but Overlooked Issue." *Training Directors' Forum Newsletter*, 1986, *1* (9), 1–4.

Zemke, R., and Kramlinger, T. *Figuring Things Out: A Trainer's Guide to Needs and Task Analysis*. Reading, Mass.: Addison-Wesley, 1982.

Annotated Bibliography

Bauer & Associates, Inc. *The Question Book: A Workbook for Designing Customized Surveys.* Ann Arbor, Mich.: Bauer & Associates, Inc., 1981.

This three-ring binder provides some general information on designing surveys, but its basic thrust is to provide pages of actual questions that could be asked on a questionnaire dealing with a variety of topics.

Bellman, G. *Quest for Staff Leadership.* Glenview, Ill.: Scott, Foresman, 1986.

While this book does not specifically focus on HRD functions, most the ideas, techniques, and suggestions are relevant.

Brinkerhoff, R. O. *Achieving Results from Training: How to Evaluate Human Resource Development to Strengthen Programs and Increase Impact.* San Francisco: Jossey-Bass, 1987.

This book describes how to evaluate training in six stages: HRD goals, program design, implementation, learning, behavior change, and organizational impact.

Chalofsky, N. E., and Reinhart, C. *Effective Human Resource Development: How to Build a Strong and Responsive HRD Function.* San Francisco: Jossey-Bass, 1988.

This book is filled with guidelines on how to build a successful HRD function. Much of the information comes from research conducted by the authors. More than one hundred HRD experts and practitioners were interviewed.

Fitz-enz, J. *How to Measure Human Resources Management.* New York: McGraw-Hill, 1984.

This book describes how to measure the results of most human resources departments, including planning/staffing, compensation/benefits, employee relations, and training and development. It is more conceptual in nature regarding the measurement of training. The concepts are sound, and the book is good.

Gilbert, T. *Human Competence: Engineering Worthy Performance.* New York: McGraw-Hill, 1978.

This is a "must read" for HRD professionals who see their role as developing performance effectiveness. The system issues to consider in developing skills are addressed.

Head, G. *Training Cost Analysis: A Practical Guide.* Washington, D.C.: Marlin Press, 1985.

This book provides many worksheets and guides to use in assessing costs of training courses.

Kearsley, G. *Costs, Benefits, and Productivity in Training Systems.* Reading, Mass.: Addison-Wesley, 1982.

This book describes in detail some models and methods for establishing a causal relationship and the detailing of Level IV results. It discusses the determination of training effectiveness and training efficiency.

Phillips, J. J. *Handbook of Training Evaluation and Methods.* Houston, Tex.: Gulf, 1982.

This book provides information regarding the conceptual framework for all evaluation, with an emphasis on results evaluation. It is a practical book, with many good ideas.

Zemke, R., Standke, L., and Jones, P. *Designing and Delivering Cost-Effective Training—and Measuring the Results.* Minneapolis, Minn.: Lakewood Publications, 1981.

This is a collection of articles, some dealing with tracking for change.

Index

A

Accountability: in collaboration, 54; in training approaches, 6, 28–29
Actions: agreed to, in initial project meetings, 74–75; from client meeting for results, 155–156
Activity. *See* Training for Activity
Affective results: concept of, 245–246; measuring, 203, 249, 250–253; timing of measures for, 253
Agreement: on actions, 74–75; in initial project meetings, 72–73, 74–77; too-quick, 158
Agway case, 110–111
Albrecht and Associates, 139
American Society for Training and Development, 8, 290
Analysis. *See* Cause analysis
Assessment: of initial project meetings, 78–79; in Training for Impact, 13. *See also* Evaluation; Performance effectiveness assessments
Attitudes and values, measuring, in learning evaluation, 203

B

Bauer & Associates, 140, 297
Behavioral checklist, 196–197
Behavioral evaluation: aspects of, 208–243; background on, 209–210; candor in, 241–242; client and business need for, 214–216, 238–239; concept of, 167; and course design and delivery, 237–238; criteria for, 214–231, 238–239; findings of, 235–238; and increased use of behaviors, 235–236; information sources for, 224–226, 229–230, 241–242; issues for, 240–243; and macroevaluation, 212; and managers, 240–241; methodology for, 218,

220–226, 239; and microevaluation, 211–212, 238–239; outcomes for, 216–219, 239; problems of, 212–213; purposes for, 210–212; response rates for, 240; results reporting in, 242; short-form approaches to, 242–243; and skill building, 217–218; summary on, 243; time needed for, 242; timing of, 226–230, 239; tracking designs for, 231–235; and variance reduction in group, 236; and work environment, 230–231, 236–237
Behavioral frequency worksheet, 198–199
Behavioral observation: for evaluation, 218, 220; for performance effectiveness assessment, 100
Behavioral observation scale (BOS), 200
Behaviorally anchored rating scale (BARS), 197–198
Beliefs. *See* Nonobservable results evaluation
Bellman, G., 297
Best-solution approach, 201–202
Binary tests, 194–195
Block, P., 50, 70, 150, 156
Bloom, B., 245, 246
Bradburn, N. M., 250
Brinkerhoff, R. O., 297–298
Business needs: alignment with, lacking, 7; for alternative training approach, 8–9; for behavioral evaluation, 214–216, 238–239; client as owner of, 41; identifying, 14–16, 73; and identifying clients, 33–47; for nonobservable results evaluation, 247–248; for operational results evaluation, 259–260; proactive identification of, 34–35; as problems or opportunities, 15, 35, 86–90, 260–261; training linked to, 57–58, 61–62
Business results formula, 11–12, 41–42, 109, 187, 210, 288–289

C

Catalogue courses, implications of Training for Impact for, 289–290
Causal links: and cause analysis, 112–113; in consultation, 57–58, 61–62; literature search for, 263–264; observations for, 264; in operational results evaluation, 262–266, 273–274; pilot testing for, 264–266
Cause analysis: agreements from, 155; aspects of, 108–131; background on, 109–110; case example of, 122–128; and causal link, 112–113; concept of, 20–22; data collection for, 118–120, 126; data comparison in, 118, 125; data review in, 116, 124; decisions in, 113–120; findings from, 127–128; information sources in, 116, 118, 124–125, 127; and learner deficiencies, 110–111, 114, 117; and manager deficiencies, 111, 114–115, 117; opinion survey distinct from, 119; and organizational deficiencies, 111–112, 115, 117; and performance effectiveness assessment, 120–122; purposes of, 114–116, 117, 122–124; and resource limitations, 120, 126–127; and skill transfer, 117, 128–130; source group size for, 118, 125–126; summary on, 131
Certification, learning evaluation for, 204–205
Chalofsky, N. E., 298
Client meeting. *See* Feedback meeting
Clients: aspects of identifying, 33–47; background on, 34–35; for behavioral evaluation, 214–216, 238–239; business needs owned by, 41; in chain of command, 41–42; characteristics of, 40–42; collaboration with, 16–17, 48–65; concerns of, 154; criteria for, 39; and decision making, 77; direct identification of, 43–44; indirect

identification of, 44–45; lacking, 45–46; level of, 40; misidentified, 37–38; for nonobservable results evaluation, 247; for operational results evaluation, 259–260; outcomes expected by, 73–74; reporting results to, 26, 42, 132–160; and situational elements, 42–43; summary on, 47; team of, 39, 41, 46
Cognitive skills. *See* Nonobservable results evaluation
Collaboration: advantages of, 54–55; characteristics of, 58–60; with client, 16–17, 48–65; as consultation style, 53–56, 60–62; and contract negotiation, 70; disadvantages of, 55–56; and feedback meeting, 150–151
Competency, demonstrations of, 195–202
Confidence and value, reaction evaluation of, 179
Consultation: aspects of, 48–65; background on, 49–50; and business needs linked to training, 57–58, 61–62; collaborative style of, 53–56, 60–62; concept of, 49; expert style of, 50–51, 60–62; pair-of-hands style of, 52–53, 60; styles of, 50–57, 63–65; summary on, 62
Contracts, in initial project meetings, 70
Cost-benefit ratio. *See* Operational results evaluation
Creative Research Systems, 139

D

Data: aspects of reporting, 132–160; case example of, 135–138; closed, analysis of, 138–140; content analysis of, 136; formatting, 141–147; open-ended, analysis of, 135–138; reporting, 153–156; statistical display of, 140–142; in Training for Impact, 25–26
Data collection: for cause analysis, 118–120, 126; errors in, 213; for operational results evaluation, 268–269, 274–275; for performance effectiveness assessment, 98–99, 106
Data comparison: in cause analysis, 118, 125; in performance effectiveness assessments, 95–97, 103
Data interpretation: for operational results evaluation, 270–272; for reporting results, 147–149
Data review: in cause analysis, 116, 124; in performance effectiveness assessment, 93, 103
Data tabulation: for learning evaluation, 189, 192; in reaction evaluation, 175; for reporting results, 134–141
Data utilization: in learning evaluation, 187–188, 193, 204, 206; from reaction evaluation, 182–183
Decisions: in cause analysis, 113–120; and clients, 77; in collaboration, 58–59; in performance effectiveness assessment, 91–102
Development, learning evaluation for, 204–205
Development costs, 267, 277
Diagnosis: aspects of, 83–160; cause analysis for, 108–131; performance effectiveness assessments for, 85–107; and results for clients, 132–160
Direct costs, 266, 276
Disagreement, by client, with results, 157–158
Discrete behaviors, evaluation of, 216–217, 218
Douglas, A., 3–5

E

Effectiveness. *See* Performance effectiveness assessment
Effectiveness rating worksheet, 200–201
Environment. *See* Work environment
Essay/open-answer tests, 193–194
Evaluation: aspects of, 161–279; be-

havioral, 208–243; formative and summative, 169, 172; frequency of use of levels of, 168–172; as front-end process, 164–165; of learning, 185–207; levels of, 165–168; of nonobservable results, 244–254; of operational results, 255–279; overview of, 163–172; reaction, 172–184; in Training for Impact, 22–23. *See also* Assessment

Expert style: of consultation, 50–51, 60–62; and initial project meeting, 77–78

F

Feedback meeting: actions from, 155–156; guidelines for, 151–152; problem areas for, 156–160; purposes of, 149–150; and reporting results, 149–153; time needed for, 159–160

Feuer, D., 8

Fitz-enz, J., 298

G

Gilbert, T., 298

Grandfather clauses, and certification, 205

H

Hawthorne effect, and behavioral evaluation, 241

Head, G., 298

I

Impact training. *See* Training for Impact

Indirect costs, 266–267, 276

Information sources: for behavioral evaluation, 224–226, 229–230, 241–242; in cause analysis, 116, 118, 124–125, 127; in performance effectiveness assessment, 93–95, 103; size of group for, 97–99, 103, 118, 125–126

Initial project meetings: and action agreements, 74–75; agreements in, 72–73, 74–77; aspects of, 66–82; assessment of, 78–79; case example of, 67–69, 79–82; concept of, 17–18; information needs for, 70–72, 73; preparation for, 79–81; problem areas for, 76–78; purposes and techniques of, 69–72; steps for, 72–76; summary on, 82

Instructors, reaction evaluation from, 183

Interviews: and data formatting, 144–146; data tabulation from, 137–138; focus-group, for behavioral evaluation, 221–222; for nonobservable results evaluation, 249–250; for performance effectiveness assessments, 99–100, 101

J

Jones, P., 299

K

Karlin, L., 67–69, 70, 79–82

Kearsley, G., 298

Kirkpatrick, D., 165, 209

Knowledge tests, for learning evaluation, 193–195

Kramlinger, T., 101

Krathwohl, D., 245

L

Lakewood Publications, 168

Leadership Style Survey, 251

Learners: deficiencies of, 110–111, 114, 117; and work environment, 230

Learning Dynamics, 251

Learning evaluation: advance notice of, 206; aspects of, 185–207; attitudes and values measured in, 203; background on, 186–187; case example of, 191–193; for certification or development, 204–205; concept of, 166; data tabulation for, 189, 192; data utilization in, 187–188, 193, 204, 206; designing, 187–191; issues for, 204–205; knowledge tests for, 193–195; and learning outcomes, 188; macro or micro, 186–187; pilot testing, 189–190, 192–193; problems with, 205–207; purposes of, 186, 187–188, 191; rigor lacking in, 205–206; skill tests for, 195–202; summary on, 207; test development for, 188–189, 192; validation and norms for, 190–191

Learning experience: and behavioral evaluation, 210, 211; and cause analysis, 109; and client chain of command, 41–42; and learning evaluation, 187; and Training for Impact, 11–12, 16

Likert scales: odd or even, 177, 223; using entire, 184

Links. *See* Causal Links

M

Macroevaluation: behavioral, 212; of learning, 186–187

Mager, R., 20, 114

Management: aspects of partnerships with, 31–82; and behavioral evaluation, 240–241; deficiencies of, 111, 114–115, 117; in Training for Activity, 7–8; and work environment, 230

Masia, B., 245

Maxxon case, 67

Meetings. *See* Feedback meeting; Initial project meetings

Mental skills: concept of, 246; measuring, 248, 249–250; timing for measures of, 253

Mezoff, B., 233

Microevaluation: behavioral, 211–212, 238–239; of learning, 186–187

Morgan, T., 220

Motorola Corporation, Hawthorne effect studied at, 241

Multiple-choice tests, 195

N

Needs. *See* Business needs

Nonobservable results evaluation: aspects of, 244–254; business needs for, 247–248; client for, 247; concept of, 167, 245–246; criteria for, 246–253; methods for, 203, 249–253; outcomes measured in, 248–249; summary on, 253–254; timing of, 253

Nu-Karparts case, 14, 16, 17–18, 19–20, 21–22, 23, 24, 25, 26, 27

O

Observation: behavioral, 110, 218, 220; for causal links, 264; objectivity of, in skills testing, 202–203

Operational results evaluation: aspects of, 255–279; background on, 256–258; and business problems and opportunities, 260–261; case example of, 272–274, 276–278; causal links in, 262–266, 273–274; client and business need for, 259–260; concept of, 167; and costs of training, 266–268, 276–277; criteria for, 259–270; data collection for, 268–269, 274–275; data interpretation for, 270–272; outcomes to be tracked by, 261–263; problems of, 274–275; purposes of, 258–259; summary on, 279; timing for, 269–270

Opinion survey, cause analysis distinct from, 119

Opportunities, business needs as, 15, 35, 86–90, 260–261

Organization: deficiencies of, 111–112, 115, 117; and work environment, 230–231

Organizational data, for perfor-

mance effectiveness assessment, 100
Outcomes: in behavioral evaluation, 216–219, 239; client expectations for, 73–74; in learning evaluation, 188; in nonobservable results evaluation, 248–249; in operational results evaluation, 261–263
Overhead costs, 267, 277

P

Pair-of-hands style: of consultation, 52–53, 60; and initial project meeting, 69, 77–78
Participants, cost of compensating, 267–268, 277
Partnerships: aspects of, 31–82; and business needs and client identification, 33–47; collaborative, 48–65; concept of, 31; initial project meetings for, 66–82
Performance deficiencies, causes of, 110–112
Performance effectiveness assessments: agreements from, 155; aspects of, 85–107; background on, 86; and business need as problem or opportunity, 86–90; case example of, 102–107; and cause analysis, 120–122; concept of, 18–20; and current business problems, 87–88; data collection for, 99, 106; data comparisons in, 95–97, 103; data review in, 93, 103; decisions in, 91–102; and future business opportunities, 88–90; information needs in, 89–90; information sources in, 93–95, 103; methodology for, 104–107; purposes of, 90–91, 92–93, 102–103; and resource limitations, 99–102, 106; source group size for, 97–99, 103; summary on, 107
Phillips, J. J., 299
Pilot testing: for causal links, 264–266; of learning evaluation, 189–190, 192–193; of reaction evaluation, 183–184
Pipe, P., 20, 114
Plunkett, J., 67–69, 79–82
Positioning: errors in, 213; of training, 35–37
"Post only" tracking design, 234–235
Pre- and posttracking design, 231–232
"Pre," "then," and "post" tracking design, 233–234
Problems: of behavioral evaluation, 212–213; business needs as, 15, 35, 86–90, 260–261; of feedback meetings, 156–160; for initial project meetings, 76–78; with learning evaluation, 205–207; of operational results evaluations, 274–275; with reaction evaluation, 172–174; with Training for Activity, 4–5
Professionals: reward system for, 291–292; skills of, 28–29, 290–291
Projects. *See* Initial project meetings
Purposes: for behavioral evaluation, 210–212; of cause analysis, 114–116, 117, 122–124; for feedback meeting, 149–150; of initial project meetings, 69–72; of learning evaluation, 186, 187–188, 191; of operational results evaluation, 258–259; for performance effectiveness assessment, 90–91, 92–93, 102–103; of reaction evaluation, 174–175

Q

Questionnaires: for behavioral evaluation, 222–224; computer software for tabulating, 139–140; and data formatting, 143–144; for nonobservable results evaluation, 250, 251–252; for performance effectiveness assessment, 100, 101; return rate for, 120
Questions: closed, 175–177; high-yield, 175–181; specific, 177–181

R

Rackham, N., 111, 220, 228*n*, 229, 241
Rae, L., 195
Reaction evaluation: alternative forms of, 182; aspects of, 172–184; concept of, 165–166; data tabulation in, 175; data utilization from, 182–183; from instructors, 183; issues in, 181–184; pilot testing, 183–184; problems with, 172–174; purposes of, 174–175; questions created for, 175–181; signed, 181; summary on, 184; time needed for, 173–174, 181–182
Reinhart, C., 298
Reports. *See* Results
Resistance, by clients, to results, 156–157
Resource limitations: and cause analysis, 120, 126–127; and performance effectiveness assessment, 99–102, 106
Results: aspects of reporting, 132–160; background on, 133; in behavioral evaluation, 242; for clients, 26, 42, 132–160; data interpretation for, 147–149; and data reporting, 153–156; data tabulation for, 134–141; formatting, 141–147; nonobservable, 244–254; operational, 255–279; and preparation for client meeting, 149–153; previews of, 152–153, 158–159; problem areas for, 156–160; summary on, 160; in Training for Impact, 13–14, 22
Return on investment. *See* Operational results evaluation
Robinson, D. G., 10*n*
Rossett, A., 220
Rummler, G., 109

S

Simulations, for learning evaluation, 196–202
Skill tests: for learning evaluation, 195–202; videotaping and audiotaping, 203
Skill transfer: barriers to, 117; and causal links, 265–266; and cause analysis, 117, 128–130; in Training for Activity, 6–7. *See also* Behavioral evaluation
Skills: building, 217–218; extinction of, 227–229; professional, 28–29, 290–291
Source group size: for cause analysis, 118, 125–126; for performance effectiveness assessment, 97–99, 103
SPSS/PC, 140
Standke, L., 299
Sudman, S., 250
Surveys: for behavioral evaluation, 220–221; opinion, 119

T

Tests: development of, 188–189, 192; of knowledge, 193–195; of skills, 195–203; standardized, for nonobservable results evaluation, 250–251
Time needs: for behavioral evaluation, 242; for feedback meeting, 159–160; for reaction evaluation, 173–174, 181–182; for Training for Impact, 283–284
Timing: of behavioral evaluation, 226–230, 239; of nonobservable results evaluation, 253; of operational results evaluation, 269–270
Tracking systems, in Training for Impact, 23–24
Trained/untrained tracking design, 232–233
Training: budgets for, 8; business needs linked to, 57–58, 61–62; conducting, 25; continuum for, 26–29; costs of, 266–268, 276–277; positioning, 35–37, 213
Training Directors' Forum, 168, 170–171
Training for Activity: approach of,

3-9; background on, 3-5; characteristics of, 5-8; problems with, 4-5
Training for Impact: approach of, 10-29; background on, 10-12; beginning, 283-293; business needs and client identification in, 33-47; and catalogue courses implications, 289-290; characteristics of, 13-26; collaboration in, 48-65; conclusions on, 293; criteria for selecting, 285-287; diagnosing needs in, 83-160; entire approach of, 283-286; evaluation and tracking in, 161-279; initial project meetings in, 66-82; management partnerships for, 31-82; moving from Training for Activity to, 1-29, 47, 62, 82, 107, 131, 160, 184, 207, 243, 253-254, 279, 293; pieces of, 286-289; skills needed in, 28-29, 290-291; structure and rewards for, 291-292; suggestions for using, 287-289; time needed for, 283-284; utilization of, 281-293

U

Utilization: of data, 182-183, 187-188, 193, 204, 206; of Training for Impact, 281-293

V

Values. *See* Nonobservable results evaluation

W

Walonick Associates, 140
Wood Panel Plant case, 272-274, 276-278
Work environment: and behavioral evaluation, 210, 211, 230-231, 236-237; and cause analysis, 109; and client chain of command, 41-42; data formatting on, 146-147; and learning evaluation, 187; questions on barriers in, 178, 179; and Training for Impact, 11-12, 16
Write-in or short answer tests, 194

X

Xerox Corporation, and skill transfer, 111

Z

Zemke, R., 101, 299